T0285813

WE MADE THEM ANGRY

TOM BROGAN

WE MADE THEM ANGRY

Scotland at the World Cup

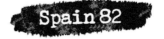

Spain 82

pitch

First published by Pitch Publishing, 2022

Pitch Publishing
9 Donnington Park,
85 Birdham Road,
Chichester,
West Sussex,
PO20 7AJ
www.pitchpublishing.co.uk
info@pitchpublishing.co.uk

ISBN 978 1 80150 090 6

Typesetting and origination by Pitch Publishing
Printed and bound in Great Britain by TJ Books, Padstow

Contents

For my mum, Catherine Brogan

Introduction

MY VERY first football memory, I realise, sounds apocryphal, as it's one of the greatest moments in Scottish football history. It was 11 June 1978. The night before, our television at home blew up as my dad watched World Cup hosts Argentina play Italy. Dad was frantic as, not 24 hours later, Scotland were due to play Holland in their final group match. If Scotland could win by three goals then they would qualify for the latter stages of a World Cup finals for the first time in their history. It wasn't a game to be missed.

On the day of the match, Dad called my uncle Pat to ask him if, or, more accurately, tell him that my dad and my mum would be coming round to his house to watch the game. To this day, Pat has very little interest in football; this is probably why my dad would use him as a patsy in the days when big match tickets were allocated in postal ballots to increase his own chances of landing a pair. 'I've been sent two tickets for the Scotland-England game,' he once said to Dad, bewildered. 'No, you haven't! They're mine!' my dad announced, having neglected to inform him of his plan.

At my uncle and aunt's house, I was handed some toys and played in the corner of the living room as the match progressed. As I vroom-vroomed my motor cars, I was suddenly shocked to hear my dad roar as I had never done before. I had heard him shout at me, but this was different; this was a roar of delight. More pressingly, I was fearful, as in leaping from his chair, Dad had sent it rocking backwards, bumping into the lamp stand, which was now tumbling towards me. I threw myself out of the way as it crashed on to the floor. I was now intrigued as to what exactly had turned him delirious. I came out from behind the chair to look at the television. What I saw was a replay of Archie Gemmill's famous second goal that night; winding past the Dutch defenders and lifting the ball over the keeper into the net then wheeling away with that raised fist that said so much about the Scottish attitude.

By 1982 I was fully committed to the Scotland cause, despite not yet attending an international match. Spain '82 was my first full televised World Cup finals. Anecdotally, I hear that the World Cup that means the most to people is the one that occurs around when they would be ten or 11. It's certainly true for me because, as a ten-year-old, it was a tournament I fully invested in. The afternoon and evening kick-off times contributed to my being able to see every match I wanted to.

When Scotland walked out into the heat of Malaga to line up against New Zealand, I clearly remember being sat in front of the television full of hope and expectation. It was a tournament that taught me all about being a Scotland fan, in just three games across eight days. There were high hopes and crashing lows.

We went into the lead in each match and began to believe, before switching off, or in the case of Brazil just being outclassed and having our hopes pushed into a dirty puddle and trampled over.

It wasn't just the Scotland games I watched that summer. Bryan Robson scoring after 27 seconds against France (I didn't even have to look up the time before writing that), the Kuwaitis walking off the field, Gerry Armstrong sending Northern Ireland into the second round, Maradona being sent off, Italy's sensational win over Brazil, the thrilling and yet horrifying France-West Germany semi-final that went on long into the night, and the final with Marco Tardelli's unforgettable celebration. Through it all, it never occurred to me that you could pick a more successful nation to follow, to admire and support evermore. No, you were Scottish, you had Scotland and the hopes and the heartache was what came with that.

I hope this book in some way captures some of the highs and lows of what it is to be a Scotland fan. – the puzzlement of why we had some of the continent's best players yet struggled to beat a team of amateurs and part-timers, how we could take the lead against the best team in the world but only make things worse for ourselves, and how, when the opposition struggled to break down our defence, we helped them out.

1

Stockholm to Belfast: Qualifying 1980/81

*'I was forced to watch from the bench
as there ensued the worst 45 minutes
of defending I had witnessed from a
professional footballer.'*

Willie Miller

THE FERRY from Stranraer docked in Belfast at 7am on Wednesday, 14 October 1981. Around 150 Scottish football supporters poured out on to the street. Throughout the day, thousands more came by sea, road and rail. One group of fans had combined their travel with their accommodation by coming over in a caravanette. Many more had looked up long-lost friends and relations in the city and were staying overnight with them. Some supporters, preempting the result, even had banners with the words 'Espana 82'.

Special leave for the 1,500 Scottish soldiers in Belfast hadn't been arranged, but those off duty were expected to make up a section of the anticipated 30,000 crowd. Rod Stewart was looking at ways to get out of interviews in London to promote his new single, 'Young Turks', so he could attend the game. 'He is as aware as anyone of the risks involved in going to Belfast,' a spokesman for his agents told the *Belfast Telegraph*. 'But that would not put him off. He would go to any lengths to try to watch Scotland play.'

They were all eager to witness Scotland secure the point that would take them to the World Cup finals in Spain the following summer. 'We don't have a single excuse to put forward if we don't succeed,' manager Jock Stein said. 'We'll be wary, of course, because organisation is such a vital part of the game today, but we want to win this one and go to the finals with a flourish.'

It was a fixture that caused much concern when the draw for the World Cup qualifying sections was made in Zurich two years earlier. Scotland went into the draw as top seeds by virtue of qualifying for the finals in 1974 and 1978. Also in Pot A were England, Czechoslovakia, Poland, Italy, the Netherlands and West Germany. Scotland were placed in Group Six. The first team added to the group was Sweden, followed by Portugal. Then came Northern Ireland. It was a draw the SFA could well have done without. Due to the political situation in the country, Scotland had not sent a team to play in Northern Ireland since April 1970, despite repeated requests from the Northern Ireland FA to do so. Since then, the nine annual Home International Championship matches had all taken place at Hampden Park.

The boycott, instigated in 1972, was not inconceivable. That year was the worst year of 'the Troubles'. January saw 'Bloody Sunday' in Derry, in which 14 marchers against internment were shot dead by the British Army. The early months also saw a bomb in Callender Street, Belfast, injuring over 60 people; a bombing of the Abercorn Restaurant, where two were killed; a car bomb in Lower Donegall Street killing seven and injuring around 100; and a series of shootings in April killing members of the Official Irish Republican Army and several British soldiers.

Northern Ireland began to play all their Home Internationals away from their own country. England and Wales shifted their 1973 Home International fixtures from Windsor Park to Goodison Park, Liverpool. By 1974, however, things were beginning to get back to normal in the city. A February 1974 letter from the Irish FA to their Scottish counterparts outlined that club matches had gone on in Belfast without a single incident; European club matches had taken place; a Canadian XI played in Belfast without problem; and assurance had been given from European Championship opponents Yugoslavia, Sweden and Norway that they would play their matches at Windsor Park. While they gave the request due consideration, it was the SFA's opinion that the civil unrest had not improved significantly enough for them to change their mind. Secretary Willie Allen told the press, 'Scotland will not go to Windsor Park during the present Troubles.'

It would be 16 April 1975 before Northern Ireland played another game in Belfast. In addition to Glasgow, they played home matches in Hull, Coventry, London, Liverpool and Sheffield, with 18 consecutive internationals being played outside their own country. Both England and Wales played in Belfast that year, with Malcolm Brodie writing in the *Belfast Telegraph*, 'At last, an era of playing all home matches away with disastrous financial results is over. The light has burst through at the end of the tunnel.'

Scotland, though, still held out. In 1976 and 1978 the SFA again cited the Troubles as the reason they would not travel across to Belfast, with the Home International games being hosted at Hampden. 'In view of the continuing civil unrest in Northern Ireland,' the SFA's Annual Report from 1978 read, 'the Association had no cause to depart from its policy of refusing to play in that country, much as everyone concerned would dearly wish to return to happier days when an international match in Belfast was an event to which Scottish football people looked forward to with relish. In the circumstances, the Irish FA has decided that its home fixture with Scotland will be played in Glasgow.'

By that time, with the infamous Wembley invasion of the Scottish fans fresh in the memory, the Irish were perfectly happy for Scots fans not to visit. Brodie wrote of the SFA, 'Their prime concern is not for the team but the fact that their now notorious fans – remember those disgraceful scenes at Wembley last May – could create problems in Belfast. It is a situation which the Irish FA reluctantly accept and one with which I agree.'

For World Cup qualifying, however, the SFA party attending the draw, president Willie Harkness, vice-president Tommy Younger and secretary Ernie Walker, all anticipated they would now have to send a team to play in Belfast. The Home Internationals had no rules insisting that countries travelled to fulfil away fixtures, and the Northern Irish had no desire to put pressure on Scotland to travel in case they pulled out of the fixture entirely. While they did lose home advantage for four internationals against Scotland, they knew that taking the home gate from Hampden boosted their coffers more than hosting the matches in Belfast would have done.

Northern Ireland's manager Danny Blanchflower was sure Scotland would have to travel. 'I think that the competition will force them to come to Belfast to meet us,' he said. 'These World Cup circumstances haven't happened before. But the world is getting smaller in the football sense, and, speaking personally, if I was a footballer now, I wouldn't baulk at going anywhere.' Tom Lauchlan, chairman of the Scottish International Selection Committee, said, 'This is undoubtedly a sensational situation. It is the strict policy of the SFA not to play in Northern Ireland. However, the alternative now would be to withdraw, and I certainly do not think we will do that.' Harry Cavan, Irish FA president, a FIFA vice-president and a member of the World Cup organising committee, was optimistic, 'We will take this opportunity to ask the Scots to play in Belfast. I'm hopeful they will now see our way.'

The SFA resolved to organise a meeting to discuss the matter while arranging with representatives from the other countries to meet in Stockholm on 3 November to arrange the fixtures. The only alternative to playing in Belfast would be to withdraw from the World Cup. There was already the suggestion that the Home International match of 1980 between the sides, scheduled as a Northern Ireland home game, be played in Belfast to 'test the waters'. Irish FA secretary Billy Drennan told the *Belfast Telegraph*, 'The priority is to get them to Windsor Park in May. On the World Cup, we're talking about matches in 1980/81.'

Cavan was concerned about the influx of Scottish supporters into Belfast and had suggested devising some scheme of ticket allocation. 'I know the difficulties, but we should be able to overcome them,' he explained.

On the subject of the draw, Stein said, 'On the whole, it's not a bad draw for us. It's a fair section, and we must think that if we play reasonably well, we have a good chance of qualifying.' The group was set to be complicated further, however. Israel had been expelled by the Asian Football Federation (AFF) in 1974 after the fallout from the Yom Kippur War when nearly every Arab FA refused to play them. Muslim countries followed suit, and in Tehran in September 1974 the AFF voted 17-13 with six abstentions to expel Israel. They had expected FIFA to kick Israel out of international football entirely, as they had done with apartheid-era South Africa in 1964. But they did not. This meant Israel could continue to play international fixtures and attempt to qualify for finals.

The Israelis resigned from the AFF in 1976. They then headed to the Asian and Oceanian zone, playing in qualifiers for the 1978 World Cup in a group containing South Korea, Japan and North Korea. Despite not being UEFA members, they were awaiting entry into the European qualifying section for the 1982 finals. In Zurich, Hermann Neuberger, president of FIFA's World Cup organising committee, said they would send a letter to the CONCACAF countries – nations from North Central America and the Caribbean – asking them to accept Israel into their section. If they refused, Neuberger said Israel would become the fifth team in Group Six. Cuban president Hector Inguanzo quickly called the plan unjust and suggested it was not up to their region to solve Israel's footballing problems. Within a week, Israel were placed in Scotland's group with FIFA saying the decision was final and not open to appeal. There was precedent for Israel to be playing in the European section as they were already admitted to the European eliminating competition for the 1980 Moscow Olympics football tournament.

'I'm not worried about having Israel added to our group,' Jock Stein said diplomatically. 'We know a little about them, and they should not be a problem.' Scotland had never played Israel before in an official international but had played in Tel Aviv during an unofficial world tour in 1967. The Scottish side, managed by Bobby Brown, won 2-1 on that occasion, with Willie Morgan and Eddie Colquhoun scoring the goals. Stein had managed Celtic in Tel Aviv in 1971 when they beat Hapoel 1-0 in a friendly.

The group began in March 1980 when Israel and Northern Ireland played out a goalless draw in Jerusalem. However, it wasn't until September that Scotland played their first match, travelling to Stockholm to meet Sweden.

Scotland went into the fixture having lost four from their last five games, losing to England and Northern Ireland in Home Internationals and Poland and Hungary in friendlies. In June, Sweden had begun their qualifying campaign by drawing with Israel at home. 'We are more than capable of getting a good start,' Stein said. 'But the players will have to work for each other and perform to the reputations they have earned at their clubs. In the past, several players have been inclined to play for themselves, and this will not be tolerated.' Stein believed that any two of the sides in the group, bar Israel, could qualify, and with Sweden already failing to win a home game, a defeat for them here would be a massive setback for their chances.

The pre-match speculation fell on where Liverpool's Alan Hansen would play after Stein said he would not partner Willie Miller of Aberdeen in defence. The thought was that Hansen would be in midfield with a licence to attack. However, when the sides lined up, Hansen partnered Aberdeen's Alex McLeish in defence with Miller in the middle of the park. Hansen had been asked to start the match in midfield, but he declined. In the *Sunday Mail*, he would later tell Dixon Blackstock that he didn't feel equipped to play a midfield role for his country. 'Naturally, if the boss had pressed me into the position, I would have had a go,' Hansen said. 'But, luckily, he understands a player's feelings and didn't pursue the matter. [The role] demands a high rate of work and aggression, which, frankly, I don't think I possess. Certainly not at international level. The heart of the defence is where I feel at home.' Stein then turned to Miller, who said he would be happy to step in. Hansen alongside McLeish would be Stein's 12th different defensive combination in 18 matches. The Scottish midfield was missing Liverpool's Graeme Souness through injury, and Miller's instructions were to nullify Mats Nordgren of Östers IF.

Although the midfield of Miller, Gordon Strachan, captain Archie Gemmill and Nottingham Forest's John Robertson took some time to exert their authority, they gradually took control of the game. Both sides looked uncomfortable on the ball at times, often conceding possession. Sweden had the best chances of the first half with Thomas Sjöberg heading wide and Thomas Nilsson having his drive saved by Alan Rough.

At half-time, Austrian referee Franz Wöhrer visited both teams' dressing rooms and warned them he wouldn't tolerate any more rough tackling. Scotland started the second half with more assurance. However, Patrick Barclay, writing in *The Guardian*, noted, 'Their passing remained prone to banality and, occasionally, sheer irresponsibility.' Andy Gray had a shout for a penalty five minutes into the half when he went down in the box under the weight of a defender, but Wöhrer, a Viennese school teacher, wasn't interested. The breakthrough came when Gordon Strachan, playing his sixth game for his country, nipped in front of a Swede in midfield to take possession. He carried the ball forward before turning and laying it off square to Gemmill. Strachan kept running down the left, and Gemmill fed him as he made his way into the box. The Aberdeen man took a touch as the Swedish defenders gathered, then hit a left-footed shot across goalkeeper Ronnie Hellström and into the net.

'Little Archie held up the return pass perfectly,' Strachan said to the *Daily Record*. 'He delayed it long enough to allow me to get into a good position in the box. When I got the ball here, I was ready at first to shoot with the right foot, and then I delayed a little myself and decided to take it with my left. I know some folk must have thought I had held back too long, but I saw a gap and changed my mind.' In the *Sunday Times*, Strachan recalled Jock Stein's reaction to his goal. 'What are you doing over there?' Stein raged. 'I told you to stay on the right.'

The goal was to give Scotland their first win in five away games and their first points in Group Six. 'It is some consolation when you have lost to a goal like that, but it was a tragic result for us,' Swedish manager Lars Arnesson told the *Record*. The team performed much like Stein had asked them to, as a unit rather than individuals. When some players had poor spells, their team-mates took up the slack. 'It's a good start for us, coming away from home and getting a victory,' Stein said. However, he sounded a note of caution, 'I can understand everyone being optimistic, but let's keep our feet on the ground. Let's sit down and look at the Stockholm game honestly and file away possible improvements.'

Scotland's next match was with Portugal at Hampden on 15 October. The sides had met earlier that year in the European Championship qualifier, where Scotland won 4-1, albeit a dead rubber in which neither side could have qualified. The Portuguese would be without the Benfica defenders Humberto Coelho and Alberto Fonseca. The latter had scored the winner when the sides met in Lisbon in 1978. Alex McLeish would be missing through injury, so Miller and Hansen would be the central defensive partnership in front of Partick Thistle's Alan Rough with Danny McGrain of Celtic on their right and Nottingham Forest's Frank Gray on the left. Souness was back to form the four-man midfield with Gemmill, Strachan and John Robertson. Andy Gray of Wolverhampton Wanderers and Liverpool's Kenny Dalglish would be up front. Stein was asked what Scotland's most significant danger was. 'Our own players – if they don't play to their full potential,' he replied. 'It's really all about the players. I pick them, but I can't win the match for them. So if they get the result we are looking for, they will deserve the credit, not me.'

Earlier in the day, Northern Ireland beat Sweden 3-0 in Belfast, the Swedes now having taken only one point from three games.

In the programme notes, Stein asked for the Scots fans to be patient. It wasn't a pretty performance by Scotland as a succession of long balls made their way towards Dalglish and Gray without any joy. It was only late on that Scotland looked like they could make a breakthrough, when Souness and Dalglish saw shots saved by Portuguese captain Bento in goal. Portugal's best chance fell to Fernandes, who got in a shot on the 80th minute that whizzed past Rough's post. As the game wore on, the 60,675 crowd looked for Stein to make some changes. 'That's the easy thing to do,' Stein said the next day, defending his decision not to put any substitutes on. 'I didn't want to upset the rhythm, and, after all, we weren't playing that badly.' Portugal were quite happy with the 0-0 draw, their players celebrating at the final whistle. The press acclaimed Bento's performance in goal as 'breathtaking'.

'Some of the moves were splendid,' said Stein. 'Many chances were made – but, the old story, none was taken. The team spirit was building up nicely. And the crowd were tremendous, not putting pressure on us but encouraging all the time. If we had gained a draw in Sweden and then won here, everyone would be happy,' Stein pointed out. 'We've just done it the other way round, and three points from the first two games can't be bad.' That was the last international for 1980, and there were a few months to prepare for the next qualifier.

'I certainly don't see the Israelis making the finals,' Stein said, ahead of Scotland's next match, 'but strangely enough, they could now be the most important side in the section. It could well come down to who takes the most points from them.'

The Scots would head for Tel Aviv in February of 1981. The Israelis were managed by Jack Mansell, an Englishman who had a ten-year playing career with Brighton, Cardiff and Portsmouth, playing twice for the England B team in 1954 and 1956. He began his coaching career with Sheffield Wednesday before embarking on a nomadic managerial journey taking in the Netherlands, USA, England again, Turkey and Bahrain before taking over Israel in 1980.

'The standard of our better players is good enough for many of them to compete in the best class in Germany or England,' Mansell told Hugh Taylor of the *Evening Times*. 'Their trouble is that they have played too long in a competition where they are outstandingly better than most of the other players. They've never had the stimulus. They can do it in a canter, so they don't bother enough and feel they know it all.' Nevertheless, Mansell believed his side could be the equal of their opponents, saying, 'We will give you a real run for your money.'

Israel had previously qualified for the 1970 World Cup in Mexico. They achieved perhaps the country's greatest-ever result there, holding eventual runners-up Italy to a 0-0 draw. A properly organised national league began in the country in 1932 with nine clubs. By 1981 there were four senior divisions encompassing 300 teams.

After a training session in the Ramat Gan Stadium, Stein kept his team selection to himself but was happy to tell the press what a tremendous shift his players had put in, 'It's easily the best training session we have had since I took over. In the past, I have had squads who trained on the Monday, and individuals said they were not sure if they could do what was asked at the time but assured me everything would be all right on the night. What a difference today. Everybody could do everything.'

The game, a 1.30pm GMT kick-off, would be live on BBC Scotland. All bar the first 30 minutes. A dispute over trackside advertising had held up the TV deal, but, by the time the issue was resolved, the broadcast satellite was no longer available for the whole match. In the days before the game the weather changed drastically, which would favour Scotland. Monday brought hot desert winds and the promise of sandstorms. However, by Tuesday evening, Tel Aviv was lashed by heavy rain and driving wind. Danny McGrain would be selected to earn his 50th cap, making him only the fifth Scotsman to achieve that honour, following Kenny Dalglish, Denis Law, Billy Bremner and George Young. However, there would be a few changes from the last qualifier. Tottenham's Steve Archibald, the leading scorer in his first season in the English First Division, started up front with Dalglish, relegating Andy Gray to the bench. 'Scotland can't leave Steve out,' former Spurs and Scotland striker Alan Gilzean said to the *Sunday Mirror.* 'He has been scoring so regularly it's got to the stage where it almost seems strange when he doesn't get a goal.' Gilzean had scored 12 times in his 22 internationals from 1963 to 1971. 'I'd love to see him in my old role of leading Scotland. I'm certain he would be a success.'

John Wark of Ipswich would be in midfield in place of Strachan. Wark had played his previous games for Scotland wide, but Stein decided to play him in the position he was used in at club level, through the middle. The latest central defensive partnership would be Alex McLeish and Nottingham Forest's Kenny Burns. 'Miller has had only two matches since coming back after a long suspension while Burns has been in great form for Nottingham Forest,' said Stein. It was a decision that left Miller, suspended for four domestic matches in January, quietly seething. 'I thought I was pretty much certain to get picked,' Miller told the *Official Scotland Podcast* in 2018. 'But for some reason, he left me on the bench and played Kenny Burns. And looking at Kenny Burns in training, my assessment of him was he was overweight and unfit, and I wasn't happy when he got the nod in front of me.'

Burns hadn't played for Scotland since December 1979, but now he was set to win his 18th cap. In his autobiography *No Ifs or Butts*, Burns recalled, 'Stein became a national icon, but I didn't rate him as a manager at all. [He] was a bit strict and didn't like us drinking. He didn't do much; he just strolled about most of the time. He was a bit sombre, and I don't think I ever saw him smile. But at least he had the good sense to recall me for the World Cup qualifier in Israel.'

Mansell picked six midfielders for his formation, although he admitted they wouldn't have the defensive discipline to play ten men in their own half for 90 minutes. Stein was adamant his side wouldn't be undone by complacency, 'There are pitfalls when players start looking for easy games, and you can bet it won't be easy for us. I have stressed to the players that they must show Israel some respect but have stressed even more that they must respect themselves and their undoubted ability.'

One thing the match wasn't for Scotland was easy. The home side pounded the Scots goal throughout the first half. Rough rushed from his line twice, first to foil Hapoel Tel Aviv's Moshe Sinai and then diving at the feet of Maccabi Tel Aviv's Beni Tabak. Scotland, wearing their red change strip, did have a couple of first-half chances, but Souness and Robertson's shots came to nothing. As the sides trooped off at the interval, it was only a great display from Rough and some desperate defending from Burns that kept Scotland in it.

In his autobiography *The Don*, Willie Miller recalls the period, 'I was forced to watch from the bench as there ensued the worst 45 minutes of defending I had witnessed from a professional footballer. It was a great puzzle how we managed to reach half-time without the opposition scoring, as Kenny was well off the pace.' Conversely, Hugh Taylor's report in the *Evening Times* read, 'It was as well for Scotland that Kenny Burns was playing a heroic part in defence.' In *The Guardian*, too, Eric Silver felt Burns had 'a strong match'.

In the dressing room, Stein ripped into his side for their performance. He was then forced into making changes. John Wark had suffered a hamstring injury. Wark hadn't been 100 per cent fit going into the match but told Stein he was. The manager was less than impressed with his player. A reshuffle was required with Willie Miller taking Wark's place and Burns moving into midfield. Not only was Miller delighted to take to the pitch, so too was his defensive partner Alex McLeish. 'Kenny was used to playing a different way at Nottingham Forest where he would run out and hold lines or play offside,' McLeish told the *Daily Record* in 2010. 'In the first half, I don't know how Israel didn't score. We got battered but somehow got in at 0-0. Jock spotted what was happening and said to Willie, "You better go on." I thought, "Thank God." Kenny was a really good defender, but we weren't on the same wavelength. It was the old adage, if it ain't broke, don't fix it.'

That wasn't the only problem Stein faced at the interval. Dalglish had been in a clash of heads and was suffering from a concussion. It was decided to give him ten minutes of the second half to see how he was. That was all the time he needed. John Robertson moved over to the right wing and, on 54 minutes, sent over a corner, which was nodded on by McLeish towards the back post. Dalglish was waiting on the edge of the six-yard box. He would later say that thanks to his concussion he could see two balls in front of him. He picked the correct one and hammered it into the roof of the net. Shortly afterwards, he was replaced by Andy Gray. The pressure from Israel, who played with alertness throughout, wasn't over, however, as Tabak had two great chances foiled by Rough.

'The first half was a shambles,' Stein said after the 1-0 win. 'Israel got to the ball first on almost every occasion. They were well organised, and they had quick players, who caused us all sorts of surprises on the soft pitch following a downpour. The real truth is we took our chance when it came along. They didn't.' Mansell knew it was one man who made the difference. 'Alan Rough was absolutely brilliant,' he said. 'Not for the spectacular saves but for the ones which really mattered when he came quickly off his line several times diving six feet towards a player's boots.'

'What's all the fuss about?' Rough asked of the superlatives he was hearing. 'If I play like that for Partick Thistle, no one takes any notice.' Rough had several superstitions as a player, one of which was to always wear his own white socks. After his last game for Thistle, he had forgotten to wash them before travelling to Tel Aviv. Rough handed them to Scotland and Celtic masseur Jimmy Steele to wash, which he duly did; he just forgot to dry them. 'There was me,' Rough said to *The Scotsman* in 2010, 'squelching around, soapy bubbles popping in the eyelets of my boots, and playing one of my best games for my country. I should have made that another wee routine.'

Steele was initially brought into the Scotland setup by Tommy Docherty. His masseur skills were developed as a physical training instructor in the RAF in the 1930s.

Stationed in Wiltshire, Steele became trainer to boxer Freddie Mills, helping him to the British light-heavyweight title. When he returned home to Scotland, Jimmy McStay, then manager of Celtic, invited Steele to join the club's backroom staff. Steele's whole career was spent without being paid a salary of any description. Always a popular figure within the Scots camp, when the squad stayed at Niteroi Cricket Club in Rio de Janeiro in 1972 ahead of a friendly with Brazil, several of the players delighted in throwing Jimmy fully clothed into the swimming pool. Only when he hauled himself out the pool soaking wet did they remember they had given him their watches and cash for safekeeping, all of which was on his person. He was let go from the Scotland setup by Willie Ormond, who found him 'too cheery', but when Ally MacLeod was appointed in 1977 he made it one of his first tasks to reinstate Steele.

* * *

The next qualifier came a month later as Northern Ireland visited Hampden Park. They had lost to Portugal by a single goal, while the Portuguese had also defeated Israel. The Irish needed to take something from the game to keep their hopes of qualifying alive. Billy Bingham had taken over as manager from Danny Blanchflower in March 1980. He would be without two of his most essential players in Nottingham Forest's Martin O'Neill and Blackburn Rovers winger Noel Brotherston. 'If you can beat us at Hampden, then I'd say you were through to the finals,' O'Neill said to the *Record*. 'But I don't see it end our chances.' Scotland would also be without regulars in the shape of injured Liverpool pair Kenny Dalglish and Graeme Souness. Andy Gray and Steve Archibald would be the front two. Kenny Burns would keep

29

the midfield position he took up in the second half of the Israel game, joined by Wark, recently voted the PFA Players' Player of the Year in England, Gemmill and Robertson. The back four was becoming a familiar sight for goalkeeper Rough with McGrain and Frank Gray the wing-backs and the Aberdeen pair of Miller and McLeish in the centre.

The Home International Championship match of 1980 had been played in Belfast, as suggested at the time of the qualifying draw. However, certain conditions were put in place for the May game. In essence, these were implemented to discourage supporters from travelling. The match was played on a Friday evening. 'Considerably lower key than the traditional Saturday afternoon,' the SFA would say. There would be live BBC television coverage in Scotland and a refusal of the SFA to accept any tickets.

The SFA's Annual Ordinary General Meeting report on 5 May 1980 finally revealed the long-standing reasons for refusing to travel. Malcolm Brodie's assertions had been broadly correct. It was not the safety of the players the SFA feared for; it was the behaviour of the fans. It was reported at the meeting, 'Had it been possible for Scotland to play in Belfast, as England and Wales have done in recent years, without the presence of thousands of Scottish supporters, there is little doubt that we would have done so, but it has been the Association's feeling that it would have been imprudent to visit upon the sensitive streets of Belfast the enthusiasm of Scottish supporters, some of whom would almost certainly welcome the occasion for reasons which have nothing to do with football. Rightly or wrongly, that is why Scotland has not visited Northern Ireland during the 1970s.' The World Cup draw had put the fear of being 'cast into the football wilderness internationally for the next four years' into the SFA. 'Much heart-searching ensued, and eventually, it was decided that the vast majority of football Scots would not wish to see their country withdraw from the World Cup and that we should observe the dictates of the ballot box.' That game went on with no incident, but the home side gave Scotland a going over as they beat them 1-0. It was something Stein reminded his players of before the World Cup qualifier, as he impressed upon them not to take Northern Ireland lightly.

At Hampden, a crowd of 78,444 paid between £5 and £7 to sit in the stand, with covered terracing at £2.50 and £2 cash at the turnstiles for entry to the uncovered terracing. Scotland began the game well enough but struggled to find a way through to goal. The midfield laboured but couldn't get the ball through to the front two often enough. Archibald hit the post with a great 20-yard shot on the turn. Then later, after Andy Gray played him in, Archibald watched as Chris Nicholl headed another shot off the line. At around the half-hour mark frustration crept in, and the Scots began chasing the game. McGrain was working hard to keep the Irish attacks at bay, and there was a shade of good fortune when a clumsy challenge in the penalty box by McLeish on Sammy McIlroy went unpunished by the East German referee Klaus Scheurell.

Scotland had a let-off early in the second half as Billy Hamilton headed against the post. Midway through the half, Rough rushed from his line to punch the ball away from Hamilton, injuring his shoulder as he did so. The game stopped for three minutes as he was treated. A goal did arrive, and it was Northern Ireland who got it with 20 minutes left. Burns conceded a free kick, with a hefty challenge on Hamilton out on Scotland's right. 'This might be a test

31

for the right shoulder of Alan Rough,' TV commentator Jock Brown said as Sammy Nelson and McIlroy stood over the ball. McIlroy flighted the kick to the far post. Rough began to move out, McLeish and Miller stood watching as Hamilton, all on his own in the six-yard box, glanced a header into the net.

It only took Scotland five minutes to draw level. Archie Gemmill played a quick free kick in the middle on to Miller who threaded a neat through ball for Wark to run on to. Wark hit it first time and slipped his 33rd goal of the season under Pat Jennings. In the aftermath, Stein threw on Asa Hartford, winning his first cap since November 1979, for Kenny Burns. With ten minutes remaining, Rough, with his right arm hanging permanently by his side, came off with St Mirren's Billy Thomson coming on for his second cap. 'It was a 50/50 ball,' Rough said later of his collision with Hamilton. 'The reason I was hurt was that he was moving more quickly than me. I didn't think it was a foul.' Wark headed over the bar a moment later. The last chance fell to Steve Archibald, who hit a tame shot at Jennings.

'I've got to say how grateful we are to the fans,' Stein said afterwards. 'They might have turned against us when we lost the goal; instead, they stayed 100 per cent behind us. They helped us come back into the game.' The Northern Irish players had some harsh words about their opponents. Southend United's Derek Spence said to the *Daily Record*, 'They appear arrogant as though they are going to stroll through it. We just roll up our sleeves. Perhaps it's their fanatical supporters that do it to them. Telling them all the time they are the greatest.' Gerry Armstrong of Watford was also critical, 'We fight for each other as a team – they seem to play as individuals. Don't blame Stein, blame the players.'

'It's rather ironic that we have never really been rated as an away team,' Stein said to the *Glasgow Herald*, 'but here we are, halfway through the section, having won two away games but having dropped two points at home. We never seem to make it easy for ourselves when it comes to the World Cup.' Stein was asked about changes he must make to the side for the future qualifiers with the home match against Israel coming up. In particular, it was noted that the pairing of Archibald and Gray up front didn't work well, with Gray failing to have a shot on target. 'I was reasonably happy with the way I combined with Steve Archibald in our first full game together,' Gray wrote in his regular column for *Shoot!* magazine. 'On paper, it may appear not to have come off as neither of us scored. But we came close with a few chances, and I'd like to think we would progress if given the chance.'

Israel at Hampden on 28 April 1981 was the next test, and Scotland were dealt a blow six days before. 'Kenny has no chance for next week,' Liverpool manager Bob Paisley said of his striker's hopes of playing in the international. It came the day after Liverpool's European Cup semi-final with Bayern Munich. Within five minutes of the start, Bayern's Karl Del'Haye raked his studs along Kenny's ankle. 'He was so lightweight in frame and ability I never thought he posed a threat as I laid the ball inside,' Dalglish said in his book, *My Liverpool Home*. 'I strongly suspect the German's intent was to remove me from the fray deliberately.' Dalglish attempted to continue. 'It is his nature to try to shrug off anything less dire than a gunshot wound,' Hugh McIlvanney wrote in *The Observer*. Despite his attempts to play through the injury, he came off after nine minutes. Liverpool secured a 1-1 draw and a place in the final without him. With his ankle in plaster, Dalglish's focus was getting fit for the May final with Real Madrid. Scotland would be without him for the second successive qualifier.

Andy Gray was pulled out of the squad with a hamstring injury after Wolves' 3-1 loss to Arsenal, further complicating Stein's striking options. Gray's club manager John Barnwell commented, 'I told him I had to be honest with Jock Stein and that I was taking him out of the Scotland squad. Andy is unhappy at the decision, but it is for his own good.' Stein himself was unhappy about the situation as Barnwell's call didn't come until Sunday morning, after Stein had heard about Gray's withdrawal through his newspaper contacts. Barnwell told Stein his secretary should have called him on the Saturday night, and the Wolves boss accepted responsibility for the confusion.

The loss of two of Scotland's regular strikers was good news for Manchester United's Joe Jordan, who hadn't won a cap since the friendly against Poland in May 1980. 'Jordan has been impressive with his club in recent matches, and is on a good scoring run at the moment,' Stein said. Davie Provan was another who hadn't appeared for his country since May of the previous year, and he would be on the opposite wing to John Robertson. 'I'm not about to go overboard and claim I'm right there in the World Cup plans,' Provan said, 'but like every other player in the country, it's my ambition to be involved. That's the peak, isn't it?'

'The boss has picked an attacking team with two wingers,' Joe Jordan said to the *Glasgow Herald*, 'and that should suit both Steve Archibald and myself. As Northern Ireland showed last month, it is very difficult for strikers to get goals against packed defences. But one of the few ways you can break down a defence of eight or nine defenders is to get behind them. To do that, you need players of creative ability and both Davie and John Robertson fit that bill.'

The most notable change in personnel for the Israel clash was the absence of skipper Archie Gemmill. 'I have chosen the best side available for a certain job, and I explained this to Archie after naming the team,' said Stein. 'The manager picks the team, and I'm not in it this time,' Gemmill told the press. 'That's something I have to accept. You have to take the bad with the good in this game.' In the programme for the match with Portugal in October 1980, Gemmill was asked what he felt was Stein's greatest forte. 'His superb knowledge of the game,' Archie replied. 'His honesty in the handling of players, and his absolute fairness to every player in the pool.'

It would turn out that the 34-year-old had played his last international. In his autobiography, *Both Sides of the Border*, Gemmill would state his exclusion from the national team resulted from an ill-advised late-night mediation with the manager. At the hotel where the squad were staying, two of the players had come to Gemmill in his role as captain, asking if he could square it with Stein for them to go out for a couple of hours. Archie headed for Stein's room and chapped on his door. Having been awakened by Gemmill's visit, Stein went ballistic, telling him that, as captain, he should be perfectly aware of what was permissible and what was not. This, Stein let him know, certainly was not. The following morning Jock made a point of chewing the Birmingham City man out again in front of the rest of the squad. As a tactic of showing the players no one was above a dressing down, Stein was well practised in it over the years.

Graeme Souness remembered the incident well. In his book *No Half Measures*, he recalled, 'I was glad that a hard game and the trip north had tired me out to the extent of having gone to bed early the night before, but he certainly made his point.' While Souness wrote of getting his head down, in Gemmill's version of events, the two players who had asked him to obtain permission to go out were Alan Hansen and Souness himself. After training, Jock asked for a private word with Gemmill. Stein told him that Asa Hartford would be in the team in his place. Gemmill recalled him saying, 'I'll make it easier for you, if you like, and tell the press boys you've got a slight injury and that I'm not risking you.' 'My reply was short and to the point, "Will you bollocks." That was the last time we spoke.' It was a sorry end to an 11-year international career that included a World Cup goal against Holland that became iconic. Of his 42 caps, 22 of them came as captain. Gemmill was inducted into the Scottish Football Hall of Fame in 2008.

Stein claimed his line-up was the most adventurous he had selected since he took over two and a half years earlier. With Rough again in goal, the back four would be McGrain, Frank Gray and Hansen partnering McLeish in the middle. Provan, making his first start after four caps as a substitute, on the right and Robertson on the left would be the wingers with Souness and Hartford in the centre of the pitch. Jordan and Archibald formed the front line. McGrain would be captain for the second time, after first taking the armband in the friendly against Poland. The day before the match, Alan Rough was voted Scotland's Footballer of the Year, beating Dundee United pair Paul Sturrock and Hamish McAlpine.

Two English-based players would be in Israel's side, Liverpool's Avi Cohen and Brighton & Hove Albion's Jacob Cohen. 'We should have won in Tel Aviv,' Jack Mansell told the *Evening Times*. 'And that man who gave you the goal, Kenny Dalglish, won't be playing this time. To be frank, nobody in the Scotland side was a danger man against us in Israel.' In his programme notes, Stein said the fans could forget about being patient, as he had asked for in previous matches, 'I'll be telling the boys to go at Israel from the first kick of the ball.' Scotland came out aggressively as the Israelis were stretched throughout the whole 90 minutes. The result was effectively wrapped up inside the first half-hour, although that's not to say Scotland didn't have a few scares before they made the breakthrough. Tabak shot over the bar before Rough blocked another shot from Tabak and a drive from Gidi Damti. Jordan, Hansen, Archibald and Gray all failed with shots before some comic defending signalled the visitors' demise.

Robertson used all his skill to goad Gad Machnes into pulling him down for a penalty on 20 minutes. Robertson took the kick himself, putting the ball in off the post. Ten minutes later, Scotland had a second penalty when Haim Bar felled Archibald from behind. Robertson stepped up again, sending Yossi Mizrahi the wrong way. 'You just knew Robbo would score whenever Scotland got a penalty,' Alan Rough said to the *Record* in 2018. 'He was brilliant at them. He was so reliable from 12 yards. Robertson and [Davie] Cooper were the best two penalty takers I have seen. I think it was because both were left-footed, and goalkeepers just couldn't get a handle on them.' Robertson had become Nottingham Forest's penalty taker during Dave Mackay's spell as manager in 1972/73. 'I've always fancied taking penalties and right through school I've had the job,' Robertson said in 1980. 'I remember vowing not to take another penalty after missing one in a cup tie for Hozier

Secondary School against Coatbridge High. We were 2-1 up when I missed and they got an equaliser. When we were awarded a penalty in the replay I was wandering up to the halfway line, but the teacher ordered me to go back and take it. I remember blasting it as hard as I could.'

After being played in by Robertson, Archibald volleyed over while McLeish sent a header on to the crossbar before the half-time whistle sounded. Nine minutes into the second period, Provan made it 3-0 when he fired a low drive past Mizrahi. Israel came back, though, with a goal from Moshe Sinai. This made the Scots determined to shut up shop, and in the closing stages, Archibald, Jordan and Souness all came close to extending the lead. However, there were no further goals and the Scots had won 3-1. 'Jordan was magnificent,' a clearly delighted Stein said afterwards. 'It was his best performance for Scotland.'

'I accept that we were beaten by a superior team,' Mansell said. 'You got goals at the right time. I thought Provan played well and so did Robertson but although our lads are improving they are still tactically naive.'

The next night Northern Ireland beat Portugal, thanks to a Gerry Armstrong header. That left Scotland top of the group on eight points, with Northern Ireland second on six. Portugal were third with five points from four games. The group was tighter than Scotland would have liked, particularly with Portugal having two games in hand.

* * *

Scotland could now forget about World Cup qualifiers as May brought around the Home International Championship. Their first opposition would be Wales at Swansea's Vetch Field on Saturday, 16 May. Stein made several changes to his side. He brought Manchester United's Gordon McQueen back after an absence of 18 months. West Ham's Ray Stewart made his debut at right-back. David Narey and Kenny Burns both came in, while another player back after a long exclusion was Leeds United's Arthur Graham, who hadn't appeared since October 1979. Stein's preparation wasn't helped by McLeish and Miller missing the team flight to Cardiff. 'I've had a word with them,' Stein said, 'and although I was certainly not pleased, despite the fact they were fog-bound in Aberdeen, I'm convinced they are in the right frame of mind.' Miller was elected to partner McQueen with McLeish on the bench. The Liverpool trio and John Wark of Ipswich would be ruled out due to their respective appearances in the European Cup Final and the UEFA Cup Final.

It was not one of Scotland's best days on a football pitch. Defensive frailties let Crystal Palace's Ian Walsh in to score twice, on 18 and 21 minutes. To make matters worse, Joe Jordan was sent off late on for an off-the-ball elbow on Terry Boyle. 'Joe always looked as if he was going to be sent off,' Stein said. 'If we had anybody with experience on the bench, we would have saved Joe by taking him off.' Boyle went to hospital with a broken nose and a missing tooth. It would be the final Scotland appearances for McQueen, Burns and Graham.

Before Scotland's fixture at Hampden with Northern Ireland, the subject of playing internationals in Belfast came up once again. England refused to travel for their match with Northern Ireland in the wake of increasing tensions in the country. The Welsh FA announced that they too wouldn't fulfil their fixture in Belfast either, as many of their players voiced displeasure in travelling. Stein thought the English FA had other things on their mind by withdrawing. 'It would suit England not to have to play the likes of Ireland,' he said. But, in what would become a prescient remark, he continued, 'They are getting too big for that and would rather face teams like Brazil.' The 1984 Home Internationals would be the last, and by 1987 England and Scotland had replaced the tournament with a three-team round-robin Rous Cup, with Brazil invited to be the third entrants. There were no fears that Scotland's October trip to Belfast was in doubt, but Stein forecast issues, 'There will be more tension in that match,' he said.

The Northern Ireland encounter came only three days after the Wales game. With Jordan suspended, Paul Sturrock, who made his debut as a substitute against the Welsh, started beside Archibald in the front line. Celtic's Tommy Burns gained his first cap. Ray Stewart was pushed into midfield with Danny McGrain returning at right-back. Billy Thomson of St Mirren would start in goal. The crowd of 22,448 was way below the attendances the World Cup qualifiers at Hampden had achieved. The fans there, though, didn't have to wait long for a goal. With just five minutes gone, Frank Gray touched a free kick to Burns, who rolled the ball for Stewart to hammer in from 25 yards. A second was added five minutes into the second half when Archibald ran in on goal, shrugging off two defenders to chip past Jennings. Stein declared the performance 'a wee bit better' than that in Swansea. Directly after the match, Rangers boss John Greig signed Northern Ireland defender John McClelland from Mansfield Town.

Thoughts now turned to Wembley and the game against England on Saturday, 23 May. Wembley was seen as a daunting place for Scottish goalkeepers. 'You must remember that not all keepers have failed there,' Alan Rough told Hugh Taylor in the *Evening Times*. Rough had already been on the winning side at the Twin Towers in 1977. 'I think about Jimmy Cowan, and he was a hero, not a villain at Wembley,' Rough said. Cowan had an outstanding opening 20 minutes against an England side containing Jackie Milburn, Stanley Matthews, Stan Mortensen and Tom Finney at Wembley in 1949 as Scotland won 3-1. 'Immense. Goalkeeping at its best,' wrote the *Sunday Post*. 'Frank Swift was his usual self. Jimmy Cowan was better. There is no greater praise than that,' reported *The Courier*. 'I was lucky to get the feel of the ball early,' Cowan said modestly afterwards. Two years later, he was also in goal when Scotland triumphed 3-2.

Rough would be between the posts, with captain McGrain on the right and Frank Gray on the left. McLeish and Miller made up the central defensive partnership. Stewart was again in midfield with Hartford while Provan and Robertson patrolled the wings. This time, Steve Archibald retained his place, playing alongside the returning Joe Jordan. Stein told Joe he wanted to see more of his performance against Israel and less of his performance against Wales. 'I certainly don't want to inhibit him,' Stein said. 'He went a wee bit over the top in Wales where he argued with every decision and went to war.'

Also at Wembley were the Scottish fans. The English FA insisted they wouldn't be selling tickets to Scots supporters, instructing English supporters who had applied for tickets not to get them for Scottish relatives. However, it didn't put the Scots supporters off, and they attended in their thousands. Ronnie McDevitt, then a 19-year-old dockyard storeman, now a popular author of books on the Scottish national team, told the *Evening Times*, 'I've been to Belgium, Poland, Hungary, Sweden and Israel. This was the easiest game I've ever found for tickets.'

'The eyes of the world will be on Wembley on Saturday. The fans must not let us down,' said Stein. An industrial dispute put tube and bus services off, meaning that many fans had around ten miles to walk to the match.

John Robertson spoke to Jim Reynolds of the *Glasgow Herald*, saying, 'Wembley holds no fears for me. I've been there four times with Forest and I love it – the big wide pitch and the atmosphere.' Robertson would be playing directly against his club-mate Viv Anderson. 'I'll do all right there,' he said. 'Viv doesn't like anyone going in tight on him.'

'When I see John Robertson play he excites me,' Bill Shankly said in 1980. 'It excites me to think about what he can do for Scotland in years to come. No Scottish side should take the field now without his name on the team sheet. It would be absolute nonsense to leave him out. He has a cute footballing brain which gives him a yard start on opponents, and that first yard is the most important in football. That's where he excels.'

'So You Tried To Ban Us Mr Croker' read a banner in the ground aimed at FA secretary Ted Croker. The official attendance was reported as 90,000, but those in the ground observed empty seats. One thing that was certain, though, was that the Scots outnumbered the English. The match itself was far from a classic. The pitch cut up almost from the start. Manchester United's Steve Coppell blazed a couple of shots over the bar for England, while Rough saved well from Glenn Hoddle's 20-yard drive. Late in the first half, a great cross from Coppell should have made it 1-0 to England, but Arsenal's Graham Rix sent his six-yard header wide. In the second half, Ray Wilkins of Manchester United shot past the post, while another great chance was wasted for England when Aston Villa's Peter Withe didn't get enough power in his header from Kenny Sansom's cross, and Miller hooked it out from on the goal line.

In the 64th minute, the goal came against the run of play. Provan found himself in space on the right. He spotted Archibald, similarly with no one around him through the centre. The Celtic man played a perfect ball through the middle and into the penalty box for the Spurs striker to run on to. Manchester United's Bryan Robson was on Archibald's shoulder, and as the Scot crossed to go goalside, the Englishman clipped his heels sending him crashing to the turf. Lying on the ground, Archibald swivelled his head to see what referee Robert Wurtz had decided. He raised his arms in celebration as he saw the Frenchman point to the spot. As several England players surrounded the referee in protest, John Robertson gathered the ball and placed it on the spot. 'It was a blatant penalty,' Robertson said to *The Independent* in 1996. 'My hands went up for it until I realised I was going to have to take it. I started panicking a bit, and it didn't help when Trevor Francis ran from the halfway line to tell Joe Corrigan where I was going to put it.'

As Robertson stood waiting to take his kick, his Nottingham Forest team-mate Trevor Francis went up to goalkeeper Corrigan and had a word with him. 'I know what he was doing,' Robertson wrote in his autobiography *Super Tramp*, 'but I said to myself, "Go your normal side," which for me meant hitting it to Corrigan's right.' Robertson did just that, and Corrigan went the wrong way. It was 1-0 to Scotland. Robertson spoke to Corrigan later, and the Manchester City goalkeeper told him that Francis had suggested Robertson would change his usual routine so to dive left. Archibald had a decent chance late on to double the lead, but there was no further scoring, and Scotland left with a famous win. Magnanimously, Ted Croker called the day 'a victory for football'.

Rough's clean sheet was the first for a Scottish goalkeeper against England at Wembley since David Cumming in 1938. 'Perhaps my experience on Saturday will be an example to Scottish goalkeepers in future,' Rough said to the *Evening Times*. 'Certainly, I feel it might take a lot of pressure off them since the so-called Wembley jinx has been lifted. A lot of English critics have been ready to doubt me in the past, but maybe now they'll give me some credit.'

Alex McLeish recalled the game for the *Independent on Sunday* in 1999, 'I played 77 times for Scotland, but when I think of how myself and Willie Miller were rubbished before this match, you would think I should never even have had one cap. It was only my ninth or tenth game for my country but the media, particularly TV, were really dismissive of our partnership because we played for Aberdeen. They didn't rate the Scottish domestic game and could not understand how Jock Stein didn't use Anglos like Gordon McQueen, Kenny Burns and Alan Hansen. Lawrie McMenemy, who was the BBC's top pundit, could not even remember my name and kept calling me "the big red-headed lad". If I had heard that, I would have been raging, but I was motivated enough with all the English papers tipping us to get murdered. Willie and I had a good teacher at Aberdeen in Alex Ferguson, but we also owed a lot that day to Danny McGrain and Frank Gray, two fine full-backs.'

Although Scotland finished top of the Home International Championship table on four points, the tournament was incomplete because England and Wales refused to play Northern Ireland, so no winner was declared.

Scotland's next international was the qualifier with Sweden at Hampden in September. By that time, Liverpool, with Hansen, Souness and Dalglish in the side, had lifted the European Cup, Ipswich with Wark, Alan Brazil and George Burley had secured the UEFA Cup, while Steve Archibald had been in Spurs' FA Cup-winning side.

There were two qualifiers in Scotland's group played in June. Sweden had won them both, defeating Northern Ireland 1-0 and Portugal 3-0. They weren't the results Scotland were looking for as the group had now become extremely close, with Sweden joining Northern Ireland on six points, just two behind Scotland.

'I can't remember the last time everything went so smoothly in the build-up to a major game,' Stein said the day before the match. 'This time, only the call-off by Graeme Souness has spoiled the perfect attendance.' It was expected that Gordon Strachan would return to the team, having been out with torn stomach muscles, but he could only find a place on the bench. Scotland would line up loosely in a 4-2-4 formation with Rough in goal, McGrain and Gray the wing-backs, and McLeish and Hansen in defence. Wark and Hartford would make up the midfield, while Provan and Robertson would be on the wings just like at Wembley. Dalglish and Jordan would be the front pairing.

Joe, now 29, had made a lucrative move from Manchester United to AC Milan in July. In the past, he had been linked with clubs across Europe, including Bayern Munich and Ajax. 'I knew this was my last chance on the continent,' he said to the *Sunday Mirror*. 'I wanted to find out how I would get on.' He made sure his move abroad wouldn't force the international manager to forget about him. 'I actually phoned Jock before signing for Milan to get his advice and ask him if it would affect my position within the national side,' Jordan told Archie Macpherson. 'He absolutely assured me that it wouldn't influence him in the slightest.'

The mood was expectant. With a largely settled team and that win in Stockholm a year earlier under their belts, the Scots were confident. 'We will show the Swedes respect, but no fear,' Stein said. The 81,511 fans at Hampden saw Provan and Robertson frequently create chances for Jordan and Dalglish. Their work paid off in the 20th minute when Robertson was fouled out on the left. He took the kick himself, sending it to the near post where Jordan had timed his run well, dived in front of the defender, and headed home. Sweden looked more assertive in the second 45 and the Scots struggled to find the timing to release the ball, or when the timing was right, they couldn't find the correct pass to play. Dalglish tested Thomas Ravelli in the Swedish goal a couple of times before making way for Andy Gray.

'We were playing poorly, really struggling,' Gray recounted in his book *Gray Matters*, 'and I came on as sub in the second half and won us a soft penalty.' There were only ten minutes left when Gray, turning away from goal, went down under a challenge from IFK Sundsvall's Bo Börjesson. Swiss referee André Daina, later to take charge of the 1985 European Cup Final, had no hesitation in pointing to the spot. Robertson stepped up and sent a right-footed kick to Ravelli's left for 2-0. Scotland had the win that put the result of their qualifying campaign in their own hands. Patrick Barclay in *The Guardian* picked out Hartford as Scotland's best man with his 'consistently inventive and accurate passing'.

'I did not think it was a penalty and I did not agree with the free kick which led to the first goal either,' Swedish boss Lars Arnesson said. Someone else who didn't think it was a penalty kick was Andy Gray. More out of bombast than an attempt to cleanse his conscience, Gray admitted to reporters that he'd conned the referee by going down easy. Stein didn't appreciate Gray's remarks. 'We don't want that sort of comment from any of our players,' Stein said. 'Anyway, Andy was wrong, he was tripped, and it was a definite penalty. He shouldn't make comments like that about any referee because what will other referees think in future matches?'

The win in Scotland's last World Cup qualifier at home meant that they had extended their unbeaten run in home World Cup qualifiers since the previous loss on 13 October 1965 when Poland won 2-1. The run, which would extend by two matches, eventually ended on 27 March 1985 when an Ian Rush goal gave Wales a 1-0 win. With two games remaining, Scotland now only needed one point to be sure of qualifying for Spain. The first chance to get that point would be the following month in Belfast.

2

A point at Windsor Park: Qualification achieved

'There were guard dogs outside the grounds of our hotel and armed plainclothes officers inside the building.'

Alan Rough

IN SEPTEMBER of 1978, Jock Stein was sat in his office at Elland Road, preparing his Leeds United side for a league match against Birmingham City, when the news came through that Ally MacLeod had resigned as Scotland manager to take over at Ayr United. Quickly, the press put Stein as the front runner in a field that numbered Leicester City's Jock Wallace, Eddie Turnbull of Hibernian, and former Netherlands boss Austrian Ernst Happel. The *Evening Times* ranked SFA director of coaching Andy Roxburgh as a 10/1 shot. They also rated Clyde's Craig Brown and Aberdeen's Alex Ferguson as possible candidates.

Stein had been in charge of Scotland previously, when in May 1965 he took over from Ian McColl, initially for two games. Celtic had permitted Stein to take over the role in conjunction with his job at Parkhead so long as Scotland were in contention for the 1966 World Cup in England. A 3-0 defeat to Italy in Naples in December of 1965 put paid to their chances of qualifying and Stein stepped down. With all his success at Celtic, including ten league titles and the 1967 European Cup, Stein was now deemed the ideal candidate by the press and punters alike. However, only the previous month he had taken over as Leeds manager. 'We've got the best in the business – the biggest name in British football,' Leeds chairman Manny Cussins told the press as Stein was appointed.

After the debacle that was the 1978 Argentina World Cup, the SFA international selection committee voted in early July on a motion to dismiss MacLeod. There was one vote, and MacLeod was allowed to stay on. His first match after the World Cup in September 1978 resulted in a defeat to Austria in the European Championship. The loss seemed to signal the end of MacLeod's reign as national team manager. When the Ayr job became vacant only a few days later, MacLeod embraced the opportunity to return to the club where he began his managerial career in 1966 and the town where he had been named Citizen of the Year in 1973. 'This gives me the chance to re-establish myself as a top manager,' MacLeod told the *Daily Express*. 'I still believe I am the best. I don't regret having been manager of Scotland. The history books will tell what I have done. The epitaph could be "He took Scotland to the World Cup".' MacLeod was the second national boss in a row to quit for a club job. His predecessor Willie Ormond departed in April 1977 to join Hearts.

In Archie Macpherson's book *Adventures in the Golden Age*, he recalls MacLeod's resignation precipitating a phone call from Macpherson's journalist colleague Jim Rodger. Macpherson was asked to give Jock Stein, apparently happy in his new job, a call.

'But as soon as he answered the phone to me, I could tell I would be speaking to an unhappy man,' Macpherson wrote. Stein knew Macpherson was going on air across the United Kingdom that night. 'Tell London that you can say something about the Scotland job and me,' Stein told him. 'You could say something to the effect that you believe I would be interested in going back to Scotland.' Macpherson went on BBC's *Sportsnight* that evening. Ahead of their highlights of Liverpool versus Nottingham Forest in the European Cup, Macpherson reported, 'The SFA only need to lift their phone to Jock Stein in Leeds and they will have their new manager.' Asked the truth of this by a reporter, Stein dismissed the statement with, 'Archie Macpherson is just flying a kite.'

Cussins was desperate to hold on to Stein. 'I am certain he will not leave Leeds,' he said. 'If a player is worth £100,000, Jock Stein must be worth £4m.' What gave the SFA hope was that Stein, still living in a city centre hotel, was working at Leeds without a contract. There was one on the table to be signed, although Stein hadn't yet added his signature. Cussins was quite prepared to offer him better terms if required. Stein was on a salary of £30,000 a year, twice what the SFA paid MacLeod.

Stein played the speculation down when speaking with Rodger Baillie of the *Sunday Mirror*. 'It would be a big thing to change again,' he said. 'I've started to settle in, and I'm looking forward to the challenge. How can I talk just now about a job I have not even been offered?' In early October, the international selection committee convened and unanimously decided that Stein was the only choice to become Scotland's new manager. The Leeds board met and reluctantly agreed to allow Stein to speak with the SFA. 'I am heartbroken,' Cussins said. 'It is not a question of money. I have made desperate attempts today to persuade him to stay.' Stein's wife Jean wasn't keen on leaving Glasgow for Leeds, and the opportunity to come back to Scotland was the ideal solution to her predicament.

'Nothing in my lifetime has worried me more than this,' Cussins said, 'not even the Brian Clough affair.' Clough's time in charge at Leeds was a turbulent period for the club, and his reign ended after only 44 days – coincidentally the exact number of days Stein was boss at Elland Road. 'The fact that this has happened after 44 days is just one of those things,' Stein said on 4 October as he left Leeds to take up the Scotland position. 'The board have done everything possible for me, and it has been a pleasure to be among them. They wanted me to stay, and I'm sure we would have been successful. I feel I have let people down, so I am leaving Leeds immediately.' Stein was handed a four-year contract, which he would sign, estimated to be worth around £25,000 a year.

'To a man everyone was delighted when he got the job,' Graeme Souness said in 2010. 'Certainly in the playing sense. Because he was the most successful Scottish manager ever, and everyone respected him. I think we were all a wee bit frightened of him as well. Some more than others. But I think he was a fantastic choice at that time.'

At his unveiling press conference, Stein said, 'We have been our own worst enemies in the past. We have to get our feet firmly on the ground and work hard. What has happened in the past must remain in the past. We now have to work together for a good future for the game.'

'The first thing he wanted to do was hose down all the expectations,' Archie Macpherson said to STV's *The Football Years*, 'to try to be more modern, more tactical, because Ally was tactically naive. He was just hopeless in terms of reading the opposition, which Stein was brilliant at. And as a consequence, he adopted an entirely new approach.'

Stein was born in 1922 in the Lanarkshire mining village of Burnbank. At 16, he followed his father George, also a son of a miner, down the pit. He started his football career at Blantyre Victoria and, at 19, joined Albion Rovers. As a coal miner, Stein was exempt from military service, and during the disrupted football of the war years he played for Rovers from November 1942 until May 1950. He made one appearance for Dundee United in April of 1943 on a temporary transfer. He turned professional when he moved to Wales to play in the Southern League with Llanelli. The switch ended 11 years of working down the mine, an experience that profoundly affected him. 'When I left,' he said to Hugh McIlvanney, 'I knew that wherever I went, whatever work I did, I'd never be alongside better men. It was a place where phoneys and cheats couldn't survive for long.'

After 18 months in South Wales, in December 1951, Stein got the opportunity to come back north. Celtic were on the lookout for an experienced central defender. They paid the Welsh club £1,200, and 12 months after signing, Stein became captain, leading Celtic to a Coronation Cup win and a league and cup double in 1954. An ankle injury, which had lingering effects in later life, ended his playing career in 1957. Stein began his coaching career at Celtic Park under manager Jimmy McGrory. The move into management came three years later when Dunfermline Athletic came calling. In his first season in charge, Stein kept the Fifers in the First Division. Then, in his second season, he made his mark. His Dunfermline side won the Scottish Cup, defeating Celtic 2-0 in a replay. By March 1964 he had moved on to Hibs, taking them to a Summer Cup win over Aberdeen.

Ten months later, Jock was back at Celtic. With the club having endured a long period without success, Stein was seen as the man to turn their fortunes around. He did so in spectacular style. Within six weeks, Celtic lifted their first senior trophy in eight years. Against Dunfermline, now managed by Willie Cunningham, Celtic went behind twice, but a goal from captain Billy McNeill with nine minutes left won the Scottish Cup. It would be the first of eight Stein would win in charge of the Celts, along with six League Cups. The league title was achieved ten times, nine in succession. Stein's crowning glory, though, was the 1967 European Cup, won in the sun of Lisbon as Celtic defeated Internazionale 2-1. In December 1970, Stein was awarded a CBE for his services to Scottish football. He stood down as Celtic boss at the end of May 1978. Shortly after his testimonial match against Liverpool in August of that year, he accepted the position with Leeds United.

In addition to losing Danny McGrain with a fractured knee, ending a run of 16 straight appearances for Scotland, the pool for the Northern Ireland clash suffered four call-offs in the weekend before the game. Joe Jordan, David Narey, Davie Provan and Rangers' Davie Cooper dropped out. A late replacement was Andy Gray. Before the party flew to Belfast, Stein spoke with him about his comments on the penalty award against Sweden. 'Perhaps that's why Andy wasn't in the travelling party from the start,' Stein told Malcolm Brodie of the *Belfast Telegraph*. 'I was very annoyed, and this is the first chance I've had to speak to him. It was a silly thing to say and I must admit I take a dim view of it. This was a show of bravado on Andy Gray's part. He isn't clever enough to con a referee, but it seems he wanted people to believe that he could.'

'That was Jock to a T,' Gray said in his book. 'I'd won him a penalty, helped the team to victory and he was dropping me for talking about it in a way he didn't approve of.'

Alex McLeish was then ruled out after failing a fitness test at Ibrox before the flight. 'It just wasn't on. We couldn't take a chance,' Stein said. 'He was honest and said that perhaps he had been too optimistic. He was most unhappy and I feel sorry for him, but I also feel he made the right decision by going home. There are other players who wouldn't have done that. But they are the ones who do not seem really interested in playing for Scotland.' Stein's squad was now down to only 16 players, although Alan Hansen would be an able deputy in defence. Northern Ireland had trouble of their own, with Bolton's Gerry McElhinney breaking his foot. Manchester United's Tommy Sloan came in for him. Brighton's Sammy Nelson and Derek Spence of Southend United also withdrew.

Stein felt Scotland would play with a positive attitude, looking for a win rather than the point that would secure qualification. Reminded that the Irish defeated Scotland in Belfast in 1980, Stein was confident that his side had become stronger, while the Irish team was probably weaker than the one that secured that 1-0 victory.

* * *

Stein was looking for composure and for the players to use their experience. 'Everyone knows what is at stake,' Stein said. 'I've spoken to the lads about how far we have come and they realise this is the big step – the game which can take the pressure from them.' Northern Ireland's Martin O'Neill called the match, 'The big one. Do or die.'

The Scottish team stayed in a hotel in Dunadry, a small village and townland three miles from Antrim in County Antrim. 'There were guard dogs outside the grounds of our hotel and armed plainclothes officers inside the building,' Alan Rough recalled in his autobiography *Rough at the Top*. Dalglish remembered similarly, writing in his 1982 book *King Kenny*, 'It wasn't the best of trips for us because of the troubles in that city. I suppose you always go there thinking that a team could become a target for terrorists, and being surrounded by security men even when you are sitting down to meals in your heavily guarded hotel doesn't put you in the mood for a game.'

Scotland lined up as: Alan Rough (Partick Thistle), Ray Stewart (West Ham United), Alan Hansen (Liverpool), Willie Miller (Aberdeen), Frank Gray (Leeds United), Gordon Strachan (Aberdeen), Graeme Souness (Liverpool), Asa Hartford (captain, Manchester City), Kenny Dalglish (Liverpool), Steve Archibald (Tottenham Hotspur), John Robertson (Nottingham Forest).

Martin O'Neill barged into Strachan in the centre circle with only five minutes gone. As the Aberdeen man looked in vain for a free kick, O'Neill made a charge down Scotland's right flank, shrugging Miller aside. Hansen blocked as he got his shot off, sending the ball out for a corner. Frantic defending by the Irish made it difficult for Scotland to create a clean chance. Archibald snapped at a shot that went high over the bar before Noel Brotherston weaved through the defence and fired inches wide of Rough's left-hand post. Souness put two shots from distance clean over the bar as the Scots struggled to find good shooting positions. Hartford and Strachan spent more time stemming O'Neill and David McCreery's build-ups than working openings for the Scottish attack. Robertson carved out some space down the left, sliding a neat ball into Archibald, whose shot curled up and over. Rough made a great interception as he pushed the ball away from Gerry Armstrong as the Watford striker attempted to get on to the end of the loose ball after Hamilton's strike had been blocked.

A typical Dalglish move created Scotland's best chance of the first half. With his back to goal, he took a ball from Robertson into his feet, turned to put distance between him and Chris Nicholl, then fired the ball into the six-yard box, where it evaded Archibald by inches. At the opposite end, with two minutes of the half remaining, the ball bobbled around the Scots penalty area, being hoofed and headed into the air, before it dropped for Sammy McIlroy to snap a shot which whizzed past the post.

In the second half, Northern Ireland made their first chance with an up-and-under high ball into the box, being met by the head of Armstrong, who nodded it into Rough's arms. O'Neill turned Souness just outside the box, down the right-hand side. His shot had enough power but Rough made the save look easy as he gathered with both hands. Scotland had a great chance when Mal Donaghy was too casual on the ball at the edge of his own box. Strachan muscled the ball off him, playing it into Archibald. The Spurs man lifted the ball with the outside of his right boot from 20 yards, but Pat Jennings watched as it sailed over the crossbar.

Although the crowd of 22,248 wasn't a sell-out, TV pictures captured one fan watching the game while standing on the enclosure roof. Hamilton and Armstrong then worked a chance between them at the edge of the box on Scotland's right. Armstrong knocked the ball to Hamilton then shielded the defenders as Hamilton fired a cross in for Nicholl to meet it with his head. The Southampton defender didn't make the desired connection, and the ball went harmlessly wide. Scotland were living on their nerves with 13 minutes left when a corner came in that was chested down by O'Neill, who fired in a shot from 12 yards. Rough got down well to block, but with the keeper grounded, Armstrong shot the rebound past him only to see Hartford kick the ball off the goal line.

As soon as the ball went dead, Andy Gray came on for Strachan. Stein recognised that Scotland needed to change the sequence of play Northern Ireland had been forcing on them. A few moments later, an overhead kick by Hamilton went wide as Northern Ireland pushed for the winner. Their next chance came in an unusual manner as Gray picked up the ball 25 yards into his own half. As Mal Donaghy pressured him, he was forced to turn back towards his own goal, where he promptly collided with referee Valeri Butenko of the USSR, falling to the ground. Donaghy latched on to the loose ball and rattled a shot off that Rough pushed away, gratefully receiving Hansen's back pass as the ball ran free.

Perhaps the best chance of breaking the deadlock came as all the Scots in the ground were looking to the official to sound his whistle. A long ball upfield by Jennings was nodded on by Armstrong to McIlroy. Racing to the byline, the Manchester United midfielder fired over a dangerous cross. Hamilton got in front of Hansen at the near post and his header was plucked out of the air by Rough, gathering the ball as it threatened to leave his grasp and fall into Nicholl's path. Then, as Rough composed himself, the referee blew the final whistle. Scotland had done it. They had qualified for their third World Cup finals in a row. 'When I hit the ground, I just looked up in time to see the referee signal the end of the game,' Rough said later. 'The importance of that save dawned on me shortly afterwards.' Jock Stein threw his arms in the air and allowed a big grin to cross his face. Irish captain Martin O'Neill sought him out and hugged him warmly. The performance was as required. Hartford, Strachan and Souness were all solid in the middle of the park.

Hansen dealt well with whatever the Irish threw at him; 'simply magnificent' was how Jim Reynolds described his display in the *Glasgow Herald*. In goal, Rough was in command when called upon. On the *Herald*'s front page, Allan Laing declared Rough the night's hero. In the *Evening Times,* Hugh Taylor went further, hailing Rough as 'a world master of the goalkeeping art'. Archie Macpherson wrote years later that the match was Rough's finest hour, 'It was an act of almost singular defiance as the Scottish defence was punctured so often that Scotland's goalkeeper ought to have been chaired from the ground for pulling out an amazing repertoire of saves.'

The Scottish players went over to take the acclaim of the 2,000 fans by now belting out 'Viva España'. 'No goalless draw could ever have been celebrated so enthusiastically,' said John Wark on the bench that night. The Irish supporters were also in voice singing 'You'll Never Walk Alone' and 'Ireland, Ireland'. At that point, the home fans in the ground and the players trooping off the pitch thought their chances of qualifying had gone. But later they heard the news that Sweden defeated Portugal 2-1 in Lisbon, meaning that Northern Ireland only had to beat Israel at home to join Scotland on the plane. Billy Bingham said, 'Scotland ran harder than they have done for a long time, and there really just wasn't much in it. But I am delighted for them.' Although Stein acknowledged luck was with Scotland on the night, he said, 'I am delighted with our team. We have proved to be the best team in Group Six, and the lads have played diligently and professionally. We got through by ourselves. We didn't have to rely on other teams to get us to the finals.'

'It was a windy night and it was Pat Jennings' long kicking which gave us as much trouble as anything else,' Graeme Souness recalled in his autobiography. '[It was] a genuine team performance, a rare professional job that got us exactly what we wanted.' Willie Miller looked back on the match for the *Sunday Mail* in 2007. 'There's a real conflict of emotions in the build-up,' he said. 'It's the game that can take you to your dreams, lift your nation to untold heights and take you to the pinnacle of your career. But there's fear of failure as well ... get the negatives out of your head – find some arrogance and concentrate on the positives. We didn't play well that night but got the job done and had Roughie to thank for that save.'

With World Cup qualification assured, there began the business of ringing some money from it. Less than a week later, SFA secretary Ernie Walker announced the official commercial drive. 'This is the third time we have been associated with the commercial side of the World Cup,' he said, 'and we have learned a few lessons. It was a fiasco in 1974, more beneficial in 1978, but this time we have taken a different tack and sold the rights to a company in return for a set fee in royalties. The emblems will be displayed on various items in time for the Christmas rush but today's announcement is unlikely to be the end.'

A mascot called Sandy – a tartan bunnet-wearing fan – and an emblem were expected to raise between £100,000 and £200,000 from their use on clothing, mugs, tea towels and other such items. Stein commented, 'Until last Wednesday we had only one aim, to qualify, but now we can look forward to the commercial aspects. The players and myself hope to appoint an agent soon and a committee from within our squad.' Bonus money had been a big problem within the squad after qualification for the 1978 finals. The mishandling of the situation led to it becoming a massive distraction when the players should have been focusing on the opening match with Peru. The SFA didn't reveal what the bonus payments would be until the players pressured them into doing so days before the tournament in Argentina began. 'We hadn't been told what incentives and bonuses we were on for the games,' 1978 captain Bruce Rioch told the *Herald* in 2018. 'There were some very unhappy players. We got to Argentina and four or five days before the game the question was raised.' Before they set off for the tournament, the players were told if they did the business they'd be well rewarded, although nothing was put down on paper. This seemed to be enough until the squad arrived in Argentina.

Mike Wilson's 1998 book *Don't Cry For Me Argentina* does an excellent job of analysing what went wrong. 'I can't remember anyone, at any time before we left, asking what the bonuses were,' Ally MacLeod told Wilson. There was a players' committee to make representations on behalf of the players. Sandy Jardine was part of the group, 'It should have been sorted out long before we left for Argentina; we should have had everything out in the open when we were in Scotland, had our debate there.' Rioch was dispatched to speak to Ernie Walker to discover the bonuses. 'The players made their point,' said Jardine. 'The bonus being offered showed disrespect; it was a slight.' Some players were irritated that the bonuses weren't big enough.

In contrast, others, happy to be with Scotland at a World Cup, couldn't have cared less about monetary compensation and were annoyed by their colleagues throwing a strop. The whole situation sewed division into the heart of the squad. It was only exacerbated once the press got hold of the story. 'I have to concede we were probably a bit naive about the bonuses,' Walker told Wilson. 'We were naive about a lot of things, I suppose. It was the first time many of us had been involved in a World Cup. We lived, and we learned.' Walker and the SFA made sure that the monetary aspect of the 1982 World Cup finals participation would be fixed in conjunction with the manager and the player committee before travelling to the tournament.

Stein found his committee from within the squad: senior players McGrain, Hartford, Miller and Dalglish. After considering a list of promoters, they appointed ProScot Services of Glasgow to look after the team's commercial affairs. Chief executive Alan McGuinness said, 'We see considerable potential in promoting the Scotland squad to the fans. Between now and next June we will try to get as many potential possibilities covered as we can.' The company, set up in 1976 and run by McGuinness and Alan

Ferguson in their early 30s, also looked after the supermarket Fine Fare. They had been involved with football previously, including the campaign to redevelop Hampden Park, MacKinlay's monthly personality awards, and the 1980 Scottish Cup sponsorship. They were confident that the national sponsorship potential would be massive if England and Northern Ireland also qualified. 'It's difficult to say how much the squad could make,' McGuinness said, 'but it will certainly be a six-figure sum.' Promotions wouldn't be signed without the approval of the players' committee. However, Stein was at pains to ensure that the committee members weren't automatic selections for the team. 'There is no point in my telling youngsters they have a chance of getting into the squad if they work hard, then in the same breath telling four others they are going to Spain if they form a committee to handle the commercial side. That is not on.'

Stein and Walker made a trip to Madrid a week after the game in Belfast. They met members of the tournament organising committee, and viewed hotels and the World Cup centres. They also checked out a pre-tournament headquarters in Portugal's Algarve. Stein was concerned that the players didn't arrive in Spain too early, fearful that boredom and anxiety may set in, 'What we want to do is give them a week in Portugal, if that is possible, at a special training camp. They'll work there privately, away from the build-up of supporters in Spain, away from the atmosphere they will have to face during the matches there.'

Stein was hopeful that Scotland would be placed in the second seeds for the finals draw. The suggestion from FIFA at that time was that the top seeds in the six sections would be hosts Spain, holders Argentina, and winners of the 1974 and 1970 World Cups, West Germany and Brazil. Then two from three – Italy, the Netherlands and Belgium – depending on qualification. 'When we know the countries we are up against I'll be making arrangements to watch them. I won't go in blind to any games,' Stein said.

The mood was now turning towards what might happen in Spain and who might be there to play a part. 'Not one of us can take it for granted that we will be going to Spain,' Asa Hartford told *Shoot!* 'It might look as if we are, it might seem that way when you see that the big man has only used 20 players in the qualifying games ... but we have to earn our places. The way we will have to do it is to keep playing our best right up until summer.'

'Obviously, if I get to Spain it will be the biggest thrill of my career,' Gordon Strachan said, 'and I wouldn't have bet on it happening last season. But I'm not there yet. I have to keep on playing well in the months between now and next summer. We all realise that. But, it's still hard to appreciate that we've qualified. It was so important to every single one of us. To the manager, players, to our whole game. And to our marvellous fans who will travel anywhere to see Scotland in action.'

There was still one game left for Scotland in Group Six and the chance to finish the campaign unbeaten.

* * *

For the final game against Portugal in Lisbon, Stein announced a pool of players he felt was practical. Although the result was essentially meaningless for both sides, he was hesitant to blood three or four new players all at once. Dundee United's Paul Sturrock was included in the squad, while on the reserve list were Aberdeen goalkeeper Jim Leighton and Celtic's Roy Aitken.

Provan and Robertson were both included, and although the aim was to get through the group unbeaten, Stein thought that with decent wide players at his disposal he could take a more adventurous approach. Provan, a Scottish record transfer when he moved as a part-timer from Kilmarnock to Celtic in 1978, was returning from injury. Still, Stein had been to watch him in his comeback against Aberdeen, and the manager rated him as 'outstanding'. 'It may be time to see what Davie Provan can do for us in a match abroad,' Stein said. 'When I have chosen him in the past, it has been matches in this country, and he has enjoyed the backing of big crowds.' Danny McGrain was still absent, the Celtic captain only just getting back to training after his injury. Alex McLeish pulled out of the squad due to an ankle knock. 'I'm only too well aware of how fierce the competition is for central defenders, and being out of the squad for too long makes you conscious of the others breathing down your neck,' McLeish said to Jim Reynolds.

In the week before the Portugal game, Paul Sturrock scored two goals in the Dundee derby as United won 3-1, and Stein was happy to announce that he would be starting in Lisbon, explaining, 'He can't be kept out on that form.'

The Scotland team flew to Estoril, on the Portuguese Riviera, around 25km from Lisbon. They would stay in the Palacio Hotel, the same accommodation that Celtic used when they lifted the European Cup in Lisbon in 1967. Stein looked at the game as the beginning of his build-up to the finals. 'This is a great chance for us to start perfecting a technique which will be a priority in the finals. We want players who want to make passes and take passes. The big thump is out.' He was keen to insist the players weren't there for a holiday, despite the 70°F temperature and views across the beach to the Atlantic.

Going against his tradition, Stein was happy to announce on the eve of the game that Miller and Hansen would be the defensive partnership. Miller had already picked up one caution during the qualifiers. Another booking in this match would see him suspended for the opening fixture of the finals. Robertson, too, was one booking away from a suspension. While Miller would find a starting place, Stein felt the match might be 'too niggly' for the Nottingham Forest winger, so he handed him a seat on the bench. 'We can afford to be adventurous,' Stein said, 'and it is the adventurous sides who will do well in Spain.'

Of the other games taking place the same night, it wasn't only Northern Ireland who needed something. England and Wales were also looking for results to take them to the finals. England and Northern Ireland only required to draw with Hungary and Israel, respectively, while Wales were required to beat USSR in Tbilisi.

The team was announced with, as usual, Alan Rough in goal. But there was to be a change before kick-off. Only hours before the match, Rough tripped and went over on his ankle on the marble stairs of the hotel. Stein asked for assurances that he was OK to play, but when Rough couldn't give his boss a confident response, Stein opted to put him on the bench and hand Billy Thomson his fourth cap. Ray Stewart would win his fifth, while Asa Hartford would be captain on his 45th appearance. Strachan was encouraged to run at the Portuguese defence. Provan, wearing number six, was told by Stein that he needed to do much better than the 'dismal' performance he'd put in at Wembley.

The match was played at Benfica's Estádio da Luz. Although it wasn't the national team's regular venue, Portugal had played all their qualifiers for the 1982 World Cup at the ground. Opened in 1954, Scotland were the first national team to visit when they played Portugal in a Euro 1972 qualifier in April 1971. This game, which kicked off at 9.30pm, would be only the 12th national match staged there.

Scotland began the contest well; in the second minute, Hansen played in Souness, who lobbed goalkeeper Bento only to see the offside flag raised as the ball nestled in the back of the net. Seven minutes later, Scotland netted a goal that did stand. Ray Stewart put a high ball into Portugal's penalty area. The defence activated their offside trap, but didn't count on a perfectly timed run by Sturrock, who brought the ball under control, then took it around the Benfica goalkeeper before walking it into the net.

Portugal almost got level in the 19th minute when Oliveira put Jaime clear, but the 19-year-old debutant fired the ball wide. Then, on 24 minutes, Souness put in a cross that Hartford knocked on, but Archibald sent his header inches past the post. After that, Portugal began to get hold of the game, and Billy Thomson had to be at his best when saving from Costa on 29 minutes.

The equaliser came four minutes later. Thomson dived to his left to push away a shot from Romeu, but Sporting's Fernandes followed up with his fifth goal for his country.

Five minutes from the interval, Frank Gray was forced off with an injured shoulder. Aberdeen's Stuart Kennedy came on for his first Scotland appearance in almost three years – his last had also been away to Portugal. He went to right-back while Stewart switched to the left.

On 57 minutes, Fernandes had his second of the night. He evaded first Hansen and then Miller before shooting past Thomson from the edge of the box. Dalglish came on for Archibald on 65 minutes, making an impact with two shots on goal. There was no equaliser though, and the final whistle sounded on Scotland's first defeat in Group Six.

Stein pointed the finger of blame for the goals at Thomson, 'I feel Billy could have got both of them.' But, conversely, Jim Reynolds wrote in the *Glasgow Herald*, 'The big St Mirren man was blameless on both occasions – the causes must go down to slack defensive work.'

Stein wasn't happy with his charges. 'The team seemed to lose the place,' he said. 'Perhaps they thought it was too easy and became too arrogant. That game showed us that what was good enough to qualify may not be good enough for the finals next summer. That will be a higher level again and we now have some idea how far we have to go.'

Gerry Armstrong netted the only goal in Northern Ireland's match with Israel, sending them through as group runners-up. Paul Mariner gave England a 1-0 win at Wembley against Hungary, putting them into the World Cup finals for the first time since 1970. Wales lost 3-0 to the USSR. With Czechoslovakia still to play the Russians at the end of November, Wales hoped a Russian win would see them go through in second place. However, a draw in Bratislava was enough to take the Czechs through on goal difference.

Scotland's finals preparations included two challenge matches, Spain in Valencia in February and at home to the Netherlands in March, and the Home Internationals in April and May. However, the players who achieved qualification weren't necessarily the 22 Stein would be taking to the finals, and he would use the forthcoming games to try some new combinations.

Dundee United and Aberdeen were both in the last 16 of the UEFA Cup in November and December. A home 3-2 win for the Dons over SV Hamburg was followed by a 3-1 defeat in West Germany to end their campaign. Sturrock and Narey were part of the Dundee United team who defeated Belgium's FC Winterslag 5-0 on aggregate to seal European football for the spring of 1982. Steve Archibald's Tottenham made the quarter-finals of the European Cup Winners' Cup by defeating Ireland's Dundalk 2-1 over two legs. In the European Cup, Celtic had lost in the first round to Juventus, but there was Scottish interest in the competition in the shape of Liverpool and Aston Villa's Anglos. Liverpool knocked out AZ 67 of Holland 5-4 on aggregate, with Alan Hansen scoring the decisive goal. Villa went through on away goals against Dynamo Berlin.

Dundee United had been managed since December 1971 by Jim McLean, who Stein had appointed as his assistant, a position McLean viewed as a tremendous honour. 'Working with Jock Stein and his players has proved to be really beneficial for me,' McLean told Alan Davidson in the *Evening Times*. 'It has given me more confidence. It has done more for me as a manager than I've done for Scotland. Jock Stein has done it all on his own. He has made all the decisions. Sometimes I might not have agreed with them all, but he's been proved right almost every time – the proof is in the fact that Scotland qualified by winning the group. I know he respects the fact that I'm not just with the squad to agree with him. He will listen to me and consider my views – but at the end of the day it's down to him and he makes the decision.'

In December, Hansen, Souness and Dalglish travelled to Japan to play for Liverpool in the Intercontinental Cup. They met South American champions Flamengo in the Olympic Stadium, Tokyo. The Brazilian side was full of internationals, including Leandro, Júnior and Zico. Liverpool, as European champions, went into the game as favourites. But it was Zico who made the difference, setting up three unanswered goals, for Nunes, who scored twice, and Adílio. Liverpool's manager Bob Paisley fumed at his side, calling them 'dead, physically and mentally'.

Dalglish wrote about the encounter in his book *King Kenny*, published before the 1982 World Cup finals. 'Naturally, I was impressed by Zico. You have to be impressed by someone who has a hand in all three of the goals scored against you. He is a phenomenal player, and he'll show that in the World Cup in Spain. They played with flair, but we let them play that way. We gave them too much respect. When you go in against the South Americans, you must respect them, but you must never be in awe of them. If you let them dictate the pace of the game, you can be in a lot of trouble, as we found out to our cost.'

It may have been wise for the national team to pay attention to Dalglish's words.

3

A Fiasco in Madrid:
The group stage is drawn

*'They've mixed it up. Would you believe
the World Cup has started with a
fundamental error?'*

Archie Macpherson

FRANCE FOOTBALL, the magazine which awards the
Ballon d'Or, released its European nation standings in early
January 1982. Scotland were ranked fifth, with reigning
European champions West Germany top. USSR and
Yugoslavia were joint second, while England were down
in 15th. Another French magazine, *Onze Mundial*, which
presented an alternative European footballer of the year
award, Onze d'Or, listed its European 11. Kenny Dalglish
was the only British player selected. In Spain, *Don Balon*
rated its top ten footballers in the world. John Wark placed
in third, behind Zico and Karl-Heinz Rummenigge, ahead
of Boca Juniors' Diego Maradona and Dinamo Tbilisi's

Ramaz Shengelia. Wark's 14 goals in the 1980/81 UEFA Cup, equalling an 18-year-old European record, was the catalyst for his placing.

With just over a week to go until the World Cup draw, João Havelange, the president of FIFA, announced that they had settled on the seedings. Scotland would be in the third pot, not the second as widely expected. In Paris, to attend the draw for the 1984 European Championship qualifiers, Havelange suggested that the seeding for second and third places would be made on a political basis resulting in the Soviet countries taking second seeding with western European and South American nations ranked third. Top seeds would be the hosts Spain, the holders Argentina, and the previous winners Italy, West Germany, England and Brazil. The second seeds would be Czechoslovakia, Yugoslavia, Russia, Hungary, Poland and Austria. The third pot would be Scotland, Northern Ireland, France, Belgium, Peru and Chile. Band four would contain Algeria, Cameroon, Honduras, El Salvador, Kuwait and the team who would be the 24th and final qualifier, the winner of the play-off between China and New Zealand. The seedings seemed to be done on a basis to suit FIFA with no solid rationale. 'It's a draw of convenience,' Jock Stein said.

There was confusion when news of the seedings reached FIFA's Zurich headquarters. Acting secretary Sepp Blatter said, 'I don't believe this can be true. I was with Mr Havelange the other day and this is not what he said. There are many things to be considered. The British teams do not wish to be together. It's the same with the South Americans. All of these things have to be counted.' There had even been reports that the entire draw had already been completed. Stein had been told that Scotland would be in a group with Italy, Czechoslovakia and Honduras. Stein used this to illustrate the disadvantage he found in Scotland being third, not second seeds; they would not play the top seeds first. 'If that, in fact, is the case, then Italy will meet the Czechs in the opening match, and we will play Honduras. I have always believed that the rabbits in the World Cup have one good game in them, and it's usually the first one – that's why I would have preferred meeting the top seeds first.' Stein, though, was comfortable with the seeding largely. 'The only thing that is certain is that nobody will win any points because of the way they come out of the hat in Madrid next Saturday. The only way you can win points is on the field.'

Belgium were not so content. They lodged a protest, seconded by France, contending that they should not have been seeded below England. As well as avoiding taking on hosts, holders, and other top sides, the first seeds would additionally have the advantage of playing all three of their games in the same venue. England, befitting that 15th spot in *France Football*'s list, had won only two of their nine internationals in 1981. Belgium had won their qualifying group, while the English finished second behind Hungary. The Belgians were also runners-up to West Germany in the 1980 European Championship. Therefore, there was no legitimate footballing reason that should place England within the top seeds. West Germany expressed sympathy but said they would not criticise the organising committee. Harry Cavan, a senior vice-president of the International Football Federation and president of the Northern Ireland FA, commented to *The Guardian*, 'I know pressure has been brought to bear on the Spanish – not by the English FA – to base England in Bilbao where it will be easier to look after their fans.' Cavan cited precedent, when in

1978, Argentina requested that Italy be placed in their group due to the number of Italians who resided in Buenos Aires. Cavan stressed that the rules allowed the committee to make a draw based not only on football form but also geographical location and commercial considerations. 'The whole tournament has got to pay for itself so commercial reasons will play their part in our thinking,' he said. He insisted that the only certainty was that Spain would be in Valencia and Argentina based in Alicante.

The organising committee convened in Madrid, while the European nations met on the eve of the draw to hear Belgium's concerns. The protests were eventually thrown out. 'England won the World Cup in 1966,' Havelange said, 'and is a country with a great soccer tradition.' FIFA were unhappy that leaks had emanated, allegedly from the Spanish organisers. 'Information has been given to the media by the organisers and they should not have done so,' Cavan said. 'It is wrong that there should have been so much conjecture before the draw. What was discussed then was to have been treated with the strictest confidence. I blame the Spaniards for all the talk since.' Havelange attempted to clarify what was going on but only confirmed most people's suspicions when he said, 'The groupings will not be manipulated. They will be directed.' Cavan said something similar. He also insisted that nothing would be settled until just before the draw took place. Asa Hartford aired his grievances to the *Daily Record*, 'The FIFA seeding system is nonsense. There's only one reason why countries such as Yugoslavia, Poland and Hungary are kept apart while France, Belgium and ourselves have to take our chances – cash comes first.'

The last team to qualify were New Zealand, beating China 2-1 in a Singapore play-off just days before the draw.

The Kiwis played 15 qualifying matches, beginning in April of 1981 with a 3-3 draw with Australia in Auckland. Their vice-president, Charlie Dempsey, was a Glaswegian who had left for Auckland in his early 30s, establishing a joinery business that would make him a millionaire. 'What we've achieved is nothing short of a miracle,' he told the *Daily Record*. 'Our entire World Cup campaign has been run on a shoestring budget. Actually, at one point, I didn't think we would have enough money to pay the players' win bonus if we qualified. From here on in every game is a bonus. Getting Scotland would be a dream for me and a few of the boys. But really just being in Spain lets people know that we play football in New Zealand. Not bad for a country of eight million sheep and only three million people.'

Jock Stein, Ernie Walker and SFA president Willie Harkness were in Madrid for the draw at the National Congress and Exhibition Hall on Saturday, 16 January. A security cordon was set up in the hall with armed guards. Over 2,500 people would be in the venue, with 500 million in 50 countries watching live on television. Both BBC and ITV made room in their teatime schedules, squeezing in the live broadcast after *Bugs Bunny Mystery Special* and *Game for a Laugh*. The *Daily Record*'s Alex Cameron was also on the ground, and he didn't much like what he was hearing. 'Brazil by the way are convinced that Scotland will be in the same section as them in Seville and Malaga,' he wrote. 'I was even asked by Brazil's leading sportswriter Janos Lengyel to act as their mole and supply the information on the Scots players you wouldn't find in the papers. I made my excuses and left. Madrid is buzzing with rumours. There are so many *official* leaks being handed out that the FIFA headquarters would sink without trace if it were a ship.' The rumours flying around incensed Blatter. 'Some of the speculation has been utterly absurd,' he said. 'How can you stage a draw before millions and determine it beforehand? It is nonsense.' The 13-year-old Prince of Asturias, Felipe de Borbon, would preside over the draw.

The organising committee met in the centre on the morning of 16 January to discuss the top six seedings, the arrangements for South American countries avoiding each other, the Eastern Bloc countries, and the British sides need to be kept apart.

The draw itself was nothing less than shambolic.

The centrepiece was the revolving drums, which were in operation each week to select the Spanish National Lottery numbers. Within the drums were miniature footballs, inside each of which would be a slip of paper containing the name of one of the teams. The task of plucking the balls from their cages fell to a team of small children, later revealed to have been orphans from a local orphanage. They would hand them up to the officials, who would unscrew the ball, then allocate a number to the name inside.

The draw began with the top seeds assigned into their groups: Italy to Group One, West Germany to Group Two and so on. Once that was completed, the next name out of the drum was third seed Belgium, who were placed in Group One with Italy. From drum B, another ball, designed in the style of the World Cup football, the Adidas Tango, was taken and passed from one child to another. The second child walked up to the desk where the delegates sat and handed the ball to Hermann Neuberger, the West German Football Association president. The TV camera hung over Neuberger's shoulder as BBC commentator Archie Macpherson looked on expectantly. 'I think I personally would hope that Scotland's name was in that,' he said, 'as they would be drawn down in a very pleasant area of Spain.' Neuberger pulled out the piece of paper for it to reveal a St Andrew's Cross. 'And it's Scotland!' Macpherson said. Neuberger handed the paper to his colleague. 'Well, would you believe it,' Macpherson said, as Sepp Blatter held the small flag up and announced 'Escocia'. Macpherson assuredly told viewers what that meant. Scotland would be included in Group Six with Brazil, where they would be stationed in Malaga and Seville.

The process now was that a number from one to 24 was allocated to the country – that number related to a place within the groups. The teams in Group One were numbered one to four, Group Two five to eight and so on. Blatter pulled out the number which would allocate Scotland's place on the board. Blatter displayed number ten. 'And they're being given number ...' Macpherson said, hesitating as he did so, a question mark entering his brain as he said the words. Scotland's name went up in the number ten position in Group Three with Argentina. The ordinarily unflappable Macpherson, who had changed gears quite elegantly from commentating on a Scottish Cup Final to a raging battle at Hampden in 1980, fell momentarily silent. 'I'm sorry,' he eventually said, 'I beg your pardon, it is a second seed, it is a second seed in Alicante. It is Alicante in fact.' That there was still confusion over what seeding teams had been allocated while the draw was taking place was a testament to FIFA's dedication to making it up as they went along. 'Quite extraordinary,' Macpherson's colleague Barry Davies said, 'they went to great lengths this morning, FIFA, to explain the procedure, and when it's come to the draw, they have not adopted their own plans.'

Davies, sat in an adjacent booth, looked across to Macpherson. He shrugged exaggeratedly, hoping his BBC Scotland colleague could clarify what was happening. Macpherson, similarly baffled, offered him a blank look in return. A Belgian official, seemingly aware that the draw wasn't going according to plan, made his way to the stage to remonstrate with the delegates. Macpherson apologised to the viewers, citing the lateness of information making its way up from the floor. The children carried on the draw as planned while the adults sat at a desk seemed to bicker between themselves. A child walked up to the desk with the next ball, holding it out, only to be ignored. Eventually, Neuberger dismissed him with a waved hand. The child trudged back to the drums to replace the ball. Neuberger was heard to chastise the child as if the pantomime had been the children's fault all along.

It wasn't long before Archie caught the mood of utter bewilderment that manifested the delegates. 'I really do think there's been some confusion down there,' he said, 'because they're going back ... with the ball. They're not too happy about that.' FIFA press officer René Courte took it upon himself to point out the errors made. Blatter then launched into a lengthy announcement, explaining what had gone wrong, not only with Scotland's allocation but also the placing of Belgium in the wrong group. 'Yes, I thought so,' Macpherson said, 'there has been a mistake.'

'Sensation is a much overused word in sport,' said Davies, 'but even, on an occasion like this, it would appear that sensation we have.' It turned out that Belgium had been drawn too early, as had Scotland. It began to fall into place for Macpherson. He had also called Belgium's place in Argentina's group correctly before the confusion attempted to overrule him by placing the Belgians with Italy. 'Scotland should have been in Brazil's section,' he said. 'I mean that was the way it was arranged prior to the draw. That's what they said they were going to do. And they've, they've mixed it up. Would you believe the World Cup has started with a fundamental error?'

In a pre-draw briefing, the organising committee had advised the media that the South American countries would be dealt with first. For this reason, they would initially leave out the names of Peru and Chile. After the groups for the first seeds had been sorted, the first name out of the hat would join Argentina's group, which would be the opening match, then the second team would join Brazil's group. Peru and Chile would then be placed in the drums. The idea was that all the South American sides could be kept apart that way. Placing Belgium in Italy's group blew this plan to smithereens as soon as it had begun. 'I think we're on the edge of a volcano, not just a congress hall,' Macpherson said before speculating that they may have to do a complete redraw. The BBC pictures showed the British players assembled in TV studios watching with bemused expressions. Kevin Keegan represented England, Pat Jennings was the Northern Irish representative, while Liverpool's Souness and Hansen were there watching for Scotland. Belgium's name was removed from Group One and added to Group Three with Argentina, while Scotland were allocated number 23, placing them with Brazil in Group Six.

The rest of the draw did not go smoothly. The drums failed to spin at one point, as well as one of the balls breaking open inside, revealing the name of Austria. Although it had been suggested precautions would be taken to ensure the

British sides stayed apart, it turned out there was no such protection. Both Scotland and Northern Ireland could have been drawn against England. The Scottish party bluntly told Harry Cavan it was his job to safeguard the British sides were kept apart, and he hadn't lived up to his responsibilities. Cavan, 22 years with FIFA, replied that he hadn't asked for assurances as it may have jeopardised England's number one place in Group Four in Bilbao.

When it was all complete, Scotland were in Group Six in Malaga and Seville with Brazil, Russia and New Zealand. It was commonly accepted that it was the most formidable group. 'I said the right things in front of the cameras,' Souness said in his book, 'while secretly wishing we could swap with either Northern Ireland ... or with England ... I didn't enjoy dinner that night and felt very low.' The newspapers had a field day with the chaos. In the *Evening Times*, Hugh Taylor wrote, 'The deplorable comedy of errors merely emphasised the widely held belief that the great World Cup draw had been fixed long before the start.' In the *Sunday Standard*, Ian Archer wrote that the draw was organised in a 'ham-fisted manner'. He continued, 'Never again, I swear, will I pour scorn on the curious way in which the SFA always ensure that Rangers never meet Celtic in cup semi-finals. It was quite inevitable that FIFA would blunder somewhere along the way because the whole day had seen intense political manoeuvring by their aristocratic leaders, with the South Americans emerging as the victors in the pre-draw moves. It was too clever by half and someone remarked that it would take a Paul Daniels to conjure up a draw they wanted. Instead, Tommy Cooper took over proceedings.' Alex Cameron, never a reporter to mince his words, summed it up for the readers of his *Daily Record* column, 'The World Cup draw with elaborate chicanery was carried out by amateurs. It was naive in conception, woefully executed and suspect because of the sheer inefficiency.'

'We couldn't have got a more difficult draw,' was Stein's immediate reaction. 'Brazil and Russia are good enough to make the final itself.' Scotland would begin the tournament against New Zealand. 'I would have preferred to open against Brazil, but some people think it's better to settle in against the weak nation in a section. We'll see.' Privately, Stein said to Macpherson, 'It's a bugger of a draw. I didn't want Brazil. I think I would have preferred the first draw.'

Scotland had played against Brazil five times previously. The first occasion was at Hampden Park in a June 1966 friendly, as the Brazilians tuned up for their World Cup defence in England. A team that included Pelé, Jairzinho and Gérson were held to a 1-1 draw, with Steve Chalmers scoring the Scots' goal. The next meeting was in the Brazilian Independence Cup in Rio in 1972. A crowd of 130,000 saw Brazil, again the reigning World Cup holders, beat a Scotland side, that included Asa Hartford, 1-0. 'Our mistake was to concede a free kick just outside the box,' the goalkeeper that night, Bobby Clark, said. 'Rivellino curled the ball in and Jairzinho's diving header was past me and into the net before I could reach it.' The third time the countries played, it was another 1-0 win for Brazil. A June 1973 friendly at Hampden Park organised for the SFA's centenary saw McGrain, Dalglish and Jordan in the Scotland line-up.

Their most crucial encounter to date was in Frankfurt at the 1974 World Cup finals. In the second match of the group, the teams finished goalless. Scotland had a great chance to go in front when Billy Bremner put the ball just past the post from inside the six-yard box. He spoke to the *Sunday Standard* about the game, 'The trouble about playing the Brazilians is that they're so good and so confident that they're almost one up before the game starts. There's no doubt at all in my mind, looking back on it now, that it's a game we should have won. I guess the best chance of the match fell to me ... but I just couldn't get to the ball to turn it into the empty net. If it had been someone like Denis Law or Joe Jordan ... their reflexes might have converted the chance into a goal, but it bumbled just past the post. I believe we made the fundamental mistake of overestimating the Brazilians that day. Sure, they'd played in every final series, and they've won the World Cup more often than anyone else, but they really weren't a very good side at that time and we missed a marvellous chance to win. And I say that allowing for the fact that this probably wasn't the best Scottish side I played in either.'

The most recent encounter between Scotland and Brazil had come in June 1977. Rough, McGrain, Hartford and Dalglish were in the side when Brazil won 2-0 in the Maracanã with goals by Zico and Toninho Cerezo. Both were expected to be in the Brazil side of 1982. Rough remembered the match, and particularly Zico's goal, well. Zico curled in a free kick while Rough was still shouting instructions to his defensive wall, which contained just about every outfield player. 'I don't know how or why we had all these players in a wall,' he said to Chick Young, 'and I remember I was unsighted. I still don't know who pressed the panic button that night, but the loss of that goal was a disaster.'

The Russians had played Scotland twice, both friendlies. An own goal by Tommy Gemmell and a strike from Fedir

Medvid gave Russia a 2-0 win at Hampden in May 1967. In June of 1971, Scotland travelled to Moscow where they lost by a solitary goal. New Zealand and Scotland had never met in an international match. The unofficial Scotland touring side of 1967 took on the New Zealand under-23 team in Wellington, winning 7-2 with Joe Harper netting a hat-trick. In 1979 the New Zealand national team played several friendly matches in Britain. The touring party, managed by the boss of the 1982 side, John Adshead, followed up a 4-1 loss to the England B team by losing 1-0 to an Ipswich team containing Scotland striker Alan Brazil. After a 5-0 defeat to Norwich, the Kiwis travelled north to Scotland. At Dens Park, the New Zealanders lost 8-1 to Dundee, with Billy Pirie scoring twice on his return after a year out injured. The All Whites team featured Sam Malcolmson, Bobby Almond, Adrian Elrick and Steve Sumner, who were anticipated to be playing against Scotland.

* * *

The Scottish players offered their reactions to the draw. 'Before the draw, we were prepared for the worst – now we must hope for the best,' said Danny McGrain. 'Brazil are worthy favourites to win the cup,' he continued, 'and as for Russia, it would have been better to have one of the other Iron Curtain countries we were more familiar with. We would much rather have been in England's section. We would have qualified from that one.' He told Chick Young in the *Evening Times*, 'My first reaction was one of horror and shock, but having time to think about it the matches can't come soon enough. Too many experienced players in the squad can remember what happened in the Argentine in 1978 and are delighted to have the chance to redeem themselves. They won't be taking anything for granted this time.'

'It is unbelievably tough,' Alex McLeish told the *Sunday Mail*, 'but the thought of playing against these sides really excites me. In 1978 we were odds on to qualify for the next phase, but this time we will be the underdogs and maybe that can work to our advantage.' Graeme Souness expressed regret that the opener was against New Zealand, 'They'll be buzzing that day, really bombing.' Alan Rough agreed, 'I don't know if it's good playing New Zealand in the first match. That's when they will be playing out of their skins.'

'The supporters can help, I think,' suggested Hartford. 'The Russians won't have anyone backing them, while our troops will be there in their thousands. It could be important in that match. I just hope the lads keep off the vino and out of jail because they could really be vital in this one. In a small, tight stadium like the one in Malaga the backing we get will give us a decided advantage.'

'Of course, being drawn with Brazil and Russia is tough,' Alan Rough said to Chick Young, 'but I have no particular fear about playing them. In Scotland, we have guys who can swerve and bend a ball like Rivellino and Zico. Players like Andy Ritchie, Davie Provan and Davie Cooper. There are lots of others too, but they don't have enough courage to step forward and say they can do it. It is a terrible thing about the Scottish nature, but they are scared someone laughs at them. In Spain, we will have our match-winners in the likes of John Robertson and Graeme Souness and it only takes two or three of our team to be right on song and Scotland will beat anybody.'

Bookmakers Coral put Brazil at 5/2 for the World Cup. Ladbrokes had them at 9/4. Scotland's odds were unsurprisingly much longer. They were 25/1 with Ladbrokes and 28/1 with Coral. Brazil were many people's favourites to win the tournament. Their qualifying campaign for a 12th consecutive appearance in the finals was predictably straightforward. They won all four matches in a three-team group with Bolivia and Venezuela. With five goals, their top scorer was Zico, Flamengo's attacking midfielder. West Germany's manager Jupp Derwall spoke to the *Sunday Mail*'s Allan Herron about Scotland's chances against them. 'Jock Stein must make up his own mind on how he is going to tackle them,' he said. 'One thing you cannot do is to mark them man for man. This is impossible as they are too fast. They have so much movement and pass so quickly; you would be destroyed. No matter what is happening in a game there are five or six players moving at the same time.'

Russia, making their first appearance in the finals since 1970, had won an uncompromising European Group Three, which included runners-up Czechoslovakia, Wales, Iceland and Turkey. The Soviets were unbeaten, scoring 20 goals and conceding just two. Russia's team consisted mainly of players from Dynamo Kyiv, Dinamo Tbilisi and Spartak Moscow. They were managed by Konstantin Beskov, the 61-year-old former Dynamo Moscow forward. At the draw, he said, 'If we are here, we are going to compete against all teams. Football is not a neutron bomb.'

New Zealand had the most arduous qualifying route of all; 15 games in eight countries. The first round was a group of five teams where they edged out Australia, scoring 31 goals, including a 13-0 victory over Fiji. The Kiwis moved on to a four-team group alongside Kuwait, China and Saudi Arabia. Kuwait won the group and automatic qualification on nine points, leaving New Zealand and China tied on six points and going into a play-off for the second spot. The neutral ground of Singapore was the setting for New Zealand to win through 2-1, with Steve Wooddin and Wynton Rufer scoring the goals.

Spain would be their first World Cup finals. Captain Steve Sumner and midfielder Bobby Almond wrote a book on their qualifying campaign called *To Spain – The Hard Way*. In it, Sumner looked forward to how his side would play at the finals, 'The last thing I want us to do against these nations is to adopt a tight, defensive role. That would not be attractive for those at home to watch on television. I want to learn more about attacking football, and only by taking the game to these teams can we do so.' Sumner was one of several British-born players in the New Zealand squad. At 16, he was an apprentice at Blackpool, moving to Preston North End and Grimsby before travelling to New Zealand to join Christchurch United in 1973. He made his debut for his adopted country in 1976 and in 1981 moved to Australia to play for Newcastle, signing later for West Adelaide. Allan Boath, Adrian Elrick and Sam Malcolmson were all Scots. Elrick emigrated when he was a child, but Boath and Malcolmson had played in the Scottish leagues. Boath was brought up in the same close in Dundee as future Scotland international Davie Dodds. Both players began with the Celtic Boys Club system in the city, moving on to Dundee United. While Dodds made over 300 appearances for United, scoring 150 goals, Boath joined Forfar Athletic in 1977, playing for the Station Park side 14 times. He emigrated to New Zealand in 1978, signing for Woolston WMC. Malcolmson had spells with Airdrie, Queen of the South and Albion Rovers.

Former Scotland manager Tommy Docherty gave his thoughts on New Zealand, 'Scotland facing them is a bit like a First Division team in England being drawn against a team from the Fourth Division. That's the gulf that lies between them. Basically, they are short of class. Honest players, yes. But few of them ever made it at home. Or would have made it.'

The Russians, it turned out, were already in Malaga. Some reports suggested they had been there at least a week, if not two weeks. They had even found time to play three bounce games against local select teams. The Official FIFA Report of the World Cup, written after the tournament's conclusion, also suggests that the Russians knew in advance where they would be based. In the section headed 'Factors Influencing Performance', the report writes, 'The USSR team were well prepared for the venues of the first final round which had been known to them for a long time.' Furthermore, Hugh Taylor wrote that when he arrived in the city, the boss of the local hotel association told him he had known for weeks that Scotland would be based there.

Stein and the rest of the Scotland party flew out to Malaga the following morning. 'I am happy with the venue,' he said. 'We had hoped to get La Coruña but Malaga was always our second choice. You expect it hard in the World Cup and we got it that way but I've no real complaints.' Quickly Stein and Ernie Walker had found accommodation with the Parador del Golf, just outside of Malaga, where the SFA would book out all 40 rooms. However, it didn't take long for some questions to be raised, and Stein was quick to deflect criticism. 'Critics have said: too near to the airport, mosquito-ridden, next to an army firing range,' Stein told the *Sunday Standard*. 'If you wanted a place where the lads could pop out for a drink or for the dancing and we could have a good time, then I've picked an absolute duffer. But if you want a hotel to prepare people for football, then it's an absolute cracker. If players can't sacrifice eight days of their lives to play for their country in the World Cup, then there's something wrong somewhere.'

New Zealand, too, had found a place to stay. Charlie Dempsey said, 'I ... didn't know that we had to make our own hotel arrangements. I honestly thought accommodation and everything was taken care of for us. Anyway, we're booked into a hotel, but I've forgotten the name of the place. It's about 40 minutes from the stadium in Malaga.' New Zealand's players were mainly amateurs, and their football organisation didn't have the resources to prepare as fully as they would have liked for the tournament. The NZ$50,000 required for the trip to Singapore for the play-off was funded by a public appeal. They had no warm-up matches planned, bar a game in February pencilled in against Hungary, so they issued a request for any British club teams willing to play against them. There was also no money for fact-finding scouting trips of the opposition. 'Everyone knows Kenny Dalglish,' Dempsey said to the *Glasgow Herald*, 'but Scotland and the rest don't know us.'

By Monday morning, travel agents across Scotland reported breathtaking sales of holiday packages to Malaga and Seville. The sales of all match tickets involving the British countries had been awarded to Sportsworld, a company based in London. Sportsworld was launched in 1980 by Hamish Ogston and Geoffrey Phillips. The 1982 World Cup was its first foray into providing travel for a major football event. Tickets would have to be bought through Sportsworld in a package which included travel and accommodation. But, ever resourceful, many Scotland fans were choosing to bypass the company, booking travel and accommodation independently and taking their chances with tickets.

The ticketing system for the tournament would become a long-running saga. A spokesman for the Association of British Travel Agents said, 'Between 3,500 and 5,000 tickets will be on sale at kiosks near the grounds involved. But that figure could be higher.'

The subject of tickets was raised in the House of Commons. Dennis Canavan, Labour MP for West Stirlingshire, asked sports minister Neil Macfarlane, 'Will the minister congratulate Scotland and Northern Ireland on qualifying for the World Cup finals – and, of course, England, which managed to scrape home by the skin of its teeth? What steps are being taken to ensure that football fans receive a fair allocation of tickets without being subject to exploitation by unscrupulous ticket touts and travel agents?' In the 1980s, the matter of hooliganism was never far away from football fans, as Canavan added, 'What steps are being taken to warn all football fans in advance to be on their best behaviour in Spain, especially in view of some of the recent examples of hooliganism on the part of English football fans abroad, who may be even more incensed when they see Scotland win the World Cup?'

Macfarlane didn't entirely take the bait when he replied, 'I am deeply concerned about the problems to which he referred. My officials are in Spain now, visiting all the centres with Spanish representatives. One of my officials also chairs a working party comprising representatives of the Football Association, the Foreign Office and Sportsworld Travel. All of these matters are under discussion, and I shall personally visit Madrid on 4 and 5 February to discuss these matters further.'

Canavan asked if, when meeting with the chairmen of the various associations, Macfarlane would ask for a larger ticket allocation to the National Federation of Supporters' Clubs, as Canavan stated it was the most responsible supporters' body covering the whole of Great Britain. Macfarlane assured him that would be one of the matters discussed.

Iain McCauley was a teenager in Dunfermline in 1982, and recalled, 'We were all sitting round one guy's house watching the draw and when we got Malaga we were all ecstatic because that was a holiday resort.' They quickly made plans on how to get there. 'Between seven of us, five Dunfermline fans and two Hearts fans, we bought a minibus,' McCauley said.

'I was in the pub in East Kilbride with my pals at the time,' said Bobby Jamieson, 'and we waited anxiously as the names were revealed, all hoping Scotland would be in Brazil's group. And so it came to pass. The decision was made there and then – we were going to Spain. Almost immediately, we commenced preparations for match tickets, travel and accommodation.' Bobby found his accommodation through an unusual route, 'My football team in East Kilbride had a twinning link with a team in Denmark, and I had made many Danish friends over the years. One of them told me his parents had a villa in Fuengirola on the Costa del Sol, and it was available if I needed it. So, that was to be our base camp for the two-week duration. The travelling party of seven souls couldn't believe their luck – a villa in the south of Spain.'

All over the country, plans were being hatched of how to get to Spain and where to stay. Some ideas were more solid than others. 'I was at Stirling University at the time,' Kevin Donnelly from Dumfries told me, 'and my original plan to get to Spain was – I had three other guys said they'd come with me, in the end none of them did but one of them could drive. What he was going to do was he was going to join the AA and he was going to disable his car on the outskirts of Glasgow, and it was that thing they had to take you to your final destination. He would say we were driving to Plymouth. So the AA would drive us to Plymouth and then we'd get a ferry to Spain. You couldn't make it up.'

It was reported that Spanish police would be taking English lessons for two hours a week until June.

The World Cup Disciplinary Committee gave in to a campaign for a bookings amnesty led by West Germany. As a result, Robertson, Jordan and Miller would all have their cautions wiped going into the tournament. It was a significant relief for New Zealand, who had Sumner, Grant Turner and Glenn Dodds all on two bookings. They would all have been suspended for the Scotland game had the amnesty not occurred.

The Scottish party moved on from Malaga to Seville. Stein was keen to inspect three pitches that had been recommended to him. He also wanted to have a look at a hotel there. Scotland would be based in Seville for only one match – against Brazil on 18 June – but Stein wanted to see the facilities for rest and limbering up. At this early stage, it was suggested that the team charter a plane from their Malaga base to Seville for the match.

A poll run by System Three (Scotland) on the national anthem was commissioned by the *Sunday Standard* newspaper. The question over whether readers thought Scotland should have its own national anthem returned

61 per cent for yes, 32 per cent for no, and seven per cent didn't know. On what that anthem should be, the poll suggested, 'Flower of Scotland' received 48 per cent, 'Scots Wha Hae' picked up eight per cent, 'Scotland the Brave' 24 per cent, 'Star o' Rabbie Burns' three per cent, 'A Man's a Man For Aw That' one per cent, with the rest of the votes split between another existent song and a new song being commisssioned.

The newspaper spoke to Ronnie Browne of folk group The Corries. 'Count us among the 61 per cent who think Scotland should have its own national anthem, regardless of the choice,' he said. 'We're obviously delighted at the choice – and delighted that so many people know "Flower of Scotland". Many people think it is a traditional song, but in fact, it was written by Roy [Williamson, a member of The Corries]. I suppose there will always be some who say that because of its connotations at some football matches it does not have the right image, or some who think that because it's a popular song it couldn't be a national anthem. But the point is that the Scottish people have taken "Flower of Scotland" to their hearts – just like "Scotland the Brave" and it's a song Scots sing when they get together.'

Scottish captain Danny McGrain said, 'First of all, let me say in general that I feel Scotland should have its own national anthem. I feel it quite strongly. And on a very personal note, let me say that when you're standing out there, and you hear the masses singing "Flower of Scotland", it does something for you – it's invigorating. That's the word for it.' Less keen on the idea was Ernie Walker, 'It's not up to the SFA to determine whether or not Scotland should have a national anthem of its own – it's really a political matter, isn't it? But personally – and I mean personally – I think it would be hopeless as a national anthem. It's more of an anti-English song than anything else.'

The national anthem was a subject that would return before Scotland's World Cup campaign began.

4

We Have a Dream: Recording the World Cup song and finding a formation in Valencia

'I've never actually seen a flawless performance by a Scottish player, but Alan Hansen came nearest to this. He was simply tremendous.'

Alex Cameron

AT THE beginning of February, Umbro launched a new Scotland kit. The home shirt introduced a V-neck design, replacing the wing collar that had been on Scotland shirts since 1972. A V-neck design had last been used in the 1960s. This V-neck was white, with a navy-blue V inside it. The shirt, of lightweight material, featured white piping across the shoulders. Although a stylish top, it was an Umbro template of the era, with Manchester City and Everton also wearing the same style.

There was also a new away strip. It retained the red shirt, blue shorts and white socks of the previous change kit. This time, though, along with a V-neck, the shirts featured blue vertical pinstripes, a style Umbro popularised on many other shirts in the 1980s. Umbro, which had provided Scotland kits since the 1950s, was an English company founded in 1920 in Wilmslow, Manchester, by Harold Humphreys, initially assisted by his brother Wallace, as Humphrey Brothers Clothing. Four years later, the company changed its name to Umbro, taking the 'um' from Humphreys and the 'bro' from brothers. During the Second World War, Umbro manufactured military uniforms and Lancaster Bomber aircraft interiors. At the Helsinki Summer Olympics in 1952, the British team wore Umbro kits, and in 1954 Roger Bannister became the first man to break the four-minute mile, while wearing the company's clothing.

At the 1966 World Cup, only one of the 16 sides – the Soviet Union – weren't kitted out in Umbro. By 1974 all the nations in West Germany were in Umbro, but in 1982 Scotland would be the only country at the World Cup wearing the manufacturer's kits. The new strips would go on sale from 1 March with prices for the shirts ranging from £7.75 to £10.95. At the launch, an Umbro spokesman said, 'I can't say how many Scots outfits we'll sell – but it will certainly be more than England. The Scots are more partisan.' The English kit was, at that time, manufactured by Admiral.

BBC and ITV agreed to split live coverage of the group-stage matches involving the home nations. The BBC would have Scotland's matches with Brazil and the Soviet Union, while ITV would screen the opening game against New Zealand.

New Zealand played a couple of friendlies against Hungary to launch their preparations, the first on 11

February in Auckland, where they lost 2-1. They had dominated play for long spells before being forced to field several reserves. Brian Turner scored their goal from the penalty spot. Three days later they went down by the same scoreline in Christchurch, Wynton Rufer the scorer from the spot on this occasion. Hungary had topped England's section in qualifying, albeit England had defeated them twice, so the Scottish press took the results to indicate that the Kiwis might not be the pushovers initially hoped.

In the middle of February, Sportsworld produced a new travel brochure. The prices for World Cup packages were a reduction on those previously advertised. Director Geoff Phillips told the *Evening Times*, 'We have a completely new range of holidays with prices down about 40 per cent.' There were also World Cup away days with flights leaving from Glasgow and Manchester for all Scotland games, bringing fans back after seeing the match. The prices for those packages, which included a match ticket, were £195. 'I hope people realise now that our prices were dictated to us by the Spanish authorities and were not our fault,' said Phillips, who explained that they could cut prices due to Scotland being based in the Costa del Sol, where accommodation was cheap and plentiful. In the original brochure, Sportsworld advertised an 11-night stay in a four-star Spanish hotel for £590, with six match tickets included. The price now was £385.

Preparations for Scotland were now focused on the February friendly in Valencia with Spain. 'Naturally, we want to take something out of the game, but we want to do so without revealing too much to everybody before we start the finals proper,' Jock Stein told Alan Davidson in the *Evening Times*. Stein was looking to the friendly as a chance to discover a pattern to implement in the games against Brazil and the Soviet Union. 'When you're playing against teams of the class of the Brazilians and Russians you need a special type of approach and you don't want to use it for the first time on the day itself. So playing Spain in their own country gives us the ideal opportunity to get the players used to it. But it's important that we don't give too much away. We'll be trying something different and maybe, in misleading the people who are watching, we can also learn something about ourselves.'

With the under-21s about to play a European Championship quarter-final against Italy, Stein thought of the fringe players who may be better placed in that match than in the squad in Valencia. That included Ray Stewart and Jim Leighton. However, he ruled out any experimentation in his squad to ensure the under-21 pool could be at its strongest. Although an early run for festivities in Spain, there weren't many Scots fans anticipated to be attending. 'There has not been a heavy demand for tickets,' said SFA assistant secretary Peter Donald. 'We don't expect more than a hundred or so to make the trip with the Travel Club.'

When Stein announced his squad on 15 February, places were found for Billy Thomson of St Mirren and Celtic's Roy Aitken, who hadn't played for Scotland since the May 1980 defeat to Poland. The notable omissions were Andy Gray, Steve Archibald and Joe Jordan. AC Milan were fighting against relegation, but despite that, Jordan wasn't finding a regular slot in the team. Sitting second from bottom of Serie A, their 3-2 defeat to Juventus on 14 February was their fourth game in a row without a win. Milan had undergone a period of upheaval with both a change of president and head coach. The club had allowed Jordan to come back to

Scotland for a break, but he had opted to stay and train. Stein had some words of assurance for Jordan, 'Things don't seem to be going well for him with AC Milan. Joe has done a lot for us in the past, and I certainly won't forget that. There is no way he is being written off. We will need touch players for the game in Valencia, and that's not Joe's style.' Stein suggested that the Netherlands game in March was more suited to Jordan's strengths and assured the media that Jordan would get his chance to play himself into the World Cup squad.

'I'm not going to claim that everything has been sweetness and light since my transfer from Manchester United to AC Milan,' Jordan said to the *Evening Times*. 'But I believe I am a better, more complete player for the experience of playing in the Italian league. It has been a difficult year personally, what with the need to adjust to a different game and in a different country. To play in Italy, you have to have patience as well as ability. The opposition will allow you all the possession you like for two-thirds of the pitch, but when you get near their goal, it is a different story. It's almost suffocating.'

Archibald's match fitness saw him left out of the pool, Stein noting that he had only played for ten minutes in Tottenham's FA Cup win over Aston Villa the previous Saturday, his first game since 5 December. 'Another month should make all the difference to his fitness,' Stein said.

'It didn't come as a shock I was not named,' Andy Gray said. 'The troubles at the club have affected me and I will have to play in midfield for the next four or five games.' Wolverhampton Wanderers were lying third from bottom in the English First Division, four points behind Leeds United. Their goalless draw with Nottingham Forest had ended a run of nine straight defeats. They were on their third manager of the season with Ian Greaves taking over from caretaker Ian Ross, who had stepped in when John Barnwell was sacked. Gray had only scored one goal in the league, with another one each in the League Cup and FA Cup. 'I will be staying put here in an effort to shake off my worries and it is pointless upsetting myself further. I would love to be back in the Scotland squad and that is my target.' Kenny Dalglish, Paul Sturrock and Alan Brazil were the selected strikers. 'It can't be bad when I can leave out men such as Jordan, Archibald and Gray and be left with three others of such high calibre,' said Stein.

Of the overall selection, Stein said, 'It's not necessarily the best 18 players who've been picked. What I'm after is a certain blend. If I were to choose only the best men, I could end up with ten defenders.' Brazil was delighted with his inclusion in the squad. 'It is a terrific feeling,' he told the *Evening Times*. 'In the past, I have only been a fringe candidate, but now that I am in the pool, I want to stay there.' Brazil had earned his two Scotland caps in the last few days of May 1980 in away friendly defeats to Poland and Hungary. 'Alan didn't do too badly in the two matches he played,' Stein said, 'but we were just beginning our qualifying matches, and with such as Joe Jordan, Kenny Dalglish, Steve Archibald, and Andy Gray available, it really wasn't a time to experiment. This will be a good opportunity to see how Alan fits in.'

Brazil celebrated in the evening by going out and playing the game of his life. Southampton, complete with Kevin Keegan, Alan Ball and Mick Channon, were the visitors to Portman Road that night. Brazil cracked in a hat-trick in the first 20 minutes. He scored twice in the second half as Ipswich ran out 5-2 winners. It was the first time since 29 March 1975 that a player had scored five in the English top flight, when Roger Davies scored all of Derby County's goals in a 5-0 win against Luton Town. 'I still can't believe it,' Brazil said as he walked off the pitch. 'My inclusion in the Scotland squad gave me a boost which couldn't be matched. It's just a dream. I'll walk outside the ground, and there will be pigs flying. The selection for the Scottish squad really perked me up, but I have never hit a hat-trick before, never mind five.' His manager Bobby Robson said, 'That's as good a performance as you'll ever see. It brought you out of your seat. He was dazzling and showed wizardry on the ball that mesmerised Southampton.' Stein's friend and Southampton boss Lawrie McMenemy called him to say, 'Brazil is brilliant. Brazil was electrifying. He scored all the goals from different positions and in different ways.'

Rangers' Davie Cooper aggravated a groin injury playing against Dundee United and withdrew from the squad. Despite Stein's doubts over his fitness, Steve Archibald was called up in Cooper's place. John Robertson developed torn ankle ligaments and was expected to be out for three weeks. 'It means I've got to change my thinking about the match,' said Stein, 'but I think we are well covered with the players we have got.'

Stein was now without a seasoned wide player. 'I like to play a winger,' he said to the *Record*. 'My plans have hinged around Robertson. But I must look for options, and I have no recognised winger now.' Wingers had long been part of Stein's footballing philosophy. 'Certainly, Celtic's best spells during my time as manager have always been when we had wingers,' he said in Celtic's match programme in 1976. 'If a team plays with wingers, they are not defensive, for, unlike midfield men, they do not have to shuttle back to clutter up at the back.' As the game was a friendly, Stein wasn't too worried about the modifications he may have to make. 'We must change our style to suit the kind of eventualities we'll meet in the World Cup. So, Robertson's withdrawal could well be a blessing in disguise. We have four games still to play before we come back to Spain in earnest. We want to make the best use of those matches.' One of those uses was for Stein to identify his striking pair. He was keen to see how Brazil played alongside Dalglish. 'If they do well, it could be the start of a World Cup partnership.'

* * *

On Sunday, 21 February, the players recorded their World Cup single, 'We Have a Dream', at CaVa Studios in Glasgow's West End. The players in the studio were Brazil, Wark, Archibald, McLeish, Rough, Frank Gray, Miller, Dalglish, Aitken, McGrain, Robertson, Strachan and Hartford. Several Scottish celebrities were also at the session, including Olympic gold medallist Allan Wells, Derby-winning jockey Willie Carson, ex-world champion boxer Jim Watt, and Miss Scotland Georgina Kearney.

Songwriter B.A. Robertson spoke to the *Record*. 'I'm living my own fantasy,' he said. 'Being a pop singer is only second or third choice to playing for Scotland. The song is a bit like "Mull of Kintyre" meets "You'll Never Walk Alone".' Robertson had enjoyed three top ten hits. 'Bang Bang' made number two in July of 1979, followed by 'Knocked It Off', which peaked at number eight in October. 'To Be Or Not To Be' climbed to number nine in May 1980. Robertson, a graduate of the Royal Scottish Academy of Music, was also a notable songwriter, co-writing much of Cliff Richard's

1979 album *Rock 'n' Roll Juvenile* and his 1981 number four hit 'Wired for Sound'.

'They put it in a newspaper in Scotland that I was doing it,' Robertson said to the *Record* in 2012, 'and then they asked me, "Ye are daein' it big man, right?"' With tongue in cheek, Robertson claimed the SFA told him, '"It better be better than whatever shite the English are daein'." I did at least fulfil that objective.' Of the day's recording, he said, 'I recall the manager Jock Stein being there but not really into it; it was a distraction, so let's get it over with.' The SFA didn't exactly allow the 1980 Ivor Novello Songwriter of the Year nominee free rein. 'I was issued with quite a long list by the SFA of what was to be allowed content-wise and what wasn't. Anything nationalistic, for example, was a definite no-no. Football was viewed by the Thatcher government as a menace, like trade unionism.'

The central vocal part – spoken rather than sung – would be performed by actor John Gordon Sinclair, star of the previous year's hit film *Gregory's Girl*. 'I am surprised but very happy to do it,' Sinclair told Ian Buchan of the *Evening Times*. 'I was phoned by B.A. Robertson's agent and asked if I would take his place.' Sinclair recorded his vocals in a London studio a couple of weeks later.

Also on the record was Christian. 'I was under the impression that B.A. would do the narration,' he said. 'I don't know why he's changed his mind.' Born in Ibrox in 1943, Chris McClure began his career at 19 as frontman for The Fireflies. They specialised in Tamla Motown and soul music. Later, they became known as The Chris McClure Section. McClure then began a solo career as Christian, releasing his debut album in 1976. The Pipes & Drums of British Caledonian Airways made up the band.

There was a plan to sell the record outside Hampden in May before the two Home International Championship matches. The SFA were happy with this, and Raymond Kildare, Christian's manager and the record's promoter, had applied for a street trader's licence.

Northern Ireland and England also recorded their World Cup singles on the same day.

Ahead of the international, Patrick Barclay's column in *The Guardian* looked at Alan Rough and how he had unjustly suffered the ribbing of English TV pundits over the years. 'It bugged me when the criticism was no longer justified,' Rough told Barclay. 'I made mistakes on TV, and Bob Wilson, in spotlighting them, was only trying to help me, but it established an image that influenced people who never had the opportunity to see me week in, week out, with my club.

'When these people joined in, it was annoying. Still, I don't worry now in the slightest; all the criticism I have taken has made me immune.'

Barclay also remarked that as a part-time player with Partick Thistle, Rough's training regime wasn't anything to be especially proud of, but noted that he had now benefited from a year-long specialised training with Erik Sørensen. The Dane had played in Scotland as a goalkeeper for Morton and Rangers in the 1960s. He had set himself up as a specialised goalkeeping coach in the 1970s, a rarity at the time, working with several Scottish goalkeepers, including Clydebank's Jim Gallacher.

'My problem is that I stayed at the same stage of development for too many years,' Rough said. 'Too often I was just doing the same training as the outfield players. The only help I've ever had, as regards goalkeeping, was from Erik Sørensen and I often wonder what might have happened if I had got it a few years earlier.'

There was always speculation that Rough would move to a full-time club, with Dundee United being the latest side to be linked with signing him. He had come close to a move to England in 1980 when it looked like Middlesbrough would seal a deal. But, in the end, they went for Kilmarnock's Jim Stewart. Rough only discovered his move was off when the *Daily Record*'s Alex Cameron told him as he came in the front door of Hampden to play against England. 'At the end of the day, you have to say, "What have I got to show for it?" and although I've got 44 caps, all players want medals. If a top English club wanted me, I'd love to go.' Rough was Scotland's most capped goalkeeper. Bill Brown had been the previous record holder with 28 caps between 1958 and 1965.

Rough started his playing career with Sighthill. He signed for Partick Thistle in October 1969 after being spotted as a 14 year-old playing in goal in a kick-about on the pitch of shipbuilders Barclay Curle on Glasgow's Crow Road. Partick Thistle's chief scout Jimmy Dickie happened to be driving past and stopped to watch. He recommended Rough to Thistle's under-16 amateur team. A Scottish youth cap, Rough established himself in the Partick team during the 1970/71 season, where he was an ever-present in the league. In the following season he started to come to notice, when, as a 19-year-old, he was in goal as Thistle shocked Celtic 4-1 in the League Cup Final of October 1971. Within days, Thistle had turned down a £50,000 bid from Hull City. He was first called into the Scotland squad the following month by Tommy Docherty for the European Championship match with Belgium. Ironically, in his last appearance before the squad was announced, he'd conceded seven goals to Aberdeen. However, Rough had to wait a few years for his international debut, keeping a clean sheet in a 1-0 win against Switzerland in April 1976.

Although Rough had come in for criticism, much of it from pundits down south, his contemporaries could recognise his class. 'I have always rated Alan as a very good keeper,' George Wood told *Match* magazine, 'and I feel that much, if not all, of the criticism levelled at him has been unjustified. If people saw him play every week in the Scottish Premier Division they would soon realise what a good keeper he is. His handling is excellent and ... he is very quick around the box. Most people would have cracked up if they were under the amount of pressure he was every time he played for Scotland. He deserves a lot of credit for the way he coped with all the criticism and still kept coming back.'

There were no surprises in the Scotland team to line up in Valencia, and Stein brushed off the lack of wide players. 'We have a few Liverpool and Ipswich players in the team and they don't play with a winger, so that fact that we don't have one shouldn't trouble us.'

Stein now saw all the games coming up as preparation for the matches with Brazil and the Soviets. He told Jim Reynolds of the *Glasgow Herald*, 'We like to play our home matches in a cavalier fashion, but that won't do against these sides in the World Cup. We'd be on our knees before half-time if we did, and we'd be skinned. What we will try tomorrow is something I tried out once before against Wales at Swansea. On that occasion, however, some of the players didn't seem keen to make it work. Now I believe I have the players to make a success of it.' The match in question was the 2-0 Home International loss in May 1981. The only three players in both starting line-ups were Rough, Gray and Hartford. With no out-and-out wingers, Stein was looking for his midfielders to get into wide positions and stretch the Spanish defence. Alan Hansen was expected to push forward from defence to turn a 4-4-2 into a 3-5-2.

Stein saw John Wark as the main man in his team, 'If John can't play in this formation, then there is something wrong. There is a heavy Liverpool-Ipswich influence in this side, and it should suit him down to the ground.' There was no expectation on Wark to defend; Stein was looking for him to fulfil his club role by coming from midfield to make mischief up front.

Stein was also hoping that with Alan Brazil's eye for goal, Dalglish could create space for him to find the target, 'In the past, Kenny has been partnered by Joe Jordan and Andy Gray, but they tend to bunch up through the middle, making it easier for defences to mark them. That should not be the case with Alan playing with him.'

Brazil was delighted to be in the starting 11. 'It sounds corny but I'm desperate to be in Scotland's World Cup party,' he told the *Daily Record*. 'I'll do anything to be in Spain again in the summer as a player. I played part of the games in Poland and Hungary a year ago and since then have been basically ignored. All of a sudden it's all changed.'

Brazil, who played with Drumchapel Amateurs and Celtic Boys Club before his move to Ipswich, had scored 18 times in the 1980/81 season; he scored just as many in 1981/82, 'I don't consider myself an outright scorer. I feel I am able to lay on chances for others, and I think Paul Mariner of England will vouch for this. I can lay off as well as shoot.' Brazil's performances for the Portman Road club, who had finished as league runners-up and UEFA Cup winners in 1980/81 and were now chasing the title again, had positioned him as a serious contender for a starting place in Spain.

* * *

The Spanish manager was José Santamaría. Born in Montevideo, Uruguay, in 1929, he had represented both the country of his birth and Spain in internationals. Playing as a centre-back, he joined Real Madrid in 1957. He won five La Liga titles, four European Cups, one Spanish Cup and the Intercontinental Cup in 1960. He was happy that John Robertson wasn't with the party. 'Along with Dalglish, I rate Robertson as Scotland's best player. It is bad luck for Scotland that he can't be here, but not for us,' he said. One of Santamaría's greatest nights as a player had been in Scotland. 'Scotland are difficult opponents. I have a special regard for their fans ever since I played for Real in the 7-3 European Cup Final at Hampden against Eintracht. I wish we could play something like that.'

The game was a hot ticket for other international managers. In the crowd were Northern Ireland's Billy Bingham, whose side were in Spain's World Cup group, England's Ron Greenwood, West Germany's Jupp Derwall, Yugoslavia's Miljan Miljanić, Italy's Enzo Bearzot, Brazil's Telê Santana, and Russia's Konstantin Beskov.

This would be Spain's 14th international at the Luis Casanova stadium since their first one there in 1925. Scotland had played at the ground before in a European Championship qualifier in February 1975. Joe Jordan had scored in the first minute before Alfredo Megido equalised in the 67th. Danny McGrain and Kenny Dalglish were also in the side that night.

'Spain will want to build up a rapport with their fans,' Stein said, 'because they play their first-phase matches in Valencia. It would be nice to upset them a bit.' The game was played on a patchy and rutted pitch. Scotland had trouble breaking down a ruthless Spanish defence in the first half. The hosts showed the benefits of their players having played regularly together for around 18 months. Wark did have a chance early on but snatched at his shot, firing it high over Luis Arconada's goal. Spain found more room in Scotland's last third of the field. Rough saved at the second attempt from Jesús María Satrústegui's shot before, on 26 minutes, the Spaniards had a penalty. Saura passed Gray on the left before sending in a deep cross which was headed into the six-yard box. As McLeish and Alonso ran in for the ball, the Real Sociedad man fell to the floor, apparently nudged over. 'He's a young player,' Stein said of Aberdeen defender McLeish after the game. 'What he needs are more and more games at this level.' Rough dived to his right as Satrústegui sent his penalty down the middle. However, the keeper's body blocked the kick. As he scrambled on the ground to get to the loose ball, Victor rushed in to drive in the rebound. Rough would explain what happened when talking to Allan Herron in the *Sunday Mail*, 'Before Satrústegui fired that first penalty kick at me, I had already decided which way to go. But I wasn't prepared for the shock when the ball hit me. I was caught – how can I put it – right in my testimonials. With the stunning effect of that shot and my feet slipping in the gravel-like surface in the goalmouth, I was unable to recover in time to block the follow-up drive.'

At the half-hour mark, Scotland had a great chance to equalise. Wark played the ball into Hansen, who had run almost unnoticed into the penalty box. From the corner of the six-yard box, he struck the ball quickly but wide of the goal when he seemed sure to score. At half-time, Archibald came on for Strachan but moved into attack as Dalglish switched into midfield. As the second half progressed, Spain began to lose their grip on the game and Souness controlled the centre of the pitch, passing assuredly. The front pairing of Archibald and Brazil looked promising as Scotland got more and more of the ball. Scotland's best chance came when attempting to cut out Dalglish's cross; Tendillo sliced his clearance almost into his own goal. Archibald and Brazil combined to set up an opportunity for Dalglish, but Arconada managed to bring the ball under control. Real Sociedad's Ufarte made a speedy run down the left with around seven minutes remaining. As he played the ball into the box, referee Bep Thomas from the Netherlands awarded Spain a second penalty after Gray impeded Saura. Substitute Quini stuck the kick away. It was 3-0 on 86 minutes when another substitute, Gallego, worked a one-two, taking him clear of McLeish. Rough came off his line and Gallego drove the ball past him as the keeper slipped.

'We made defensive mistakes but also created goal chances which we didn't take,' Stein said after the final whistle. 'However, playing against a team like Spain we found out some truths about the reality of football at world level. Spain defend well and go forward cleverly on the break. I'm concerned about the fact that we're not scoring enough goals. But I can never see us as high scorers in the World Cup. If we can get a couple and not lose more than this I'll not be too unhappy.'

Stein felt the referee didn't have a good night either, 'We made mistakes defensively, but I think the referee was wrong with the second penalty. Frank Gray didn't really touch the Spanish winger. I couldn't see why the referee gave the penalty. Heads went down then and we lost a bad third goal. However, we now know the kind of things referees do at this level. I honestly believe that if we were playing Spain tonight at Hampden we could reverse the result.'

Most people at the game agreed that the standout was, perhaps surprisingly, given that he played in the Scottish defence, Alan Hansen. In the *Evening Times*, Alan Davidson wrote, 'A truly world-class performance from Alan Hansen. This lad can play all right, and the great thing about him is that he knows he can.' In the *Daily Record*, Alex Cameron said, 'I've never actually seen a flawless performance by a Scottish player, but Alan Hansen came nearest to this. He was simply tremendous.'

'Alan was the best man on the park,' Stein said. 'I have never seen a Scottish player give a completely faultless performance in an international match, but Alan came as near to it the other night as anyone else.' Danny McGrain said to the *Sunday Mail*, 'What about Alan Hansen? He proved to everybody he can play at the highest level. He was brilliant.'

'He turned in a display against the Spanish in their own backyard that was reminiscent of Franz Beckenbauer at his brilliant best,' John Wark wrote in his autobiography *Wark On*. Hansen acknowledged his performance in his 1999 book *A Matter of Opinion*, 'Ridiculous as it might seem, my best game was the 3-0 defeat by Spain in Valencia in February 1982. Because of the space Spain allowed me when I was in possession, I was able repeatedly to involve myself in our attacking play – so much so that Ruud Krol, the famous Dutch sweeper … paid me the compliment of describing me as Scotland's most important player.'

Someone who begged to differ was Patrick Barclay in *The Guardian*, 'Hansen, though as tall, skilful and constructive as Spain's impressive Alesanco, was simply not equipped by experience to be an international sweeper.' On Stein's tactics, Barclay was scathing. 'Scotland's experiment with man-to-man marking was a waste of time,' he wrote. 'The players did not appear to have been told how the system should work and, in their confusion, produced a feeble hybrid of continental and British defence that served only to help the World Cup hosts build confidence with a flattering 3-0 victory.'

'I didn't know I had the temerity to criticise Jock,' Patrick Barclay told me in 2021. 'I remember us playing Austria and a guy called Pezzey was the man of the match for them. [He was] a sort of libero similar to the Italian Scirea or Morten Olsen of Denmark and I felt Hansen could have been ours, but the bedding in of the system should have been done years in advance and I felt although he had a good game in Valencia, once we got to the World Cup it was a half-baked system.'

Barclay went on to expand on his views about the sweeper system, 'Bear in mind also, Scottish players are much harder to coach. Or were in those days definitely. Maybe not now, but were much harder to coach in those days. They all fucking fancied themselves. They were good lads, but they weren't disciplined footballers like the Italians or Danes or Swedes. Their attitude was terrible really. It's the discipline that was involved in the man-to-man marking. At that time I thought of that system as being a footballer and a load of markers who had to be absolutely rigid – and I still believe that is what Stein should have done. Ours weren't good enough. I felt that the only way we could play it was by giving Hansen freedom to play, to be our playmaker in the way of Olsen for Denmark and Beckenbauer for Germany and all that. And others had to be German like Buchwald or Briegel – people who would kill. Who would go at half-time up the tunnel with their opponent and stand at the door while they had a piss and then accompany him out again. That was the way I felt. I didn't think that we had got it right.'

Rough was far from happy with the second penalty award. 'Spain's second penalty goal in Valencia was illegal. I'm convinced of that,' he said. 'And Quini should have been ordered to retake the kick. I was on the line and had decided in which direction to go for the ball as the Spaniard made his run-up to the penalty spot. But then he checked his stride, and I was thrown out of gear. Quini changed his direction and his mind – but I was left flat-footed so that when he did strike the ball to my right, I was left flat-footed and immobile. Breaking the run is a favourite Spanish trick – but it is not allowed under the rules. The Spaniards did this twice against England in the European Championships in Italy in 1980. On the first occasion, scorer Dani got away with it. The second time, six minutes later, the referee ordered a retake, and Ray Clemence made a fine save. I feel I should have been given a second chance.'

Rough also felt that he bore the brunt of the Spanish fans' ire. 'You name it, they threw it,' he said to the *Glasgow Herald*. 'I pity the opposing keepers when they have to play there in the opening matches this summer. I was pelted with oranges, tomatoes, coins, bits of wood, and even chocolate bars. It can really upset a goalkeeper's concentration.'

The verdict from the international managers present was positive. England's Ron Greenwood said, 'There weren't three goals between the teams. Scotland played much better than the 3-0 scoreline suggests.' The Dutch boss, Kees Rijvers, commented, 'The Scots did enough to show me we'll have to play to our best to win at Hampden. I liked their style.' Telê Santana, though, wasn't impressed, 'Russia are technically far superior to Scotland. The Soviets have better team players, have been training for a long time and are all ready.' As a concession, Santana added, 'The Scots fight much harder than their Soviet counterparts.'

'The Dutch referee was taking charge of his first international, news that didn't surprise us because the two penalty decisions were both a bit dodgy,' John Wark wrote in his autobiography. Nevertheless, Wark felt that the game was undoubtedly one of his best performances for his country. 'The manager put me in a central position alongside Graeme Souness and instructed me to get into the opposition box as often as I liked. It was going well for over an hour, but when Steve Archibald came on for Gordon Strachan, we had to change the system.'

On the flight home, Stein defended his side and the choice of opposition. 'We could have played a team like Iceland and kidded ourselves on. But we would have learned absolutely nothing. For instance, what have England learned by beating Northern Ireland 4-0 this week? We took on the host nation in front of their own noisy support and we have seen the influence that can have on referees. Well, we might as well get used to it, for it's going to be like that when the finals get underway in the summer. To lose 3-0 is not a good thing and we're not proud of it. I know our fans who were not at the game will be saying that we took a drubbing, but the truth is we played well and at times exceptionally well.'

With lessons learned in terms of both players and tactics, Stein's attention now turned to the Hampden friendly against the Netherlands in late March.

5

Preparations Continue:
A change of hotel in Spain and
a win over the Dutch

'It's going to be a difficult tournament in
Spain this summer for everyone – except
Brazil. I agree with Mr Stein that the
Scotland–Russia game on the 22nd of June
could decide which of us goes forward.
It will be very hard.'

Konstantin Beskov

AT THE beginning of March, Jock Stein and Ernie Walker flew out to Spain to look at the squad's hotel. Although Stein had given assurances previously that the location was suitable, the trip threw the hotel selection into doubt. Having spent time at the Parador del Golf hotel, five minutes from Malaga airport, the SFA were now looking at alternative venues. The concern was that they were not getting the best deal possible. Prices had risen from £18 to £70 a night, and Scotland's quote had now jumped from £12,000 to £70,000. The SFA president Willie Harkness spoke to the *Daily Record*, 'One or two things have concerned us about the Golf Hotel at Malaga. We were aware it was on a flight path but had been given assurances there were no planes at night. The Malaga area is also troubled in the summer with mosquitoes. Nothing has been decided definitely yet but everything will be gone over fully at our International Committee meeting on Monday. We want to make sure we are getting value for money.'

Harkness told the *Glasgow Herald* that his main concern was that the players had the best facilities, best food and best accommodation, 'The Parador has a lot of good things going for it, but it may be wiser to base ourselves nearer Seville, where we play Brazil in our second match.' On the price increase, Harkness said, 'Of course, there is a limit to what the SFA can spend, but there is no way we will scrimp concerning our World Cup arrangements.'

At the International Committee meeting, the decision was made to move hotels. 'We have terminated the arrangement in Malaga because we are unable to agree a realistic figure,' said Walker.

As an alternative, the SFA first turned to a five-star retreat at Cadiz, 233km from Malaga, but then another hotel came into the picture – the Golf Hotel in Sotogrande. 'We want the best for Jock Stein and our players,' Harkness said. 'The Golf Hotel is excellent – if we get the proper terms.' By 9 March, Scotland had booked the 50-room hotel out at £45 per night per room. 'We made up our mind that we would not be ripped off,' Walker said. 'We gave the previous choice of hotel until today to come up with a reasonable offer. They didn't, so we changed.' Stein was delighted with the new location, 'We had a problem at the other hotel about a training pitch. Here, though, I was able to lay out three training pitches, one to the exact dimensions of the ground at Malaga. We shall have privacy. And the people who run the hotel are used to having footballers. Real Madrid play in a tournament down there every summer, and that's where they stay.' Fifteen minutes away from Gibraltar, but 114km (70 miles) from Malaga, it was suggested that the team could fly from Gibraltar Airport to Malaga and Seville. That would, unfortunately, turn out not to be the case.

The Hotel Sotogrande was an exclusive 4,400-acre estate developed into expensive private holiday villas. It stretched four miles from the foot of the Sierra Almenara mountains to a mile-long strip of Mediterranean beaches where the Rock of Gibraltar loomed on the horizon. Sotogrande itself was established by Joseph Rafael McMicking, his wife Mercedes Zobel, and their nephews Jaime and Enrique Zobel. McMicking served as a member of General MacArthur's staff throughout the Second World War, attaining the rank of colonel in the United States Army. After the war, he became a self-made millionaire, establishing one of California's first venture capital companies. Impressed by the luxury Forbes Park estate in Manila, in the Philippines, McMicking liked the idea of building something similar. So he commissioned a search for a suitable location, which was required to have unspoiled beaches plus access to an airport. This area of Cadiz province seemed to fit the bill. After coming to see for himself, McMicking, with the assistance of his two nephews, eventually decided to buy the Finca Paniagua estate in the municipality of San Roque. They began developing the area in 1962. The McMickings moved to Sotogrande to live, and other residents in the early days included George Moore, the president of the First National City Bank in New York, and some of his friends such as Jackie and Aristotle Onassis, opera singer Maria Callas and politician Spiro Agnew.

The SFA negotiated a discount for their 13-night stay. The hotel manager, Ian Bateman, a 34-year-old from Ipswich, told the *Record*, 'It's somewhere between the full price and the deal I offer tour operators.' In 2014, Bateman spoke about how the Scotland team came to stay at the hotel. Bateman had heard the SFA had booked into Málaga's Parador, 'I got in touch with the Scottish FA's secretary and offered Sotogrande as a more private alternative. They were initially a bit sceptical, but when he and coach Jock Stein came over and inspected the facilities they were bowled over.' The Sotogrande complex comprised two 18-hole golf courses, a nine-hole course, six tennis courts and several swimming pools. 'As a training centre, its potential for us is tremendous,' Ernie Walker told the media. The two golf courses were designed by Robert Trent Jones, an English–American golf-course architect, one of which was considered among the best in Europe. The major course, to which Henry Cotton was once attached, opened in 1965. At Stein's instruction, a pitch the size of Malaga's ground was marked out on the polo field with goalposts borrowed from the local football team.

The location was certainly an improvement on Scotland's accommodation at the 1978 World Cup. They were based then in Alta Gracia, a city in the province of Cordoba in Argentina. The team's headquarters were nicknamed 'Château Despair' by the accompanying media. The players had next to nothing to do at the camp as there was no games room or other form of entertainment. 'Time hung very heavy,' Joe Jordan recalled. The players would train in the morning, have lunch and then be left to their own devices the rest of the day. 'Most of the lads just whiled away the hours chatting about this thing and the other,' Jordan said. 'Personally, I don't think I've ever read as many books in my life.' The hotel had a tennis court with no net or rackets and a swimming pool with no water. 'I really think the 1978 World Cup was the competition which made it better for every Scotland World Cup team afterwards,' squad member Joe Harper told Mike Wilson. 'We were bored. We had about 20 videos with us, which, after about four days, everybody had seen.' The Sierras hotel had poor training facilities. 'The so-called training pitch was hard and rutted,' recalled Kenny Burns, so the decision was made for the squad to train in Cordoba, a 40-minute journey away. 'It was a joke,' Don Masson said. 'We would go 20 miles to the training camp, then back to the hotel, with nothing to do. The rooms were a shambles, dirty. It was a complete debacle from start to finish.'

The disorganisation in Argentina was why the players and the SFA were aware that getting things right off the park was vitally important to getting it right on the pitch. 'Jock Stein, with all the experience and knowledge he has gained over the years, won't allow boredom to affect his players in Spain, that's for sure,' Jordan said. However, it wasn't long before the residents voiced their apprehension about a squad of footballers pitching up in their exclusive resort. Anne Russo, administrator of the 450 strong residents' association at Sotogrande, told the *Sunday Standard*, 'Already I have had several members of the community here expressing their concern. We have asked for a letter from the management detailing what extra precautions are to be taken while the Scots are here.' Her family owned the Queen's Hotel in nearby Gibraltar while Mrs Russo had been a resident in Sotogrande for ten years. Ian Bateman responded, 'I'm sure the residents don't really think that tartan hordes are going to stagger down from Torremolinos to wreck the spas, dig up the polo pitches and camp on the 18th green.'

Back at home, the press was full of speculation that Jock Stein had been sounded out about going to the New York Cosmos on a yearly contract rumoured to be anywhere between £135,000 and £200,000. Stein was quick, though, to scotch the rumours. 'It's completely untrue that I have any notion of leaving Scotland,' he said. 'My one concern is managing Scotland in the World Cup finals. My mind has not been swayed from that target for some time, nor will it be. I was only one of several who were asked, but I said right away that I wasn't interested. Since I joined the SFA, I've had good relations with everyone, and I don't want to spoil that in any way. I am Scotland's manager and intend to stay in the job.' Brazilian Julio Mazzei, interim coach at the Cosmos, would continue throughout the 1982 season, eventually being appointed permanently in 1983.

Getting on with World Cup preparation, Stein headed out to Athens to watch Russia take on Greece. The Russian boss Konstantin Beskov spoke with Alex Cameron of the *Daily Record*, 'It's going to be a difficult tournament in Spain this summer for everyone – except Brazil. I agree with Mr Stein that the Scotland–Russia game on the 22nd of June could decide which of us goes forward. It will be very hard.' Cameron pointed out to Beskov that Telê Santana stated that Russia are technically better than Scotland, but the Scots had more fighting spirit. 'Well, I don't know if he really said this or even meant it,' Beskov replied. 'I feel the two countries are even. As for fighting spirit, I've never noticed any difference when the two teams have met in the past. Certainly, when I saw Scotland in Valencia recently, they were unlucky to lose 3-0. It was a level game.'

Beskov was also the coach of Moscow Spartak. His assistants were the manager of Dinamo Tbilisi, Nodar Akhalkatsi, and Valeriy Lobanovskyi, manager of Dynamo Kyiv. Beskov said, 'I didn't get a chance to speak to Mr Stein after the World Cup draw in Madrid. But I hope to put this right after the match with Greece. The Greek team is being built but I feel they will give us a hard 90 minutes. That is why we have flown from Moscow.' Beskov shared the impressions he formed from watching Scotland against Spain, 'It would be bad for Scotland if Alan Hansen and Kenny Dalglish were hurt. I was particularly impressed by them in the game in Valencia.' That match wasn't Beskov's first experience with Scotland, 'The two penalties given against Scotland seemed to bring back memories of the night I played for Moscow Dynamo against Rangers in 1945. Yes, I remember it well. There was a big crowd and a very good atmosphere. The 2-2 draw on the night was fair. We had a great tour of Britain and the match in Glasgow was the one I remember most. When I'm in Glasgow looking at Scotland, I'd like to renew acquaintances with Rangers. I respect Scotland very much. They are a fine team, and I can see they are being well prepared.'

David Kipiani was missing from the Russian squad, but Beskov would not be drawn on the attacking midfielder's absence. The Dinamo Tbilisi player was one of the most stylish players in the Russian team. Voted Soviet Footballer of the Year in 1977, he had only recently returned to football after a leg break. Kipiani had put Liverpool to the sword in the European Cup in 1980 and led his club to the European Cup Winners' Cup in 1981.

With several changes to their usual line-up, the Russians won the match in the Nikos Goumas Stadium 2-0 with Fyodor Cherenkov of Spartak Moscow and Leonid Buryak of Dynamo Kyiv the scorers. Stein felt that the Russians were disguising their real form, but the trip allowed him to see that they had strength in depth, as they used four substitutes throughout the game. 'Shengelia looks so sharp up front,' Stein noted. However, he wasn't impressed with Oleg Blokhin. 'He only looked half interested in the task at hand,' Stein said. 'When they really did play, and it was only in short spells, I could see they were an accomplished group of players.' He elaborated to Jim Reynolds on a few of the Russians. On Shengelia, Stein said, 'I think he showed that he could really live up to his nomination as Russia's Player of the Year. He also played in short spells and showed tremendous acceleration. The type of player who is very difficult to mark because he drags defenders all over the field.' Of Blokhin, Stein wondered if Beskov utilised him in midfield to confuse Scotland or if that could be an alternative role for him, 'He played only in fits and starts and certainly was only a shadow of the player I expect to see against us in Malaga playing in his most productive role, wide on the left and attacking.' Stein wanted to see more and was therefore intending to travel to Villa Park to see Dynamo Kyiv take on Aston Villa in the second leg of their European Cup quarter-final. The Kyiv side had seven players who were sure to be in the Soviet squad for Spain. 'It will give me a chance to see some of the Russians under real pressure. They won't be able to hide anything

WE MADE THEM ANGRY

in that game,' Stein said, although he wasn't worried about Scotland's opponents spying on his players, adding, 'It's time for building and trying to find a couple of players to challenge for places.'

* * *

Several of the Scottish squad were in action in European competition in early March. Scotland's last European contenders were Dundee United. David Narey scored their first goal in a 2-0 home win over Radnicki Nis in the UEFA Cup. Paul Sturrock was also in the line-up. The Anglos were also in action on the continent. Hansen, Souness and Dalglish were all in the Liverpool team who beat CSKA Sofia at Anfield by a single goal in the European Cup quarter-final. Hansen, though, picked up damage to his ankle ligaments, which would lead to him missing the League Cup Final the following week. 'That's a blow for us,' Jock Stein said. 'It looks like he will also miss Scotland's game against Holland at Hampden on March 23, and I would not hide the fact that Alan is one of our key men for Spain.'

Steve Archibald picked up a booking as his Tottenham side beat Eintracht Frankfurt 2-0 at White Hart Lane in the European Cup Winners' Cup. Allan Evans was missing from the Aston Villa side as they drew 0-0 with Dynamo Kyiv in Russia. Three Scots played in the English League Cup Final at Wembley on 13 March. Archibald opened the scoring for Spurs in the 11th minute before Ronnie Whelan equalised with three minutes left. In extra time, a second goal from Irish international Whelan and a last-minute third from Ian Rush gave Liverpool the cup. It would be the second winners' medals in a row for Kenny Dalglish and captain Graeme Souness.

122

Stein's squad for the Netherlands game included Allan Evans, Tommy Burns, Billy Thomson and Jim Bett. Uncapped Evans had been named only as a standby player in a previous World Cup pool. 'I've always maintained that a few places need to be filled before the finals,' Stein said, 'and these players know that. It's up to themselves. Tommy Burns has shown a bit in the past. Evans is quick and good for his club and Bett has been impressive for his club and the under-21 side. Now they will get a chance to show me what they can do.' Evans described his inclusion as 'a big surprise', adding, 'I thought any chance I had of making the World Cup pool had gone.'

'He is good in the air and quick on the ground,' Stein said of Evans. 'And I have no worries about bringing him into the pool at this stage. He has plenty of experience at the top with Villa.'

Along with Hansen, winger John Robertson was also absent due to an injured ankle. Burns was seen as a possible replacement in the wide position. Joe Jordan was back in the pool, not having played for his country since the win against Sweden in September. 'We have to try Joe sometime to see what he has to offer.' Having consulted with his assistant Dundee United manager Jim McLean, Stein opted to leave Paul Sturrock out of the squad. With United still in Europe, Stein, confident he knew what Sturrock could do, didn't want to land him with more games. Stein was careful not to disturb the under-21 side with their second leg against Italy coming up. 'I strengthened it for the match in Italy last month, and it would not be fair to interfere with it now with the boys having come so close to a place in the semi-finals,' he said.

The 34-year-old Johan Cruyff, in his second spell with Ajax, was named but swiftly withdrew from the

Netherlands' 16-man pool. He claimed it was because he had heard of his inclusion from a third party and not from Dutch manager Kees Rijvers. This was the second time Cruyff had pulled out of an international squad in succession. A year previously, he withdrew from the World Cup qualifier against France. On that occasion the dispute related to the branding of the Dutch shirt. Cruyff insisted that he wouldn't wear Adidas while personally sponsored by Puma. He admitted that the dispute had still not been settled. A few days later, Cruyff would receive a letter from Rijvers informing him that he would now be banned from the international side. 'For me, the chapter on Cruyff has definitely been closed,' the manager said.

Cruyff hadn't played for his country since October 1977 and wouldn't appear again. The Dutch squad, though, was littered with talent. Ruud Krol, now plying his trade with Napoli, was named alongside Ipswich Town's Arnold Muhren. The goalkeepers were Hans van Breukelen of FC Utrecht and Piet Schrijvers of Ajax. Also in the squad was Simon Tahamata of Standard Liège and AZ 67's John Metgod. The Dutch had narrowly missed out on qualification for Spain. In a group with France, Belgium, the Republic of Ireland and whipping boys Cyprus, they had got off to a bad start losing 2-1 in Dublin, then 1-0 in Brussels. After that, they didn't lose in the group again until they got to Paris for their final fixture. A win would have seen the Dutch qualify, but they went down 2-0, and France went on to beat Cyprus to seal the runners-up spot to Belgium.

Rijvers had been impressed by Alan Hansen in the match against Spain. He told the *Record*, 'He is a player of real international ability – a world-class player if you like. He is a very modern player, a defender who can come forward into attack and who can play with skill when he does leave defence. Hansen was magnificent, probably the best player on the field. I'm certain he will be outstanding in the finals. It was a disappointing display by Scotland in Valencia, but I don't think it will reflect on what the team might do this summer. In Hansen, they had an extra point as far as I am concerned. I have seen him with Liverpool but never playing as well as he did in the role he had with Scotland.'

From the village of Sauchie in Stirlingshire, Hansen excelled at several sports as a youngster. He represented Scotland at volleyball and was also a squash player and an accomplished golfer, playing off a handicap of two. Hansen once turned down a trial at Hibs as it clashed with the Scottish Boys' Stroke Play Championship at Montrose. At the time, he was more intent on becoming a golfer. 'But I was persuaded that there was a more promising future for me at soccer,' he said in 1975. At 15, he went for a trial at Liverpool, but the club turned him down. The rejection letter, signed by Geoff Twentyman, read, 'It was decided after trials that you did not reach the standard required. Thank you for attending.' Undeterred, he signed for Partick Thistle in the summer of 1973, establishing himself in the first team in the 1974/75 season, playing 26 league games. In Alan's first season at Firhill, brother John, who played in the same side, said, 'If he is groomed the right way, I see him developing into another Gordon McQueen. He has all the ability to go a long way.'

Alan's under-23 debut came in Gothenburg as Scotland beat Sweden 2-1 in April 1975. Another two under-23 caps followed. When the age level changed, he won four under-21 caps in the Toulon Tournament of 1977. In the

Anglo-Scottish Cup, Hansen played in the Thistle defence as they drew 0-0 with Bolton. In the second leg, Hansen scored the only goal of the game. He made an impression on his opponents as they tabled a bid of £80,000 but Bertie Auld turned it down flat.

It was Liverpool who matched Thistle's valuation of £100,000 and Hansen's Anfield manager Bob Paisley judged him the most skilful centre-half he had seen in the British game. 'I sometimes wonder whether or not he is really a Scot,' Paisley said. 'There are no rough or rugged edges about him at all, no violent streak, no simmering temper. He is a joy to watch. Alan has always been an excellent footballer, a beautifully balanced player who carries the ball with control and grace. His talent is rare for a defender.'

Hansen made his first-team debut for Liverpool against Derby County at Anfield towards the end of September 1977, prompting journalist Don Evans to note, 'The man of the match, the lad who made his debut for Liverpool and came off a new Spion Kop hero, was the young Scot, Alan Hansen.' With the central defensive pairing of Phil Thompson and Emlyn Hughes already established, Hansen's opportunities were limited during his first full season on Merseyside. But he still appeared in nearly half the league matches, 18, and several cup ties. If disappointed to miss out on the League Cup Final team narrowly defeated by Nottingham Forest after a replay, his consolation came in being picked in the starting line-up that would successfully defend the European Cup at Wembley against Club Brugge in the last match of the 1977/78 campaign. Hansen played left-back in that final but replaced Hughes in the centre of defence early in the 1978/79 season. After Hughes left for Wolves in 1979, Hansen started to make the position his own on a permanent basis. In May 1979, the same month he won his first English First Division title, he made his Scotland debut with John Wark and George Burley as Wales won 3-0 in Cardiff.

Stein headed to Villa Park for Aston Villa's European Cup tie. The night before, he saw Wolves beat Leeds United 1-0 at Molineux. Frank Gray, who rejoined Leeds for £300,000 in May 1981, was the only one of his players on show that evening, although, now out of favour, Kenny Burns was also in the Leeds side. Kyiv lined up with five players expected to be in Spain: Sergei Baltacha, Anatoliy Demyanenko, Andriy Bal, Oleg Blokhin, plus Viktor Chanov, back-up goalkeeper to Rinat Dasayev. The attendance of 38,579 saw Gary Shaw put Villa in front on four minutes. A second goal came four minutes from the end of the first half when uncapped Scot Ken McNaught leapt to head in a Gordon Cowans corner. The Villa defence were seldom in any trouble in the second half, and they saw out the match to make the semi-final. Elsewhere in Europe, Dundee United were knocked out of the UEFA Cup after a 3-0 loss to Radnicki Nis. Liverpool's hold on the European Cup ended after losing 2-0 in extra time to CSKA Sofia. Steve Archibald and Tottenham had better luck as, although they lost 2-1 on the night to Eintracht Frankfurt, they made the semi-finals of the European Cup Winners' Cup with a 3-2 aggregate win. Archibald, however, picked up another booking that would see him suspended for the first leg of that tie.

'I'm certainly much happier having seen Dynamo Kyiv at Villa Park,' Stein said the following day. 'In Athens last week the Russians were seldom under any pressure, but their World Cup men were given a severe test in Birmingham and, quite frankly, I didn't see anything to frighten us.'

The match was played on a heavy pitch, which had been sanded in order to get the game on. Stein admitted that these conditions didn't suit the Russians, 'They couldn't play those neat little one-twos, but there were flaws and they showed they could make the same mistakes as any other side.' Stein had previously voiced a theory that the Russians didn't enjoy playing with a packed crowd closing in on them. 'They were obviously uneasy with that crowd roaring on Villa. Well, it will be worse in Malaga, because the crowd will be even closer to them and we could have something like 20,00 Scottish fans right behind us. Because they were not impressive against Greece and they lost against Villa doesn't mean I'll underestimate them. They have ability and they have shown it in many games. But they don't fight back well when they find things going against them. They don't like being pressured.'

In *The Guardian*, Charles Burgess quoted a Russian journalist who had told him of the Kyiv side, 'They play like robots and cannot change their pattern of play if things are not going their way. The implications for the national side are dire and it is only the inclusion of the more carefree players from Dinamo Tbilisi that will give us any chance.' Allan Evans agreed that Villa's success could be good for Scotland, 'With so many men in the World Cup squad, it must give the Russians plenty to think about, being beaten so comprehensively by a British side. We simply closed them down quickly, they didn't like it and began to give the ball away. Scotland can do the same.' Kyiv and Russia's star man failed to impress Evans, who said, 'I was rather surprised by Oleg Blokhin's performance. We all know that on his day, he is a great player, but he didn't give us any problems.' Evans felt that the Soviets wanted room on the pitch to build their moves. 'They like space to play short passing movements, which will get them into dangerous positions. We didn't give them that. We realised in Russia that they didn't like being shut down when they got possession. It worked for us out there, and we did it again at home. What it meant was that they were forced into making hurried, inaccurate passes and giving the ball away.'

Evans started with Dunfermline United, the nursery team of Dunfermline Athletic. He signed for Dunfermline on an 'S' form in May 1971, turning professional in December 1973. His early progress in the first team was hampered when he broke his leg against Rangers in only his second appearance. That kept him out for six months, but he established himself in the first team in 1974/75, playing 25 league games. 'I was a centre-half at Dunfermline for three years, and then our centre-forward picked up a bad injury,' he said in Ipswich Town's match programme in 1980. 'They couldn't afford to buy a replacement and moved me up front. I did quite well and scored a hat-trick the day Villa sent a scout to watch me, but I always thought of myself as a defender.' Evans scored 13 times in 37 league games in 1976/77 as Dunfermline finished third in the Second Division. That hat-trick came on the final day of the season against Stranraer. Evans told the Aston Villa website, 'Villa and Leeds United had sent a scout to watch our goalkeeper Hugh Whyte. I was playing as a striker at that time and I scored a hat-trick in the first 15 minutes. From there I was pulled into the manager's office and told of the interest. It was arranged that I go to the Villa for a trial first and then to Leeds the week after. I was a big Leeds fan at the time because they had so many Scotsmen in the side – Bremner, Lorimer, the Grays and Jordan. But even though the trial at

Villa was physically demanding I'd shown enough for Ron Saunders to offer me a contract. I made the decision to say yes to Villa and forget about Leeds.'

Villa paid an initial £21,600, with an additional £10,800 coming after he had made ten first-team appearances. Six goals in a reserve match against Sheffield United a week before Villa's UEFA Cup quarter-final against Barcelona in March 1978 suddenly put Evans forward as a first-team contender. He played 15 minutes against Johan Cruyff's side. Coming on at 2-0 down, he helped his side claim a 2-2 draw. There were three league games as a striker before he was moved into the heart of the defence. Evans became a rock in that position, helping Villa to the First Division title in 1980/81, playing 39 games and chipping in with seven league goals. Villa's subsequent European Cup campaign had firmly brought him to Jock Stein's attention. Evans's performance against Kyiv pleased Stein. 'I hadn't seen Allan play for some time,' he told Jim Reynolds, 'but had some glowing reports about his form. Not from his own manager, because that's not the way I work, but from managers who had seen him in opposition to their own sides.'

The 26-year-old was buzzing from being included in the squad for the Netherlands match, 'My plans were to stay at home this summer and watch the whole of the World Cup on television, but now I'm in a bit of a whirl. Mr Stein's call-up on Monday came as a complete surprise. I just couldn't believe it at first, but now I'm well aware what this could mean to me.'

Stein also suggested that there may be room for a couple of Evans's team-mates. 'It certainly isn't too late for people to force their way into my squad,' he said when Chick Young asked him about Ken McNaught and Des Bremner.

'It was a good team performance by Villa but the Scottish lads certainly impressed me.' The draw for the semi-final paired Villa with Belgian champions Anderlecht, while Spurs would face Barcelona in the last four of the Cup Winners' Cup.

* * *

The Scotland squad assembled in Troon after the Saturday fixtures. Allan Evans had the weekend's stand-out performance despite his Villa side going down 3-1 to Ipswich. Town boss Bobby Robson described him as 'a hero in defence', adding, 'If Evans hadn't been there, the Villa defence would have crumbled.' John Wark scored Ipswich's first goal, with Alan Brazil also in the team. Gordon Strachan's performance against Dundee United was Scotland's star turn of the day. He set up the first goal in Aberdeen's 2-1 win for John Hewitt. Joe Jordan's AC Milan went down 2-0 to fellow relegation battlers Como. Milan supporters went berserk, and captain Fulvio Collovati was taken to hospital, having been hit on the head by a rock. Police had to fire tear gas to get the Milan fans to disperse. The squad suffered two withdrawals as Graeme Souness and Asa Hartford dropped out. Souness sustained a back injury in Liverpool's win over Sunderland, while Hartford played against Everton for Manchester City but picked up a calf injury. Stein opted not to draft any replacements.

On the morning of the match against the Dutch, Tuesday, 23 March, the Foreign Office reported that an Argentinian commercial group, Davidoff, a scrap metal business, had illegally landed on the Falkland Islands, a British overseas territory, the previous week. The 60 workers had now established a camp there and had hoisted the

Argentinian flag. The Foreign Office deemed this a serious infringement of British sovereignty of the Falklands. The British Embassy in Buenos Aires said that the Argentine firm was dismantling a British-owned whaling station with the knowledge of the government. Still, it acknowledged that they had been warned to follow official immigration formalities on several occasions. A field party from the British Antarctic Survey team was sent to investigate, using the naval patrol ship HMS *Endurance*, operating off Adelaide Island, within three days of sailing time from Port Stanley. At this point, the incident was a matter only for bureaucratic discussion, a British Embassy official being quoted as saying, 'It is just a piece of silliness.' But it would soon become far more serious and cast a shadow over the involvement of the British nations in the World Cup.

At Hampden, Allan Evans and Jim Bett made their international debuts. Bett's selection was the first time a Rangers player had been picked for Scotland since Ally Dawson came on as a substitute in Poland in May 1980. 'The more people challenging the better,' Stein said, 'and I want the men who play … to justify their selection and put the pressure on others. At this stage, players should be hoping and working to go to Spain, not expecting.'

Joe Jordan was also back in the team. 'Of course, it has been a worry,' Jordan said of his and his club's struggles. 'But I've felt all along Jock Stein was not the kind of man who would listen to other people's views. It's smashing to be in the team. It's the biggest lift I've had in weeks.'

'Although Jordan has missed our last few matches,' said Stein, 'I have said all along that he would not be forgotten. I think this is the game in which he should be given his chance, rather than the one in Northern Ireland next month. And if he has a good hour, then that will be useful, for he can be tucked away and used in certain matches.' Moreover, Stein felt that the World Cup would require two separate sides, explaining, 'What will do in one game won't necessarily do in another.' For this reason, he felt that missing some regulars could be seen as a blessing.

In the Dutch side, John Metgod of AZ 67 was seen as Krol's eventual successor at sweeper, and good things were expected of Wim Kieft, who had been scoring goals for Ajax. The referee was Englishman George Courtney. For the first time 'Scotland the Brave' would be played in place of the national anthem. In his programme notes, Stein wrote, 'In tonight's game and in the Home Internationals with Northern Ireland, Wales and England I'll still be experimenting up to a point. Yet I still want the nucleus of our side to play together as much as possible before our World Cup ties.' A crowd of 71,848 turned out at Hampden, taking great delight in taunting the Netherlands, who in the words of Andy Cameron's 1978 hit 'Ally's Tartan Army', 'didnae qualify'.

Evans acquitted himself well, robbing Keift early on, then blocking a later shot from the striker. On 13 minutes Scotland won a penalty. Out on the left, Bett played a high ball in for Jordan. However, Ronald Spelbos got there first, knocking the ball away with his hand. The referee had no hesitation in awarding the penalty. With no John Robertson in the 11, Leeds United's Frank Gray stepped up. He placed the ball just inside Hans van Breukelen's left-hand post as the keeper dived to his right. Scotland extended their lead nine minutes later with what Alex Cameron in the *Daily Record* would call 'one of the best goals ever scored at Hampden'. Dalglish gave Archibald the ball in midfield.

Kenny moved forward and received the return, switching possession to Jordan. A back-heel from Jordan found Dalglish in an instant. Two defenders tried to pounce. The Liverpool striker dragged the ball clear, veered to his left to avoid a challenge and chipped it over the keeper. 'It was soccer of such high skill that surely nobody will ever again suggest that Dalglish should be left out of a Scottish team as long as he can put one foot in front of the other,' wrote Cameron.

Metgod thought he had a goal back a minute later after heading in a cross but turned to see the linesman raise his flag for offside. Holland repeated the move on the half-hour as Gray was beaten down the right. Ajax's Frank Rijkaard crossed and Kieft, unmarked, headed into Rough's left-hand corner. Scotland let Holland in again minutes later when Narey was short with a back pass. But when Muhren put his cross in, there were no takers. Spelbos seemed to knock Jordan over in the box shortly after, but Courtney wasn't inclined to award a second penalty.

Dalglish and Archibald, the star performers in the first half, were withdrawn at half-time as Tommy Burns and Alan Brazil came on. Burns played Gray in as the Leeds man saw his shot well saved by Van Breukelen. Holland came back at the Scots, and Evans was forced into heading over his own crossbar, then Krol hit a swerving drive from 25 yards which Rough was equal to. Scotland had a great chance to extend the lead on 56 minutes when Brazil and Jordan got into a tangle with only the keeper to beat. Brazil got a shot off but it trickled wide. Rough was there to save Scotland on 62 minutes when he got down well to a Muhren header. Strachan replaced Jordan with four minutes left.

The 2-1 win delighted Jock Stein. 'We won a game against quality opposition,' he said. 'We've won and at the same time tried out two or three players, and we scored as good a goal as we would ever want. There are still one or two things to sort out, of course, but that's what these games are about.' Jordan could not be faulted for his work rate, and Stein was pleased with his performance, 'Joe did exceptionally well considering that he had a hard game on Sunday before travelling here.' Ruud Krul commented after the match, 'Joe Jordan was very good. I was glad to see that. Joe has had problems in Italy, but I play there too and I know how difficult it is. [At AC Milan] no one supports him. But I saw a different Jordan at Hampden. This is not the player I have seen in Italy. He caused us a lot of problems, myself included. Playing like that in the World Cup could cause anyone problems.' Boss Rijvers wasn't unduly concerned by the defeat, 'We had a few youngsters in the side and they found it difficult to settle early on. We tried a new style in the second half and I was quite pleased with how it worked out.' He had one note of caution though for Scotland in Spain, saying, 'You will need Alan Hansen of Liverpool in the defence.'

Although a good win, the newspapers believed that Scotland didn't look comfortable for the game's entirety. Reporters were sympathetic to the Dutch's claims that their disallowed goal was a good one, and many felt that the shine went off Scotland's display when Dalglish left the field. However, a win over a side like Holland, albeit one in transition, has to be looked at like a good thing. There were many individual performances to inspire confidence. Narey, in midfield, shackled Arnold Muhren so well as to render him ineffective, Miller and McGrain were both excellent at the back, and Evans and Bett both had solid debuts.

Stein defended Rough, who took some criticism for the Dutch goal. 'Our bad goalkeeper once again proved that he is as good as anyone, playing for any country,' he said. 'Apart from his saves, his cutting out of long balls through the defence and his handling were excellent. It's a great credit to him how he can pick himself up for the big occasion.'

The lack of goals was also something Stein was not keen to hear about from pundits. 'That's because we don't take on easy matches,' he said. 'Look at the friendlies we have played in recent seasons – Poland, Hungary, Spain and Holland. Nobody would expect us to score a lot of goals against that type of opposition. If we wanted to score four or five we would play against the likes of Norway, Cyprus or Finland. We could turn on the fancy stuff, but we would learn absolutely nothing. We just don't take on easy games.' Stein declared the experimental team a success and now looked forward to preparing for the Home Internationals.

The following evening the under-21s drew 0-0 with Italy at Pittodrie in front of 16,000 to put the youngsters through to a European Championship quarter-final with England.

The national team and its various squads looked in as promising a condition as it had at any time in its history. However, the focus now for Stein and the full squad was the Home Internationals. Although traditionally competitive fixtures, the question was if Stein would treat them as such or simply as trials for Spain.

6

Back to Belfast: Stein continues to tinker, and a boycott threat emerges

'We could bank on a fully fit John Robertson doing a vital job for us in Spain, but we're certainly not banking on the one we saw in Belfast. It's really quite simple – he either gets himself properly fit or we change our style and play without him.'

Jock Stein

BY THE beginning of April, the Davidoff scrap workers, intent on dismantling a disused whaling station on the South Atlantic island of South Georgia, part of the Falkland Islands group, were still in place; 'illegally squatting' according to the British government. Argentina had sent three warships and their only aircraft carrier to the area to face down HMS *Endurance*, recently condemned to the government breaker's yard in the latest round of defence cuts. The government stressed that they were looking for a peaceful solution amid criticisms that the British maritime defence policy was ill-equipped to defend the Falkland Islands. The Lord Privy Seal Humphrey Atkins MP told a cabinet meeting on 1 April, 'It would not be an easy task to defend a colony which was 8,000 miles distant from the United Kingdom and 3,500 miles from the nearest airfield of the use of which the British government could be assured.'

By the evening of 2 April, Argentina announced that the islands, a British sovereign territory since 1833, were under Argentine control.

There was now speculation that due to holders Argentina's involvement, the situation in the Falklands may lead to the home nations withdrawing from the World Cup. Ernie Walker admitted to the *Glasgow Herald* that the Falklands situation had been discussed at a regular SFA executive committee meeting, 'Everyone seems to know a lot about this matter except the three British football associations taking part. We have discussed the situation. Obviously, we can only await developments. If the situation deteriorates badly, we will be guided by Her Majesty's government. There is no doubt that there is a dire threat to the World Cup.' Government sources admitted that, even if they wanted to, they would be unable to prevent the home nations from travelling to Spain. An official at the office of the sports minister Neil Macfarlane said, 'As always in this country, the government has no powers over the actions of the football associations, so we cannot stop them.' English FA secretary Ted Croker said that they had not discussed the matter at any level, 'It is much too early to even think about such a situation.' A FIFA spokesman could not offer any solutions, saying, 'We have no information so far, so there can be no answers to any hypothetical questions.'

The SFA continued to make preparations for the tournament and appointed John Little, former chief constable of Tayside, as security liaison for the World Cup. His brief would be to advise Spanish police and Scots fans in Malaga.

The *Daily Mail* reported that a special British cabinet committee would discuss whether the home nations would withdraw from the World Cup. The committee was headed by Douglas Hurd, minister of state at the Foreign Office. Hurd led an ultimately unsuccessful campaign for Britain to join with the USA in boycotting the 1980 Moscow Olympics following the Soviet invasion of Afghanistan. He would examine Britain's sporting links with Argentina. The *Mail* speculated on whether the committee would look at withdrawing the countries or if they would attempt to put pressure on Argentina to be expelled from international events, as South Africa was. The Common Market had imposed a trade ban on Argentina, and the fears were that if those countries also boycotted the World Cup, the tournament would lose France, Belgium, Austria, West Germany and Italy.

The World Cup single 'We Have a Dream' was released on Monday, 15 April. The launch took place at a Glasgow casino with B.A. Robertson and Danny McGrain waving flags for the cameras.

In England, Asa Hartford's manager at Manchester City, John Bond, launched a stinging attack on him after City's 1-0 defeat to West Ham United at Maine Road in the First Division. 'If Asa thinks he's entitled to play in Spain on the strength of the way he's been performing over the last couple of months, he's in trouble,' Bond began. 'I don't know how up to date Jock Stein is on the situation, but I would respectfully suggest that he gets here quickly and has a good look at what Hartford is doing, or rather not doing for City. Frankly, I don't see how Jock Stein can pick him. I'm getting fed up with watching a player of his ability contributing next to nothing. He's going to have to prove to me that he isn't over the hill. If he can't, then he'd better start looking for another job pretty soon.' Bond pulled his side in for a Sunday training session after the defeat to the Hammers, branding them 'pathetic'.

Hartford was born in Clydebank in October 1950. His playing career began with Drumchapel Amateurs. Wolves had been interested in taking him down south, but West Bromwich Albion secured his services. They came to hear about him through their midfielder Bobby Hope's father. Hope and Hartford had both gone to Clydebank High School. At this time, Scottish clubs couldn't approach schoolboys, so the Baggies could snap him up without competition from local teams.

Hartford made his league debut in February 1968 against Sheffield United and from the 1968/69 season he had firmly established himself in the team. In November 1971, Hartford was on the verge of a £177,000 transfer to Leeds United. He had a training session with his new team-mates before going through a medical. In an era where most club doctors were volunteers, and medical checks were 30-second check-ups of blood pressure and weight, Leeds had a far more rigorous procedure and the medical showed that Asa had a hole in the heart. The transfer was off, and doubts were raised about his football career. 'I can't believe there is anything wrong with me, and I refuse to believe I won't be playing again,' Hartford said.

He went back to The Hawthorns, and WBA arranged a second medical examination. A Birmingham doctor confirmed the diagnosis but suggested that it shouldn't stop Hartford from playing. He was back in the West Brom team the following Saturday. Asa had been on the verge of the Scotland team as interim manager Tommy Docherty had him in his plans for the match with Belgium in the same month, but he was left out due to the diagnosis. Hartford would make his Scotland debut in April 1972 under Docherty, against Peru, and in 1974 he signed for Manchester City. He was part of the team who won the 1976 League Cup with a 2-1 victory over Newcastle United in the Wembley final. He joined European Cup holders Nottingham Forest in the summer of 1979 for £500,000 but his career there lasted for only 63 days. After three league games, Asa fell foul of boss Brian Clough. 'Asa is finding it extremely difficult to fit into a side which clicks in every department,' Clough said after a 4-1 win over Coventry City. 'At the moment, he is like a dog after a bone. He is running about all over the place without any discipline in his play. He has never played disciplined football in his life. It is bound to be worrying him, but it is certainly not worrying me. If he is no good, he will go.' Forest got their money back a few days later when Everton snapped him up. A return to Manchester City followed in the autumn of 1981.

'It's not the time for experiments,' Stein said before naming his squad for the Home International against Northern Ireland in Belfast. Joe Jordan wouldn't be available as AC Milan would not release him for what they considered friendly internationals. However, Hartford and John Robertson, both suffering from loss of form at club level, were aware that this was their big chance to ensure they were on the plane. 'I know how much it means to me to have a good game at Windsor Park; if I'm chosen, that is,' Hartford said.

'It's been a frustrating season for me, what with injuries, loss of form and squabbles with Nottingham Forest manager Brian Clough,' Robertson said to the *Evening Times*. 'Now I've got to do my best so that I can be sure of a place in the final 22 for Spain.'

In the week leading up to the squad announcement, Andy Gray hit three goals in three games for Wolves, leading to his manager Ian Greaves saying, 'If Andy can continue scoring goals I'll be getting in touch with Jock Stein, and I think Jock will listen to me, for I've known him for 20 years.'

'I thought my chance had gone,' Gray himself said. 'The best I was thinking about was a place in the 40. However, I dare not build my World Cup hopes too high. To give myself the slightest chance I must score at least a goal a game until the end of the season. Reputations are quickly forgotten when it comes to picking an international team, so I must build myself another. If people think my best days were behind me they are wrong. We have a fight on our hands at Molineux to get clear of relegation and perhaps that will help bring out the best in me.'

* * *

The *Sunday Telegraph* reported that diplomatic sources in Whitehall had disclosed that if Argentina took part in the World Cup, there was no expectation of Scotland, England or Northern Ireland to play. The newspaper's sports editor David Grice wrote that initial moves had been made to persuade the European Economic Community to join forces to eject Argentina from the competition. The newspaper speculated on where the loyalties of the competing nations would lie with the suggestion that, in addition to the Common Market countries, New Zealand, Chile, Cameroon, Algeria and Kuwait would all side with the home nations. The paper expected that the Eastern Bloc countries, the Soviet Union, Poland, Czechoslovakia, Hungary and Yugoslavia, along with Peru and El Salvador, would support Argentina. Honduras and Brazil, it was thought, would remain neutral. Should it come to it, the situation would put Spain in an unfortunate position. Typically pro-South American, it was currently on the fringe of Common Market membership.

In the House of Commons, Dennis Canavan, MP for Falkirk West, asked the secretary of state for the environment what matters he intended to discuss at his next meeting with the football authorities about arrangements for the World Cup. Neil Macfarlane replied that his main concern in the World Cup arrangements was to advise the Spanish authorities on possible hooliganism 'by a minority of British supporters'. Canavan asked if the minister would clarify his previous written response, 'in which he urged a sports boycott of Argentina, especially as Scotland, England, Northern Ireland and Argentina are all in the World Cup finals? Does he agree that a boycott of the World Cup would not help the oppressed people of the Falkland Islands but could damage international relations if we allowed a Fascist dictator, such as Galtieri, to spoil one of the greatest international sporting competitions in the world?' Macfarlane responded, 'There is no question of a boycott. Therefore, I have nothing to add to the written answer that I gave.'

Sir Hector Monro, the MP for Dumfries, who was previously the minister for sport until he was dropped after opposing the withdrawal of the British team from the Moscow Olympics, addressed Macfarlane. 'Does my honourable friend accept that many of us agree with his advice? We must hope that FIFA will realise that many European and Commonwealth countries would not wish to be involved in a tournament with Argentina. Should not FIFA take the responsibility of removing Argentina from the World Cup if the present position continues?' Macfarlane stated that he could not anticipate what action FIFA may take, 'As matters stand now, we have no objection to British teams taking part in international competitions where Argentina may also be represented. However, our position must be kept under constant review in the light of changing circumstances. I have nothing more to say now.'

Denis Howell, the MP for Birmingham Small Heath and another former minister for sport, spoke next, 'Does the minister accept that if resolution 502 of the Security Council has not been honoured by the time of the World Cup, the government must consider what principles will govern their advice?' United Nations Security Council Resolution 502 was a resolution adopted by the United Nations Security Council on 3 April 1982. The council demanded an immediate cessation of hostilities between Argentina and the United Kingdom and a complete withdrawal by Argentine forces. The council also called on the governments of Argentina and the United Kingdom to seek a diplomatic solution to their differences and refrain from further military action. Howell continued, 'The Labour party would support the proposal by the honourable member for Dumfries that, in such circumstances, the right course would be for FIFA to exclude Argentina.' Macfarlane responded, 'Many millions of British people would think it strange if our three teams were not to participate in the World Cup because of the action of an aggressive nation. All those matters are being kept under the closest review. I cannot comment on any events that may take place during the next few weeks. However, I am in close contact with the representatives of the football authorities, both nationally and internationally.'

On Monday, 19 April, Scotland's under-21s took on England at Hampden Park in the semi-final of the European Championship. Just over 16,000 turned out at Hampden, but it was a relatively flat occasion as the young Scots went down 1-0. In the last minute, Ray Stewart and Mark Hateley got into a tussle on the byline. 'A stupid, senseless fracas,' wrote Joe Melling in the *Daily Express*. They traded punches and were sent off, ruling them out of the second leg.

When Jock Stein announced his squad for the match with Northern Ireland, there were two surprises. In goal, George Wood was recalled, having not played for Scotland since the 3-1 defeat to Argentina in June 1979. Wood had been enjoying a good spell at Arsenal, keeping Pat Jennings out of the team since December 1981 and achieving ten clean sheets from 20 league games. In defence, uncapped Arthur Albiston, an ever-present for Manchester United in 1980/81 and 1981/82, was named. Tommy Burns found himself called in as an overage player to the under-21 squad.

The sending off in the under-21 game had seemingly done for Stewart's chances of joining the World Cup squad. 'Ray disqualified himself from the return against England,' Stein said, 'so there seems no justification for promoting him to the full squad. No player deserves promotion after being sent off.' A disappointed Stewart spoke to Joe Melling, 'Mr Stein had a chat with me this morning,' he said, 'and told me he would not tolerate such behaviour. I was going to be in the squad until that sending off. I could not argue because it was a stupid thing to do. It was in the heat of the moment.' It would land Stewart with a three-match UEFA ban, which would leave him eligible for the Home Internationals and the World Cup but ineligible for the first three games of Scotland's Euro '84 qualifying campaign. With Spurs coming up to a European Cup Winners' Cup semi-final second leg and the FA Cup Final, Steve Archibald was left out of the squad. Paul Sturrock could now make his claim.

At Spurs, Archibald had been working with two psychologists, John Syer and Christopher Connolly of The Sporting Bodymind, a sports psychology consultancy. The 45-year-old Syer was Scotland's first national director and coach of volleyball. He moved to California in 1979 to study psychology. His business partner, 34-year-old Connolly, was an American. Archibald explained to Harry Reid of the *Sunday Standard* what he was getting out of the work, 'I still chase and harry all over the place, but then in the box, when I need composure, it's suddenly available for me.' Archibald had been told to visualise, with great intensity, times in the past when he has felt composed. In this way, he could summon up that quality when he needed it, according to the theory. He said, 'I'm a totally different person now. Basically, I'm uptight. Before, I was always edgy, always biting my nails. I've now a full set of nails for the first time since I was eight. I'm more sociable. I hope I'm more likeable. I don't shut off like I used to. I think back to the past and can see that at times I was a bastard.' In an interview with *The Times*, he added, 'When I'm not scoring goals, I'm tense, and that is when injuries seem to occur. Lack of confidence is akin to fear in that it is related to the past or the future at the expense of the present. "How" questions bring us back to the present.' Archibald said it was even improving his driving, 'I'm slower now. In fact, my wife is faster – I find myself telling her to slow down.'

There was trouble on the terracing at Stade Emile Versé in Brussels at Aston Villa's European Cup semi-final with Anderlecht. Rival fans behind the goal fought, holding the game up for six minutes, while several spectators were carried off on stretchers before a cordon of baton-wielding police ended the fighting. With Evans, McNaught and Bremner in the side, Villa came away with a 0-0 draw which meant they were in the final where they would face Bayern Munich in Rotterdam on Wednesday, 26 May. Anderlecht mounted an ultimately unsuccessful campaign to have Villa thrown out of the tournament. Rene Eberle, secretary of UEFA's Disciplinary Committee, said, 'It is a fact that we on the continent are fed up with the behaviour of your English football fans. We do have some little trouble of our own, but always it seems to be the English who create the major incidents.' In the Camp Nou, Archibald's Spurs missed out on a place in the European Cup Winners' Cup Final as they lost 1-0 to Barcelona.

In the other semi-final, Standard Liège defeated Dinamo Tbilisi. That night, the Russian side contained five members of the expected World Cup squad. Dutch international Arie Haan, part of the Standard Liège line-up, told the *Evening Times*, 'I've a tip for Scotland. Don't fear the Russians.' His advice was not dissimilar to what Allan Evans and Jock Stein had observed from Aston Villa's match with Dynamo Kyiv. 'In Soviet football, players like Kipiani, Shengelia and Chivadze are used to space, and they look like world-class players. But they had no space against us, and they were bad. If Scotland close down on them by tackling quickly and firmly, they can squeeze Russia out of the group,' said Haan.

Frank Gray was released from the Scotland squad two days before the Northern Ireland game. His Leeds side, lying second from bottom of the First Division, had a match with Aston Villa the same night. It wasn't Allan Clarke at Leeds who had asked for Gray to return; Jock Stein had contacted the Yorkshire club to offer his services. 'No way would we have asked for Gray's release had Jock Stein intended to play him against Ireland,' Leeds assistant manager Martin Wilkinson said. 'We had already made plans to cover for Frank.' Like Alan Hansen, Gray had an older brother who had been capped for Scotland before him. Brother Eddie won 12 caps from May 1969 to November 1976. Also, like Hansen, Gray started his career with the same club as his sibling.

'It was touch and go whether we would get him,' Don Revie, manager of Leeds from 1961 to 1974, said to *Football Pictorial*. 'Around 28 other clubs were also interested, among them Rangers, Celtic, Manchester United, Manchester City and Arsenal. All put forward that argument about two brothers rarely making it big with the same First Division club, and it was hard to argue against this. But as far as Frank was concerned, I kept telling him about the three Milburn brothers, John, James and George, who all played for Leeds in the 1930s.' Frank joined Eddie at Elland Road and made his debut in February 1973 as a substitute for Mick Bates in a 2-0 loss away to Leicester City. He played six times that first season, his final appearance coming in the European Cup Winners' Cup Final against AC Milan in Thessaloniki. Leeds lost 1-0 in an infamous match, which led to UEFA banning Greek referee Christos Michas.

Originally a forward wearing number 11, Gray played only sporadically until the 1974/75 season, where he moved into defence and made the number three shirt his own. 'It was Boxing Day 1974, Terry Cooper and Peter Hampton were injured, so I agreed to take on Burnley's Leighton James,' Gray told *Match* in 1982. The 1974/75 season ended for Gray with an appearance in the European Cup Final as Leeds went down to Bayern Munich in Paris. That season, Gray had played *against* Scotland at Hampden. Leeds warmed up for that final with a match against the Scotland under-23 side. The Leeds team with Gray and Jordan lost 3-2 to a Scottish side, including Alan Rough, David Narey and substitute Willie Miller.

Gray made over 300 league appearances for the Yorkshire club until his move to Nottingham Forest in the summer of 1979. He won the European Super Cup while at the City Ground as Forest defeated Barcelona 2-1 on aggregate. At the end of the season he played in his second European Cup Final, this time being on the winning side as Forest defeated Hamburg in Madrid. Winning five under-23 caps between 1974 and 1976, Gray's full international debut was in April 1976, a 1-0 win over Switzerland, a match in which his brother didn't feature. They had both been in squads together but never played alongside one another for Scotland. Frank's second cap didn't come until Stein's first match in charge against Norway in October 1978.

Gray's removal now meant that the stage was set for Arthur Albiston to earn his first full cap. 'Since I was brought into the squad I've heard talk about Spain, but it's not something I'm dwelling on, although I'd obviously love to be there,' Albiston said to Alan Davidson.

Souness and Strachan had now dropped out of the squad with injuries, while Celtic's Davie Provan had been drafted in.

* * *

The Scotland squad were staying at Troon before travelling to Belfast. But, aware that every player was at the end of a long season, with still a lot of work ahead, Stein prescribed a training ban. 'The players won't do any training until we arrive in Northern Ireland,' he told the *Belfast Telegraph*. 'They will have a workout at Windsor Park, and then I'll name my team. Meantime, they will spend their time at Troon soaking up the sea air and playing golf.'

With England having already played two of their three games in the Home International Championship and winning them both, Scotland were the only nation who could stop them from winning the title. 'We will be looking for something special from John Robertson who has missed the last three games,' Stein told the *Record*. 'Asa Hartford doesn't have to prove anything to me, but he might feel this is the time to prove something to his club boss and maybe himself.' Of the opposition, Stein said, 'It really doesn't matter who plays for Ireland, they always show the same fervour. This is not just a warm-up game for Spain. It's a big challenge, and what a tonic it would be for us if we won the British Home Championship [as the Home International Championship was also known] before we travelled to the World Cup.'

But Stein was eager to ensure everyone knew this would not be an easy game, 'This will be a real tough international, a game played in earnest. Ireland will be all out to restore morale after two heavy defeats and cheer up their fans at home.' In recent months, Northern Ireland had lost 4-0 to both England and France.

The Irish were forced into making some changes in their squad. Injuries forced withdrawals from Pat Jennings, David McCreery, Terry Cochrane, Tommy Cassidy, Chris Nicholl and Jimmy Nicholl. However, Bobby Campbell of Fourth Division Bradford City was drafted into the squad. He had scored his 25th goal of the season against Crewe on the previous Monday night. The Irish FA lifted the ban he had been serving after crashing a car while with the youth team in Switzerland in 1975. Five players from the Irish domestic league were also called up. 'Billy Bingham has fulfilled his promise to give us a chance,' Linfield centre-back Roy Walsh said. 'Now, it is up to us to make the most of it.'

Tommy Burns spoke to the *Daily Record* about missing out on playing for the full side and being chosen as an overage player for the under-21s. 'This is still a chance for me to prove myself and reach Spain,' Burns said. 'At first, I was upset at not being in the first team. I thought I had done enough, perhaps, to be in it. Since then, I have spoken to Danny McGrain, and he has told me that Maine Road will be a better place to play. Danny says that there is a bad surface at Windsor Park and rarely a good game there. So, maybe I'm better off in this game. I think this will be my last chance. Looking at things, I am an outsider right now, otherwise, I'd probably be at Belfast. But if I play well in this game, maybe I could get to Spain. The team manager has said that the final 22 will probably be the players he picks for the home internationals – I'm still hoping I'll be in that squad. If I'm not, it won't be the end of the world, but I will be disappointed.'

A 1-1 draw with the Scots' goal coming from Graeme Sharp would see England through to the final. The star man in a Scotland shirt was Tommy Burns. 'I thought Burns was quite outstanding,' Manchester City boss John Bond said. 'His all-round display was one of the outstanding features of the match and Scotland's performance.'

'It's not up to me to tell Jock Stein what to do,' under-21s boss Ricky McFarlane said, 'but Tommy can't have done himself any harm. It's a measure of how seriously he took the match that he was sick at the result in the dressing room later.'

Paul Sturrock was named the Scottish Writers' Player of the Year, and said, 'It has been a long, hard season for me – but a rewarding one. At the start of the year, it was my ambition to get into Jock Stein's squad and I knew it could only be achieved by consistency. Even though my form shaded off a bit midway through the season, I'm still trying for that place in Spain.'

A Brazilian camera crew was in Belfast to film Scotland training. Stein had no problem allowing them access, saying, 'There was no reason why the Brazilians should not film us in action. After all, we did not show them anything in practice as we concentrated on defence, and it was just a relaxed runaround.' Stein's team selection included two wingers in Robertson and Provan, and he was looking to play an open, attacking game, 'With due respect to the Irish, this is the one in which we shall be opening the door a bit and going after a few goals.' He made sure the players selected had an incentive by announcing that there were still two or three places in his final 22 for Spain he hadn't yet settled on.

The bookies put Scotland at 11/8 to win the match with Northern Ireland at 7/4. Scotland lined up in their new red away kit, while Northern Ireland were in their traditional green. While a fierce wind came in off the Irish Sea, the Scots looked good in the first half as they kept the ball well and used it nicely. McGrain had an assured 90 minutes but Albiston seemed uncomfortable against Noel Brotherston's dribbles. Scotland went ahead in the 32nd minute, after Brazil and Dalglish worked well to create space. Brazil got his shot off, and when Jim Platt saved, John Wark followed up to knock the ball in. But Stein's suggestion that this was a night of goals for Scotland came to nothing as Northern Ireland forced Scotland into errors in the second half. An Irish team with only four players from the English First Division gave Scotland several problems, while Donaghy and McClelland worked well together at the centre of their defence. John Robertson was a big disappointment as he flitted in and out of the action. In the *Evening Times*, Hugh Taylor went as far as to call his performance 'distressing'.

Northern Ireland's equaliser came ten minutes into the second half. Brotherston, who had shared digs with Souness when they were youngsters at Tottenham, beat Albiston and Robertson and slipped a through ball for McIlroy to latch on to and hit a low shot into the corner of Wood's net. McLeish slipped when making a pass back on 73 minutes, and Wood saved well from O'Neill's shot. McLeish came off for Hansen in the 76th minute, while Robertson was withdrawn for Sturrock with nine minutes left. In the case of the Nottingham Forest winger, Stein took him off before he was sent off as he got himself embroiled in several minor incidents with Irish defenders.

Wood cemented his position as Alan Rough's deputy with a solid performance. Evans showed up well while McLeish seemed off form. In midfield, although he got the goal, Wark didn't have a particularly good game, while Hartford played well without being flash. Dalglish was already on the plane, while Brazil seemed to have done enough to join him. So there were still places up for grabs, with two more internationals still to come before the 22 for Spain was announced.

'We were in control in the first half and then let things slip,' Stein said. 'We were unsettled at the back.' Stein was not happy with the performance of John Robertson. 'Robertson will have to prove his fitness or else he won't be in our final 22,' he said. 'It would be wrong to say I based my plans on Robertson. I'll be asking him if he's fit but certainly not if he isn't. In Belfast, he simply wasn't doing the kind of things everyone knows he can. And he was getting involved with the opposition in situations where he normally laughs and gets on with the game. His fitness problem isn't one of weight. He has been off with an ankle injury and now his club aren't really fighting to win anything which doesn't help.'

Robertson was well aware he didn't have a good game, admitting, 'My Belfast form was a shock even to me. It's up to me. I didn't think I was doing so badly in the first half against Northern Ireland but the manager left me in no doubt about what I must do.'

'He used to get past people and give himself time to make passes, but he's not doing that now,' Stein said to the *Glasgow Herald*. 'And when it wasn't happening for him in Belfast, he started to get involved in niggling incidents. When players start niggling it spreads right through the whole team and that's something we don't want happening in Spain. He is fully aware of how I feel. I have told him what I think and he knows it is up to himself. When he returns to his club we'll see where his heart lies – whether he is prepared to reach the standard of fitness I want. We could bank on a fully fit John Robertson doing a vital job for us in Spain, but we're certainly not banking on the one we saw in Belfast. It's really quite simple – he either gets himself properly fit or we change our style and play without him.'

Robertson was born in Uddingston in January 1953. Kenny Dalglish once quipped of the town, 'It's famous for John and a mass murderer of the 1960s [Peter Manuel]. But people there never talk about John.' Robertson started out playing with Drumchapel Amateurs. As a teenager, he earned four youth caps and four schoolboy caps. It was while playing for Scotland Schoolboys against England at White Hart Lane that he was spotted by Bill Anderson, assistant to Johnny Carey at Nottingham Forest, who was there on a routine scouting mission. 'John was a little left-winger and although he was only 14 you couldn't fail to be impressed by his terrific football brain. Even at that age he used the ball so well and saw things so quickly. It was obvious to everyone and although lots of clubs were sure to be after him, I decided we had to make a big effort,' said Anderson.

Anderson also spotted the talents of Souness that day, and although he brought him down to Nottingham and took him to the FA Cup Final, he couldn't secure the youngster's signature. Anderson headed to Uddingston to speak to Robertson's parents. He said, 'John's father was not too keen on the idea of him coming to Nottingham, but his grandmother swung things my way. I found out later that Jock Stein [then manager of Celtic] arrived at the house about an hour after I left, but he had missed his chance.'

John signed professionally with Nottingham Forest in May 1970, making his debut as a substitute against

Blackpool in the First Division in October that year. Forest suffered relegation in 1971/72. Although Robertson was an established first-team player in the following seasons, he was heading for an unremarkable career in the Second Division. Carey was then replaced as manager by Matt Gillies, who gave way to Dave Mackay in November 1972. The former Hearts and Spurs man appreciated Robertson's apparent talents as he tried to build a side that would win promotion. However, a knee injury during a 1973 pre-season game with Benfica in Lisbon derailed Robertson's career. As Robertson recovered from a cartilage operation, Mackay left to be replaced by Allan Brown. Brown didn't rate Robertson, placing him on the transfer market and saying, 'He could leave here now and make a fool of me, but that's a chance I've got to take.' No one came in for him. Then in January 1975, Brian Clough arrived at the City Ground.

Clough's assistant Peter Taylor had a look at Robertson on the training pitch. 'I decided he had a slovenly approach and cried out for discipline. I told him what I thought and that if he had the skill that people were telling me about, then he had better do something about his attitude,' Taylor said. John did change his attitude and became a mainstay of the Nottingham Forest team that gained promotion from the Second Division and won the Anglo-Scottish Cup in 1976/77.

'I remember him in his younger days,' Stein said in 1980, 'when he was playing in midfield and I always got the impression he was kidding people a bit. Then Cloughie arrived to sort him out and it's my responsibility to do the same thing for Scotland.'

In 1977/78, Forest won the First Division with Robertson playing in every match, scoring 12 goals along the way. They also lifted the League Cup with Robertson scoring the winner from the penalty spot. Forest went on to greater success in 1979, Robertson supplying the cross for Trevor Francis to score the goal that won the European Cup against Malmö in Munich. Robertson himself scored the winner for Forest's second European Cup a year later against Hamburg in Madrid.

West Bromwich Albion's Brendan Batson, who Robertson revealed in 1980 was his most difficult opponent, said, 'He turns defenders inside out if he gets the chance, but if he can't do that, he drops off and tries something different. It's always difficult to go tight on John or to hold off him.' Robertson came into the Scotland side during preparations for Argentina. He made his debut in the Home International Championship in May 1978 against Northern Ireland at Hampden in a 1-1 draw.

Robertson wasn't the only player moving away from a place in the World Cup squad. Alex McLeish, too, did not have a great game in Belfast. 'I know McLeish is struggling,' said Stein. 'He is not having a particularly good time at club level either. But I tried to give him a pat on the back by playing him against Northern Ireland. Now time is running out for him to do something.'

All these players could be confident that they had little time to play themselves into Stein's plans. A provisional squad of 40 was soon to be announced, which would be whittled down to the travelling 22. 'There are so many men in my squad who still have a lot to play for at club level,' Stein continued. 'We must wait first of all to see if they all come through without serious injury, then after they have had a short rest, we will be able to judge the position much better.'

Some unsettling news came in from Spain as suggestions emerged that Argentina were about to stage-manage a boycott threat of South American nations from the World Cup. It was thought this would put pressure on FIFA into forcing the home nations to stand down. England boss Ron Greenwood said he was resigned to his side pulling out if war started in the Falklands. 'When your country is faced by a crisis as grave as this,' he told the press, 'there are more important things to worry about than football.' The SFA, though, were refusing to panic. Stein said, 'We are going as usual. We haven't heard anything from the government.'

The situation was about to get worse before it would get better.

7

The Final Preparations: The Falklands crisis escalates and the Home Internationals conclude

'I wish to make it clear the SFA have no plans to withdraw from the World Cup. We are still in the competition and intend to stay there pending any advice from the government, which we would have to consider.'

Ernie Walker

ALEX FLETCHER, the minister for sport in Scotland, held a press conference about the Falklands crisis at Love Street where he was presenting a cheque for £270,000 from the Football Grounds Improvement Trust. 'If the situation escalates,' he said, 'I can't see Scotland or Northern Ireland playing in Spain. And, even more so, England. The government doesn't want to interfere. However, if there isn't a settlement on the Falklands – and we hope there is – a directive will emanate from somewhere.' A meeting was scheduled for 13 May between the government and the football organisations. 'We are going on as usual,' Jock Stein said. 'We haven't heard anything from the government.'

In early May, Stein set off for New Zealand on a scouting mission. The Kiwis would be playing three matches against the League of Ireland across four days in May in both Rotorua and Gisborne. Before he left, Stein visited Anfield to see Liverpool defeat Nottingham Forest 2-0. Graeme Souness failed to make his return from injury, although he assured his national manager he would be fit for Spain. Dalglish and Hansen did play, the former setting up the first of Craig Johnston's two goals, while John Robertson put in a mediocre performance.

Stein was accompanied on his journey to New Zealand by broadcaster Archie Macpherson. Stein's trip, according to Macpherson, was to 'cover his political rear'. Stein was aware his predecessor Ally MacLeod hadn't taken the time to personally watch Iran or Peru before the 1978 World Cup. Stein wanted to make sure he would avoid the flak MacLeod took when the results went against him. Macpherson successfully pitched the idea to BBC London of making a TV programme about the journey, allowing him to travel along with a TV crew.

On the eve of their departure, British forces bombed Port Stanley Airport in the Falklands. The escalation of the tensions made Stein very uncomfortable. He called Macpherson at home, the broadcaster recounted in his book *Action Replays*. 'I don't think we should go,' Stein said. 'This war could get nasty and they'll end up cancelling the World Cup or we'll withdraw. Something's bound to happen. I think it'll be a waste of time to go away out there now.' Macpherson felt that Stein was really trying to bounce the notion off him, in order to get his response. Macpherson's counsel was that if the trip were cancelled at this late stage the press would sniff out the reason why, giving Stein a set of questions he would be better off not answering. Stein took Archie's advice and the pair set off for New Zealand by way of America.

Macpherson admitted in 2018's *Adventures in the Golden Age* that he really wanted to enhance his credentials with BBC London during the excursion. He also admits that, while he knew Stein had much more tactical nous than MacLeod and he really would get little out of watching New Zealand play an Irish select team, he just didn't have the nerve to steer him away from the plan.

At the Albany Hotel on 2 May, Harry Cavan presented Paul Sturrock with the Scottish Football Writers' Association Player of the Year trophy. Sturrock had a great season with Dundee United, playing 53 games in all competitions and scoring 24 goals. 'In all honesty, he has been the country's only totally outstanding name this World Cup season,' Danny McGrain wrote in his *Shoot!* column. The Scottish Players' Player of the Year, announced a few days later, was someone not even on the fringes of national selection, Airdrieonians' Sandy Clark.

Cavan commented on the political situation, 'I cannot see the British government ordering Scotland, England and Northern Ireland not to go. I was in West Germany last week with all the heads of FIFA, and the Falklands troubles weren't even mentioned. I would have thought it was an excellent chance for a discussion. Now, no meetings are scheduled. Scotland, Northern Ireland and England are really under contract to play, and, with a basic £40m at stake, I certainly can't see the tournament being abandoned.'

That day the situation in the Falklands worsened. The sinking of the cruiser *General Belgrano* by HMS *Conqueror* caused the first major loss of life in the Falklands War, with 368 Argentines killed. Stein heard the news at a hotel in San Francisco. 'C'mon, we're getting the hell out of here back home,' he told Macpherson. 'I told you it could get right out of hand. Get on the phone and get us a flight back home tomorrow.' The following day, however, Stein had cooled, and the pair spent the time as tourists. As they headed to the airport to fly to New Zealand they discovered that HMS *Sheffield* had been sunk with the loss of 20 lives. In the airport, Jock turned to Archie and said, 'I don't think I could face up to this. We could have a world war on our hands. People are getting killed and we're going to be fartin' about amongst the Maoris. It'll look bad, us out there making films and young men getting maimed and slaughtered. It's bad.' Macpherson replied, 'I'm going on. With or without you.' He insisted he would find a way to make a film in New Zealand on his own. Macpherson headed into Departures, ordered a drink and sat down. When he looked up he saw Stein approaching. 'I couldn't let you go on your own,' the Scotland manager said.

The meeting between the British football associations and the sports minister on 13 May, originally intended to discuss containing hooliganism in Spain, would now consider the situation in the Falklands. The SFA hoped for some guidance on their participation in the finals. Willie Harkness said after the SFA's Annual General Meeting, 'We are sitting on the fence at the moment and hoping that everything will turn out all right.' No official communication had been received from the government. In other business, the meeting re-elected the office bearers: Harkness, vice-president Hibernian's Tommy Younger and treasurer David Will of Brechin City.

Harkness had played for Queen of the South throughout the 1930s and 40s, having brief spells with Ayr United, Stirling Albion and Carlisle United. After retiring as a player he went back to Queen of the South to become scout, shareholder, manager, director and chairman. He took over from Rankin Grimshaw as SFA president prior to the 1978 World Cup. His four-year tenure was extended by 12 months with the agreement of Tommy Younger, who was scheduled to take over, so that Harkness could see Scotland through to Spain.

The relationship between the Falklands and the World Cup got more complicated when the Scottish Professional Footballers' Association decided to become involved. 'We are not prepared to sit back and even consider participating in a tournament with a country which has killed our brothers,' SPFA secretary Harry Lawrie wrote in a letter to Margaret Thatcher, the prime minister. 'It would be a terrible insult to the relatives of those killed in the South Atlantic if we got involved with an Argentine team in any sporting capacity.' Lawrie requested that Thatcher order the removal of the three British sides from the World Cup. The SFA described the request as 'utterly irresponsible'. Ernie Walker said, 'It is not for sporting organisations to try to tell the government what to do.'

The English PFA rejected the request from the SPFA to countersign the letter. Its chairman, Alan Gowling, told the *Glasgow Herald*, 'It's a bit premature. We have already said we would support the government in whatever they decide.' Gowling, who telephoned the SPFA to let them know, continued, 'If we took a decision now, we could find the Falklands thing resolved and ourselves out of the World Cup.' The earliest England could meet Argentina would be at the third-place play-off stage, if both lost semi-finals, or the final if both won. It was possible, however, for Scotland to play Argentina in the second round. Scotland captain Danny McGrain was also on the SPFA committee. 'Any action is premature, I would think, until the government gives a lead,' he said.

The government's position up until this point had been to stop British sportsmen competing one on one against Argentinians but to allow competition in multinational contests. Billy Drennan, chief executive of the Northern Ireland Football Association, did not support a boycott. He told the *Daily Mirror*, 'I'm not interested in what [the SPFA] has to say – they have nothing to do with it. England, Scotland and Northern Ireland have signed formal contracts to compete in the World Cup finals.' Ernie Walker added, 'The situation is obscure, to say the least. Football is one of the least important aspects of the crisis at the moment. We are talking about war and people are dying.' In his opinion column in the *Daily Record*, Alex Cameron wrote of Lawrie's letter, 'It is a good moral stand. For how could Britons play football and risk meeting Argentina while men's lives are at stake in a fight for freedom?'

All three nations would obey any government order to boycott.

Graeme Souness told *The Guardian*, 'If the decision is up to me, I would not go as long as the situation remains as it is. The World Cup is important, but nothing could be more important than what is happening.' Souness was also quoted elsewhere in the English media saying, 'Whatever the government say won't make any difference to me. There are people being blown to bits and drowning in the South Atlantic. How could you think about football if that is happening?' Asa Hartford and John Robertson both said they would be happy to be guided by the SFA.

In Madrid, the head of Spain's organising committee, Raimundo Saporta, said if the British teams were unable to participate then FIFA's replacements would be Sweden and Portugal for Scotland and Northern Ireland while Romania would substitute for England. New Zealand's minister of foreign affairs, Warren Cooper, said his nation supported a British boycott. New Zealand had supported Britain over the Falklands by expelling the Argentine ambassador and invoking a trade embargo. Charlie Dempsey, vice-president of the New Zealand administration team, confirmed the squad would go to Spain if the British sides pulled out.

* * *

Scotland's official World Cup song, 'We Have a Dream', entered the UK charts at number 24, selling 100,000 copies over its first weekend. Midweek figures added 62,000 sales just prior to the squad's performance on *Top of the Pops*. 'It's ages since a record has shifted as quickly and it's not just Scots who are buying it,' a record label spokesman said.

In his book *The Rough and the Smooth*, Alan Rough recounted the experience of recording the show, 'For some reason, the BBC decided that we had to fly down the night before the live broadcast, so we enjoyed an evening's plush hospitality, prior to arriving at the studios at midday for a rehearsal. What the producers didn't tell us was that they wanted to put us through our paces three times prior to appearing live at 7.30pm. Perhaps inevitably, this was asking for trouble, given that we all knew the lyrics.' Rehearsals completed without a hitch, the players repaired to the BBC bar. 'By the stage we were close to going on air, several of the players were out of their faces,' said Rough. 'Looking at the clip today you can see us all swaying to the music, with several of the more sober characters stopping the others from falling down. John Robertson had been asked to hold a football, but he was completely plastered and so glassy-eyed that he had forgotten the words of the song and was reduced to a state where he was lurching in front of the cameras, slobbering nonsense. He can't remember a thing. John Gordon Sinclair and B.A. [Robertson] were true professionals, and served up an excellent live version, which helped the song towards the summit of the charts.'

It's not the way Sinclair remembers it. Speaking to STV's *The Football Years* in 2010 he recalled, 'There was a whole crowd in there that started cheering, so I didn't hear the eight-bar introduction, and we were miming as well, so my voice started coming out [of the speakers] and I hadn't started speaking and I think the squad behind me were pretty much the same. They were opening their mouths and nothing much was coming out except alcohol fumes.'

Songwriter Robertson told the *Daily Record* in 2012, 'My abiding memory is that it got me on to Concorde. I was in Nashville, working I think. In those days, the chart was announced on Tuesday morning. You had to get the song rerecorded Wednesday daytime for the taping of *Top of the Pops* Wednesday evening, to be broadcast Thursday. If you didn't get *Top of the Pops*, you weren't on the telly, so it was a big deal, and the episode couldn't be done without me, so they put me on Concorde out of Washington.'

Other Scottish acts in the Top 40 that week were The Associates at number 35 with 'Club Country', Simple Minds at 15 with 'Promised You a Miracle' and Ph.D. at three with 'I Won't Let You Down'. Paul McCartney and Stevie Wonder held the number one position with 'Ebony and Ivory'. Robertson has mixed feelings about the song, 'I performed my one-man shows at the Edinburgh Festival four or five years ago. I didn't plan on doing ['We Have a Dream'] but when I was in the midst of my sensitive singer-songwriter moments, a voice from the back called out, "Hey, big man, could you not dae somethin' a bit mair upbeat?" I said we could have a go at "We Have a Dream" if he fancied it. A proper bear down at the front then said, "Brilliant, that's the only fuckin' reason I'm here." I got the hint then it had become part of Scotland's cultural fabric and sang it every night afterwards. It plays well in Scotland because it has a rousing chorus and seems to be shortbread tin nationalism but it pokes fun at itself.'

On *Top of the Pops*, John Gordon Sinclair was out front belting out his parts while B.A. Robertson and Christian stood in front of the swaying World Cup squad, as yet to be officially announced. Fringe players Jim Bett, George Wood and Jim Leighton made up the numbers with Asa Hartford, Frank Gray, Alan Brazil and Steve Archibald front and centre. Archibald made some history that evening by also appearing with Tottenham Hotspur's FA Cup Final squad and Chas and Dave singing their song 'Tottenham, Tottenham', which was at number 30 in the charts. His Spurs team-mates Glenn Hoddle and Ray Clemence also performed double duties by singing on England's World Cup song 'This Time (We'll Get It Right)'. The episode, presented by Simon Bates, also had in the studio British

R&B artist Junior, Depeche Mode performing 'The Meaning of Love', Ph.D. with Bridgeton-born Jim Diamond on vocals, Tight Fit, Patrice Rushen, Joan Jett, Bananarama with Fun Boy Three, and McCartney being interviewed alongside his wife Linda.

After the *Top of the Pops* appearance, the song climbed to number 13. 'We Have a Dream' would peak at number five, spending nine weeks on the chart, five of them in the Top 20.

On Sunday, 9 May Alan Rough's testimonial brought in a 14,000 crowd to Firhill to see Celtic beat a Scotland XI 8-3. The Scotland 11 lined up as Rough, Brian Whittaker, Frank Gray, David Narey, Kenny Burns, Dixie Deans, Alan Brazil, John Wark, Paul Sturrock, Asa Hartford and John Robertson, with Donald Park the substitute. Burns, Brazil and Park were the Scotland scorers, while Davie Provan scored two of Celtic's eight. Almost 20,000 were at Ibrox the same afternoon for Sandy Jardine's testimonial as his Rangers side beat Southampton 1-0.

In New Zealand, Jock Stein saw 19 Kiwi players in two games over 24 hours. He said, 'I have virtually seen two New Zealand sides. The trip has been well worthwhile. New Zealand are a very physical side, and although they have no real stars they are well organised.' New Zealand won both games against the League of Ireland by a single goal. With a further two games to go, Stein decided to cut short his trip and head home as the government began making noises about the World Cup. Macpherson wrote that there was really not much they could ascertain from matches played on rough pitches with rugby markings. 'All we could tell was that, technically, they were about the level of a decent junior side in Scotland,' he said.

The situation in the Falklands was leading to increasing fears that the British teams would be forced to withdraw from the World Cup. Stein wanted to be involved if there were any talks looking at withdrawal. 'I can't really see it coming to that,' he told Australia's *The Age* newspaper, 'but I would at least like the chance to be in on discussions should the question arise.' However, SFA assistant secretary Peter Donald insisted Stein's return was unconnected with any pull-out threat. The worries centred around Neil Macfarlane's decision to cancel a press conference launching a government advice booklet for fans going to Spain. He said, 'It would be inappropriate to go ahead with the launch at a time when doubts have been expressed about British participation in the World Cup.' A reception planned at 10 Downing Street for the English, Scottish and Northern Irish squads had also been cancelled. The government's official line was this was because of a fixture pile-up due to the bad winter. The government had no power to ban the home nations from playing, only to offer strong advice, as it did in the case of the 1980 Moscow Olympics. An editorial in *The Guardian* read, 'It seems inconceivable that a prime minister who tried to talk our athletes out of going to the Olympics because of Afghanistan should not now do her very utmost to keep British teams away from Spain while Argentina remains included.'

The war cabinet were meeting in London, while in New York the United Nations secretary-general Javier Pérez de Cuéllar was in discussions with the Argentine representative and the British ambassador Sir Anthony Parsons. It was thought that a breakdown in talks would lead to a task-force assault on the Falklands, which would, in turn, lead to the advice that British nations should withdraw from the World Cup. Neil Macfarlane wrote to the Prime Minister to say, 'Up until a week or ten days ago I have taken the line that it was up to the football authorities to decide whether they should participate. However, the loss of British life on HMS *Sheffield* has had a marked effect on some international footballers.' In addition to Graeme Souness voicing his concerns, English players Kevin Keegan and Trevor Brooking had also admitted to having some misgivings. 'They feel revulsion at the prospect of playing in the same tournament as Argentina at this time. Much has appeared in the sporting pages and much more will appear the longer these hostilities continue,' Macfarlane wrote.

Keegan said that it would be 'hypocritical' to play against Argentina in Spain. 'We can't expect our lads to go to the Falklands and be killed, as they were on HMS *Sheffield*, and then face Argentina at football.' Brooking told the *Daily Mirror*, 'I feel strongly about it. I support the principle that people should be against acts of aggression like Argentina's in the Falkland Islands. There are some things more important than football.' Brooking was backed by Alan Gowling, chairman of the PFA. Harry Lawrie, the secretary of the SPFA, said, 'We are wholeheartedly with our English colleagues. There is no way we would wish to play with people associated with all the fervour of taking lives. We will call a special AGM of our players to discuss this vital question.'

The Republic of Ireland were setting out on a South American tour with a game against Argentina on 18 May. Arsenal and Brighton withdrew their players from the squad. 'I don't feel it is right our players should have anything to do with Argentina,' Gunners boss Terry Neill told the *Daily Mirror*. Coventry's Gerry Daly said he wouldn't travel, while

Liverpool intimated that Mark Lawrenson and Ronnie Whelan wouldn't be going. Manager Eoin Hand travelled to England to sound out club managers. He found that they considered the prospect of their players travelling to Argentina utterly preposterous. Hand spoke to Manchester United manager Ron Atkinson about his three Irish players. Atkinson told him the FAI could 'fuck off'. 'I told him I needed his official response,' Hand recalled for the *Irish Times*, 'and he said, "Fuck off, that's my official response."' A week before the match the Argentina game was pulled from the Irish tour schedule.

Mike Norris, a director of Sportsworld Travel, was keen to make clear that Scottish fans would not get refunds on their match tickets should the team be forced to withdraw. 'Scots fans would still get match tickets, but they would see Scotland's replacements, Sweden,' he said. 'We are selling holidays to the World Cup. Whether British teams go or not is immaterial.' The rumour mill was buzzing with suggestions that pulling out would see the teams banned from the 1986 World Cup, and even that FIFA would insist on one British representative team in future. A suggestion of fines in the region of £1m was also being thrown around.

At FIFA, Sepp Blatter insisted that any replacements must have two weeks' notice; for that reason FIFA requested the British nations make their final decision by the end of May. For Ernie Walker, it was business as usual. 'We have done nothing to suggest that we will not play in the finals next month,' he said. Walker also insisted Stein had returned from New Zealand as scheduled and not because of any uncertainty over the team's inclusion. 'I wish to make it clear the SFA have no plans to withdraw from the World

Cup,' Walker continued. 'We are still in the competition and intend to stay there pending any advice from the government, which we would have to consider. We are bound to issue a list of players to FIFA by the weekend and we'll be doing just that. We are aware of the difficulties and the problems and the government are aware of the position we find ourselves in. But the fact is that we have qualified for the finals and as qualifiers, we must proceed with naming players who would then become eligible to play.'

Stein was due to announce a 40-man preliminary squad. 'I may make two important switches in the 40,' he said to the *Record*. 'This is because of what has been said by players. I need experienced men on standby in these circumstances. The situation has changed a great deal since I went to New Zealand. I'd be silly not to call on the experience of players who've helped win a championship and are now in the European Cup Final.'

Stein also spoke with journalist Ken Gallacher about the threatened boycott. 'I wouldn't have gone halfway round the world to see New Zealand if I wasn't going to Spain, would I?' Stein said. He indicated he would talk to his players about the Falklands, but added, 'I won't be going out of my way to talk to any individuals who have already indicated their views.' Kenny Dalglish added his opinion on the situation, 'As Argentina appear the aggressor any pressure from FIFA on teams to withdraw should be aimed at them. Obviously, it's not good for them not to defend their title, but I still feel FIFA should ask them, rather than us, to pull out.'

* * *

On the morning of 14 May, Stein announced his 40-man squad:

Goalkeepers: Alan Rough (Partick Thistle), George Wood (Arsenal), Jim Leighton (Aberdeen), Billy Thomson (St Mirren), Jim Stewart (Rangers)

Defenders: Danny McGrain (Celtic), Stuart Kennedy (Aberdeen), Frank Gray (Leeds United), Iain Munro (Sunderland), Ray Stewart (West Ham United), Arthur Albiston (Manchester United), George Burley (Ipswich Town), Alan Hansen (Liverpool), Alex McLeish (Aberdeen), Willie Miller (Aberdeen), David Narey (Dundee United), Allan Evans (Aston Villa), Paul Hegarty (Dundee United), Roy Aitken (Celtic)

Midfielders: Graeme Souness (Liverpool), Asa Hartford (Manchester City), John Wark (Ipswich Town), Gordon Strachan (Aberdeen), Tommy Burns (Celtic), Jim Bett (Rangers), Bobby Russell (Rangers), Iain McCulloch (Notts County), Des Bremner (Aston Villa), John Robertson (Nottingham Forest), Davie Provan (Celtic), Davie Cooper (Rangers), Arthur Graham (Leeds United)

Strikers: Kenny Dalglish (Liverpool), Joe Jordan (AC Milan), Andy Gray (Wolves), Steve Archibald (Tottenham Hotspur), Alan Brazil (Ipswich Town), Paul Sturrock (Dundee United), George McCluskey (Celtic), Derek Johnstone (Rangers)

The squad included 20 home-based Scots. Four of those chosen were uncapped: Leighton, McCluskey, McCulloch and Russell. Several of the players selected hadn't earned a Scotland cap for several years. Bremner had played once before, against Switzerland in April 1976, while he was still a Hibernian player. Jim Stewart had two caps, one while with Kilmarnock in 1977 and his second while he was at Middlesbrough in Jock Stein's first match in charge, a 3-2 win over Norway in 1978. Derek Johnstone had been included in the 1978 World Cup squad at a time when he was the in-form striker, although he didn't get a game in Argentina. His last appearance for Scotland was against Belgium in December 1979. Hegarty and Munro both hadn't appeared for their country since the game against England in May 1980. Roy Aitken also hadn't played for Scotland since May 1980, when he won his fifth cap against Poland. That 1-0 defeat was also the last time George Burley had played for the national team. Burley had been out for around 15 months with a serious knee injury. Kenny Burns and Archie Gemmill were the only players that had featured in the qualifiers who were not selected.

'We have picked players in this 40 to cover as many eventualities as possible,' Stein said to the *Record*. 'These players have helped us reach Spain, and you don't just throw them aside. But they must be playing well. There is no way we will take anyone who might be a passenger. That should by then be the framework of the 22 for Spain. But we have until 5 June to name the final pool.' On individual players, Stein said that Derek Johnstone was there as a big centre-forward was just what was needed for the New Zealand game and it would provide cover in case Joe Jordan wasn't available. Similarly, Davie Cooper was there, as John Robertson's form for Nottingham Forest hadn't been great. The squad would be cut to 24 for the games against Wales and England, with it being reduced to a final 22 after the England match on 29 May.

On the subject of the Falklands-driven boycott, the *Daily Record* ran an opinion poll, 'Play or Stay?' The newspaper asked fans to tick Yes or No then send the coupon into its offices at Anderston Quay. The *Record*'s poll produced what its editorial described as 'an astonishing runaway support for Scotland to play in the World Cup'. The results came in as 89.92 per cent in favour of playing while 10:8 per cent voted to stay away. In total, 1,061 votes were received. It broke down as 954 voting to play with 107 opting to stay. Ernie Walker and Jock Stein were asked for their views on the result. 'These are most interesting facts,' Walker said. 'It is something we will take into account should we be called upon to make a decision about not going. The correspondence we have had ourselves has been very much in favour of Scotland competing. Our position is that we are going to Spain. All our efforts are geared towards doing well in the World Cup. If we receive any request from the government then we would have to consider it, but the *Record* poll provides very interesting statistics.' Stein said simply, 'The *Record* poll figures are very interesting.'

New Zealand played a further three games against the League of Ireland XI, drawing 0-0, losing 2-1 and finally winning 1-0 in Invercargill.

Joe Jordan's AC Milan side went into the last day of the Serie A season needing not only a win, away to Cesena, to avoid relegation, but for Genoa to lose as well. Despite pounding the home team's goal Milan were 2-0 down midway through the second half. They found it within them to stage a late comeback, with Jordan pulling a goal back before a 20-yarder from Francesco Romano levelled the score. A fine solo goal nine minutes from time by Roberto Antonelli gave Milan the win they required. With Napoli leading Genoa 2-1 going into the 85th minute it looked as if Jordan's side had narrowly survived the drop. But a bizarrely conceded corner, thanks to Napoli keeper Luciano Castellini throwing the ball over his own shoulder with no one near him, led to a Genoa equaliser and Milan were relegated to Serie B. They had only scored 21 league goals all season, Jordan responsible for two of them. It certainly wasn't the form of a World Cup striker, but Jordan's reliability over this and previous campaigns in a Scotland jersey was in his favour. 'I will be making no decisions until after the World Cup,' Jordan said to the *Herald* about his club future, 'but, as I feel now, I would like to stay with Milan.'

On 19 May in the House of Commons, Tam Dalyell, MP for West Lothian, asked Neil Macfarlane, 'if he has since reviewed the question of participation by Scotland, England and Northern Ireland in the World Cup'. Macfarlane's response was, 'I keep the position under constant review.'

'At least in relation to Scotland,' Dalyell replied, 'where most of us in the industrial belt have a rather different perception of the whole Falklands issue than the Southern English, will the government make an effort to ascertain the views of the Scots on the task force before pressurising the SFA to withdraw from the World Cup?' Macfarlane said, 'I cannot give any assurances or guarantees on that topic or that approach. At this stage, the government see no objection to the three British teams taking part as planned in the World Cup finals next month. I have said previously, both inside and outside the house, that many millions of people would find it odd if we, as the non-aggressor nation, were not taking part in the World Cup finals.'

Sir Hector Monro, MP for Dumfries and Macfarlane's predecessor in the role of sports minister, raised the question of Argentina being thrown out of the World Cup, saying, 'They are the aggressor, not us. We should be going and they should not.' Macfarlane stated he understood the point, but that he didn't know of any dialogue that had taken place to that effect within FIFA. He added, 'The Brazilian president of FIFA has made it clear that Argentina will not be excluded from the World Cup.' Macfarlane summed up the matter by saying, 'I think that all honourable members will share my view that, at the moment, this is a matter that has to be held under constant review and that ultimately it is a matter very much for the football authorities. I am reviewing the matter day by day. I cannot answer hypothetical questions about what might happen over the next seven to ten days – I have no means of knowing – except to say that the British government see no objection at the moment to the British teams going to the World Cup finals next month. I hope that the competition can continue under normal circumstances. I wish to make it clear to the house that I have put no pressure on the three British football associations. The matter is under constant review.'

Sir Robert Armstrong, the cabinet secretary, addressed PM Margaret Thatcher with his concerns on the matter, 'Argentina would see British withdrawal not as putting any pressure on them but as an opportunity to make propaganda. The United Kingdom – not Argentina – would be the country set apart.' The secretary of state for the environment, Michael Heseltine, also wrote, outlining how he saw the options. Heseltine felt that the situation would be reviewed in line with events in the South Atlantic, that British concerns centred on the possibility that British supporters could be provoked, and that any decision to withdraw would be made at a senior political level. He also hoped that Argentina might be excluded from the tournament, although accepted that FIFA would be unlikely to insist upon this. Heseltine additionally raised the issue of possibly insulting Spain, primarily in relation to the tense situation regarding Gibraltar, ahead of the opening of its border, which was due on 25 June, and concerns were also raised about the possibility of having to compensate the football associations of Scotland and Northern Ireland. 'The Scottish and Northern Ireland Football Associations could be bankrupted,' he wrote. 'Whilst there might be no legal obligations on Her Majesty's government for compensation, there could be a moral one. In the present international situation I believe that ministers can continue to argue strongly that Argentina is the aggressor nation and that the onus of withdrawal lies in that direction and not with us.' In summing up he offered, 'My present view is that Her Majesty's government should not yet suggest withdrawal to the football authorities, be that we should be ready to adopt that course, at short notice if the situation worsens and in the light of public opinion.'

Cabinet papers show that Thatcher felt that if Scotland reached the second round 'it would be helpful if FIFA could arrange that they did not play Argentina'. An offer was made to George Younger MP, the secretary of state for Scotland, in consultation with the secretary of state for the environment, to consider an approach to FIFA to have them rearrange the World Cup groupings to avoid such a scenario.

Dinamo Tbilisi's David Kipiani, left out of Russia's preliminary squad for Spain, retired from football at the age of just 30. The attacking midfielder, Soviet Player of the Year in 1977, was quoted as saying, 'I had two dreams – to win a European trophy and to play at the World Cup. I have accomplished the first one, but the second is out of reach because I will be too old in 1986. Therefore, there is no reason to continue playing.'

Stein trimmed his squad of 40 down to 24 for the games against Wales and England. Cut were Billy Thomson, Jim Stewart, Stuart Kennedy, Iain Munro, Arthur Albiston, Paul Hegarty, Roy Aitken, Jim Bett, Bobby Russell, Iain McCulloch, Des Bremner, Andy Gray, George McCluskey, Derek Johnstone, Davie Cooper and Arthur Graham.

Stewart, Kennedy, Munro, Bremner, Johnstone and Graham wouldn't play for Scotland again in their careers. Neither Russell, McCulloch nor McCluskey would go on to earn a full Scotland cap. It's remarkable when you consider both Russell and McCluskey were instrumental to their Old Firm clubs winning leagues and cups throughout the 1980s. Aitken and Cooper would get further chances to play in the World Cup finals in years to come.

Perhaps the most disappointed of this group was Andy Gray. 'If missing out on the 1978 World Cup had been a big blow, 1982 was even worse,' he wrote in his book *Gray Matters*. 'Although I was at Wolves and we weren't a great side, I'd played in nearly all the qualifying matches and thought I'd done well. I was sure I'd be spending my summer in Spain, so when Jock called me at home and said he'd decided to take Paul Sturrock instead, I was flabbergasted.' Gray admitted, with hindsight, that his domestic form had been patchy, 'I was the sort of forward who was completely reliant on service, and in a poor team that was sometimes in short supply.' Gray's Wolverhampton Wanderers had been relegated from the English First Division having finished second from bottom. He would go on to play, and score goals, for Scotland again, but this would be the nearest he got to a major finals.

UN peace talks with the United Kingdom and Argentina failed, ending any hopes of a diplomatic solution to the

Falklands crisis. Three thousand British troops landed at San Carlos Water with a view to establishing a beachhead for attacks on Goose Green and Stanley.

* * *

Both the Scottish Cup Final and the FA Cup Final had players from the Scotland squad involved. Aberdeen with Miller, McLeish and Strachan in the side took on Rangers, while down south Steve Archibald's Tottenham played Queens Park Rangers. Those not involved in the finals gathered at a hotel in Glasgow before moving on to Turnberry to prepare for the match against Wales on Monday, 24 May. Aston Villa's Allan Evans would be missing as he prepared for Villa's European Cup Final against Bayern Munich two days later.

The Scottish Cup Final was one of the better games of recent years. Rangers went in front through John MacDonald, only for McLeish to bend in an equaliser from the edge of the box. In extra time the Dons were dominant with a Mark McGhee header putting them in front. Gordon Strachan marked a fine performance with a tap-in to make it 3-1 before Neale Cooper blasted in the fourth from almost on the goal line after he had broken clear of the defence. In *The Guardian*, Patrick Barclay wrote, 'Over 120 minutes the outstanding influence had been that of Strachan, whose brilliance must have put an even keener edge on Jock Stein's anticipation of the World Cup.' The game at Wembley wasn't so eventful as the two London clubs played out a 1-1 draw, which meant a replay on Thursday, 26 May.

On television, the night of the cup finals, was the play *The Game*, written by Paul Pender. STV would screen it in opposition to BBC Scotland's *Cup Final Sportscene* highlights. The play was set during the 1978 World Cup finals and saw a group of Scotland fans watching the games. Starring Freddie Broadley, Billy Riddoch, Drew Dawson and Janette Foggo, it was directed by Bill Gilmour and produced by Sandy Ross. Made by Granada Television, it was originally staged at the 1979 Edinburgh Festival. 'Undoubtedly some Scots will react very badly to what they see on television tonight,' Riddoch told the *Daily Record*. 'It is the sort of play you will love or hate. Hopefully, if you stick with it you will enjoy it.'

John Wark was sent home from Turnberry after breaking down in training with what Stein called 'a quite serious knee injury'. It would rule him out of both the Wales and England games and cast doubt on his involvement in the World Cup. He was sent back to Ipswich to see his club's doctor. Steve Archibald was out of contention due to the FA Cup Final replay. 'With Archibald committed to the cup final it looks as if I must ignore him for both internationals and that does him no favours at all,' Stein said. Danny McGrain had a cold, so Stein thought it better not to risk him, handing the captain's armband to Graeme Souness for the first time. John Robertson would be left out, but Stein stressed this was due to him being worked hard in training in readiness for the England game and not because of concerns over his form.

On the eve of the Wales match, Stein spoke to the *Sunday Mail*. 'I'm going to try something completely different,' he said to Allan Herron. 'It is the natural instinct of Scottish players to go forward. In the past, this has cost us games. I want to expose ourselves deliberately in this match against Wales, but this time I want a safety factor at the back. I intend fielding all the good readers of a game in this match.

I want to show people that we Scots are not just a team of hard tacklers who can play a bit with the ball. I want players to adjust and tactically change their style. It's a system we may continue against England and into the World Cup.'

Newly promoted Watford beat New Zealand 1-0 in Christchurch in the first of three matches between the sides. John Barnes scored the First Division side's goal. The second encounter, in Wellington, was drawn 1-1 with Wooddin scoring for the Kiwis.

Ray Stewart and Tommy Burns would find places in the team, with Dalglish in midfield, and Brazil and Jordan, winning his 50th cap, the front two. A crowd of 25,284 turned out at Hampden in drenching rain to watch a game played at a middling pace. Souness was the lynchpin in the Scottish side, controlling the play throughout the first half. The move to the game's only goal, in the seventh minute, started deep in Scotland's half with a pass from Narey to Brazil. Brazil timed his pass to Hartford well and the midfielder ran on to hit the ball perfectly away from Dai Davies.

At the back, Narey and Hansen showed their partnership had promise. The midfield showed up well with Dalglish having an outstanding first half, Hartford playing well and Tommy Burns 'the revelation of the night' according to the *Daily Record*. The real problem for the Scots was turning midfield creativity into goals. As Jim Reynolds in the *Glasgow Herald* put it, 'That dreaded knack of turning easy chances into woeful misses remains with Scotland. A legacy handed down by our international sides for the past decade or more.' In the 28th minute, Dalglish held the ball up, and slipped it through to Burns on the gallop. With time to pick his spot, Burns instead went to hammer the ball and sent it flying over the bar. His disappointment was obvious as he held his head in his hands. Alan Rough was rarely called on to make a save, but he had to be alert on the half-hour as Robbie James found space, hitting a drive that Rough got down to save. In the second half Souness stepped back into defence to play as sweeper, a role he played assuredly. Burns showed his class with a range of passing, displaying accuracy and composure. His intelligent running off the ball was also a feature of his night's work. Burley and Sturrock came on for Stewart and Jordan on 72 minutes. Liverpool's Ian Rush and Welsh substitute Ian Walsh were both foiled by Rough late on.

It was far from a convincing victory. 'We were strolling approaching half-time,' Stein said, 'but we strolled through the second half in a different way altogether. There was no reason why we shouldn't have built on that excellent start when we had some good passing movements and created chances.' Stein suggested that Narey was 'not along for the ride', and while he admitted a few players enhanced their chances of making the final World Cup squad, the manager noted, 'And one or two didn't.'

Welsh boss Mike England said, 'Dalglish gave us a lot of problems early on. He is an incredible player, but when we did close down on him after that early spell I didn't think Scotland looked as good.'

The delayed launch of the government's guidance leaflet for fans travelling to Spain took place the same day. Although not a confirmation, this could be seen as an indicator that the government was not intending to advise the teams to withdraw. The leaflet, titled, *Amigos Espana '82* was published jointly by the Department of the Environment and the Scottish, English and Northern Irish football associations. It offered helpful advice such as 'Don't trespass on the pitch', 'Don't take drink into the stadium', and 'Booing, whistling and other forms of disrespect during the playing of the national anthems could lead to a spell in jail'.

In Rotterdam, Aston Villa defied the odds to beat Bayern Munich and lift the European Cup. The Germans launched attack after attack on the Villa goal, with Allan Evans and his fellow Scot Ken McNaught outstanding in defence. Although Villa started well, Bayern began to turn the screw, and it was against the run of play when in the 67th minute Tony Morley crossed for England striker Peter Withe to tap the ball in for the final's only goal. The result meant another four Scots had European Cup winners' medals: Evans, McNaught, Des Bremner and Andy Blair, an unused substitute. Evans had played himself into serious contention for a starting place in the back four in Spain. 'I know it's up to Mr Stein but I'm fit and ready to play if he picks me,' Evans said afterwards. 'It's still a little bit hard to believe that we won the European Cup – I suppose it takes time to sink in. But, what I'm thinking about now is playing against England and I'm hoping I get that chance. It's the match that everyone dreams about. I think that any Scot will tell you that the big one is the one against England. I'm no different from anyone else.'

Archibald was the next Scottish player to play in a major final that week. 'I'd like to get a goal or two to keep my face in the picture,' he said to the *Record* on the eve of the game. 'If I have a bad game and don't score, Jock Stein will be under pressure.' While the 1981 FA Cup Final replay between Spurs and Manchester City was a classic, the 1982 vintage, as Spurs took on Second Division QPR, paled in comparison. It was settled in Tottenham's favour by a sixth-minute Glenn Hoddle penalty.

At Glasgow's Apollo Theatre, The Rolling Stones played to a sold-out audience. Singer Mick Jagger walked on stage wearing a new Scotland shirt to loud applause. Jagger, though, wasn't the first musician to show off the new Umbro strip. Five-time Grammy award winner Glen Campbell posed in the kit for the *Sunday Mail*. His dad, Wesley, was born in the Borders and Campbell was always keen to play up to his Scottish roots. 'I know Rod Stewart is a big fan,' he said, 'but the strip I have is the only one in America. Rod will probably get his in Spain. I'd love to be there as well, but I can't because of commitments. But believe me, I'll know the score in every match almost at the same time as they have it in Scotland. I'll be with Jock Stein and the boys every step of the way.'

Jock Stein and Ernie Walker attended the Newspaper Press Fund luncheon in Glasgow where they both looked ahead to the finals. 'It's all about the players,' Stein said. 'If they do well then so do we. The SFA and all the officials involved make their best possible preparations, but once the game starts it is up to the players out on the field. I have spoken to the players about responsibility. We want none of the problems involved in the '78 finals in Argentina. I think the SFA have done everything possible to make sure the players live in the best possible accommodation. The most important people in the game are the players and we have treated them accordingly.'

On the subject of the Argentina debacle in 1978, Stein commented that his predecessor Ally MacLeod undeservedly took the blame for the failures in the tournament, when Stein felt that it was the players who were culpable. 'I hope we can come back from Spain with a higher reputation than when we went,' Stein said. 'We hope events on the field give the writers more to write about than things off the park.' For his part, Walker was keen to emphasise that Scotland would definitely be taking part in Spain. 'A great many people have had a great many things to say as to why we should not be there,' he said. 'Suffice to say that the office bearers are determined, having considered all the options, that Scotland will compete in Spain, given, of course, we do not encounter some dramatic turnabout.'

* * *

The speculation about the Falklands-induced boycott was finally ended towards the end of May when Neil Macfarlane addressed the issue in the House of Commons. He responded to a question from John Carlisle, MP for Luton West. 'I am grateful to my honourable friend the member for Luton West,' Macfarlane began, 'for giving me the opportunity to end recent press speculation and to place clearly on the record, once again, the government's views on our participation in the World Cup.' Macfarlane indicated that the government had never raised any objection to the nations' participation, nor had it suggested any boycott be implemented.

He continued, 'It is the government's policy to discourage all sporting contact with Argentina, either here or in that country at representative, club or individual level. Outside these two countries, we see no objection to British teams or individuals competing in any international events where Argentina may be represented. This policy applies to all sporting events. There are a number of reasons for this stance. It is the Argentines who are the aggressors and who

186

stand condemned in the eyes of the world through United Nations resolution 502.

'We in the United Kingdom are the innocent party and, as I have said on several previous occasions, I feel that it would be grossly unfair to penalise our sportsmen and women by denying them the right to participate in international competition abroad simply because the guilty party, Argentina, does not withdraw from such competition. Certainly, Argentina has so far given no indication that its football team will not be going to Spain. In addition, as I have said before, there must be many millions of people in this country who would think it strange if our teams withdrew from the World Cup because of the actions of Argentina, which is solely responsible for the battle of the Falklands.'

Macfarlane suggested that perhaps FIFA or UEFA could have looked at the possibility of excluding Argentina from the tournament, but said that was for the football associations to have pursued, 'I must emphasise that, however the government view this situation, the final decision on whether to participate in the World Cup finals is one for the football authorities and their players. Certainly, the authorities have made clear their wish to participate in the World Cup finals. It has, however, been reported in some papers that a few individual footballers – and perhaps one or two administrators – have queried the morality of participation. Again, should any player feel that strongly on the issue, the decision whether to go must rest entirely with him.'

Macfarlane had also seen the earlier *Daily Record* poll on whether Scotland should stay at home or go to Spain. He said, 'Public opinion on this issue, like so many others, is difficult to gauge accurately. Certainly, there are indicators such as the recent poll by a Scottish newspaper, which showed that 90 per cent of those asked favoured their team's participation in the World Cup. Like my honourable friend, I have had – as one would expect – much correspondence on the matter. Virtually everyone who has written to me has favoured our teams going. Some have made the very valid point that bearing in mind the love of football by the average Argentine citizen, any withdrawal by the United Kingdom teams would be greeted with great joy in Argentina and be regarded by them as a moral victory over us and presented by the Argentine government as an indication of world opinion against Great Britain.'

Macfarlane quoted some of the letters, all saying that a boycott would be a boost for Argentina. He also 'emphatically denied' that he had been quietly pressing the football authorities behind the scenes to withdraw. The launch of the guidance leaflet for fans earlier in the week was a sign, Macfarlane said, that his department was looking to tackle the potential problem of hooliganism in Spain, indicating he expected the nations to be there. He concluded, 'I repeat that the final decision on whether our three teams participate in the World Cup finals lies solely with the football authorities, and their players. The government see no objection to their taking part. I hope that this statement will end all future speculation and I am sure that the House will join me in wishing our three teams great success.'

The Scottish players who had voiced some concerns now made it clear they had no hesitation in travelling. Graeme Souness said, 'I suppose everyone was concerned when things looked so bleak. It looked as if the government would advise us not to go, but it hasn't happened. It seems the men in the Task Force want us to go and play. I've even talked it over with my dad. I'll be going.' Danny McGrain spoke to the *Record*, 'The poll the *Daily Record* conducted made me reconsider. Players are sometimes accused of being selfish. It concerned me as much as anyone else. Your poll made me realise most people in the country wanted us to play in Spain. Now the government is saying so I'll be up there.'

In 2012, when cabinet files were made public due to the 30-year rule, despite having commented publicly at the time, Kenny Dalglish told the *Daily Record*, 'I was oblivious to any talk of pulling Scotland out. It probably stands to reason that the players would be the last to know. Big Jock Stein didn't mention anything like that and I'm surprised to be hearing that such talks had been taking place. It's all hypothetical talking about it now, but I don't think it would have gone down well if the Scotland team had been withdrawn. But I think footballers are there to play football and the politicians can get on with their thing.'

With fears of a boycott now abated, the Scotland squad remained at Turnberry to prepare for the match against England, while England settled in Troon. Stein got good news from Ipswich where John Wark had been passed fit. As the player headed north to join the party, Stein said, 'This is the best news any manager could get while preparing for the World Cup finals. It's very likely that John Wark will be in my travelling pool of 22 for Spain.'

On the subject of his starting 11, with practically every member of his squad having played another match that week, Stein commented, 'There will be bumps and bruises and we want to check on everyone before thinking about the team. Scotland will be going full out. It is a match we want to win. The fans won't allow us to take it easy. After all, if we win we will be British champions and it would be nice to go to Spain with this title.' Stein said the only name on his team sheet, with days before the match, was Alan Rough. 'It's one I want to win,' Stein added. 'I think Ron Greenwood will approach the game with caution and will be pretty happy with a draw. I won't. I want to win this and I want to win it with a bit of style. I don't want to see any hacking or dashing about. I have a lot of players who need a lift, who need a big game, who need a prestige game. England at Hampden is such a game. I will field my best team against England, but I may not necessarily field my best players.'

Earlier in the year, England manager Greenwood had commented, 'I don't like the idea of meeting Scotland so near to the World Cup finals and I don't think Jock does either. There's too much tension.' There was a suggestion that the two managers felt that playing a competitive match of this nature so close to the tournament was counterproductive. 'Contrary to what some people say, I'm really looking forward to Hampden on Saturday,' Greenwood said a couple of days before the game. 'I've carried the can for proposing that the Home International Championship format be changed this year in view of the World Cup. I can tell you it was the Scots – Jock and Ernie Walker – who approached us.' Greenwood asserted that the game wasn't a friendly in his eyes, 'Every Englishman wants to win this particular fixture, simply because they know the Scottish players in the English league will rub it in for a year if they don't. Maybe we don't treat the thing as passionately as you Scots, but we certainly like to beat you.'

Stein was named as the £500 winner of the MacKinlay's Personality of the Year award, chosen by a panel of Scottish football writers. He had also won the prize in 1977.

All 24 members of the squad had been kitted out with the official clothing for the trip to Spain, but Stein had resolved his two to be cut would be known shortly after the England match. 'I know it will be hard on the two left out,' he said, 'there are no shysters in this squad, no one has come along for the ride.'

* * *

England sat on top of the group going into the game with four points, with wins over both Wales and Northern Ireland. Scotland were a point behind. Stein announced a team the press described as 'mysterious-looking' and 'smacks of the experimental'. Frank Gray, the only player who had started all eight World Cup qualifiers, was out as were Strachan and Robertson. Stein's programme notes for the game said he wanted to see Robertson playing, 'He has had problems with injury and his club have not had a good season so he needs to get used to the big time atmosphere again.'

McGrain moved to left-back to accommodate Ipswich Town's George Burley at right-back. 'I have now played 38 matches since my knee injury,' Burley said, 'but as pool after pool was picked for the internationals and I wasn't included I thought my chances of World Cup football were slim. I never gave up hope completely and now that I'm here, I must have a wee chance.'

Evans, who had played in the European Cup Final on the Wednesday night, had made it into the side, but Archibald, who had played in the Thursday's FA Cup Final, was left out. Archibald, it transpired, only made it to Turnberry on Friday evening when he was expected earlier in the day. 'He could have been here at ten o'clock this morning if he had been of the same breed as the other fellow,' Stein said. Evans had made his way from Rotterdam to Ayrshire by two o'clock the afternoon after his final. 'All I did was switch a few flight schedules,' Evans said to the *Aberdeen Evening Express*. 'There was a champagne reception laid on for us in Rotterdam, but I don't smoke or drink and all I wanted to do was join up with the rest of the Scotland lads. The manager asked me to get to Scotland as soon as I could and I just carried out instructions. On reflection, it probably helped me get into the team.'

The game on Saturday, 29 May was the 100th meeting between the sides. In the programme, Ernie Walker wrote a 'plea to fans', saying, 'Supporters will be colourful, enthusiastic and kindly disposed towards people of other nationalities. They will make friends readily with the Spanish people and no doubt be a credit to Scotland. Sadly, but unfortunately inevitably, the behaviour of a minority of those who travel will not reflect well upon our country. Overindulgence in drink will lead some to resort to the usual aggressive, disagreeable conduct which all decent Scots deplore.' Walker said the SFA and the government had done everything they could to ensure this behaviour didn't take place. He asked in his notes that 'the true supporter of Scotland who has no desire to see his country shamed in the eyes of the world' should do everything possible to 'keep things low key'.

England had the first shot on target with a minute on the clock when Rough saved well from Trevor Brooking. Terry Butcher shot over the bar a few minutes later, but England

Scotland colleagues Alan Brazil and John Wark playing for Ipswich in September 1981.

Graeme Souness on the ball against Israel in Tel Aviv in February 1981.

Graeme Souness and Steve Archibald celebrate with John Robertson after he had scored against Israel at Hampden in April 1981.

Danny McGrain captains Scotland against Spain in Valencia in February 1982.

Steve Archibald on the ball in Belfast the night Scotland achieved qualification.

The toepoke – David Narey watches as his shot flies into the Brazil net.

'Did anyone think he was going to do that?' Éder chips Alan Rough for Brazil's third goal.

Willie Miller pays close attention to Ramaz Shengelia in the game against USSR.

Joe Jordan celebrates scoring against Sweden in the qualifiers.

Having endured a farce of a draw, Jock Stein stands with Northern Ireland boss Billy Bingham and England manager Ron Greenwood in front of the final groups.

Christian is out in front of the Scotland squad who had been making good use of the green room at the Top of the Pops recording in May 1982.

Physiotherapist Hugh Allan with manager Jock Stein as Scotland play Wales in May 1982.

The Scotland team line up for the game against the USSR.

Alan Hansen shouts instructions in the game against New Zealand.

Gordon Strachan challenges USSR's Andrei Bal.

John Wark scores Scotland's second against New Zealand.

John Robertson lines up for the game against USSR.

Graeme Souness, Kenny Dalglish and Steve Archibald celebrate as a free kick from John Robertson (out of pic) hits the back of the net for the fourth goal against New Zealand.

took the lead on 13 minutes when a Trevor Brooking corner was headed at goal by Butcher. His Ipswich team-mate Burley knocked it against the bar, but with the Scottish defence flailing, Paul Mariner headed into the empty net, silencing the 80,529 crowd, composed entirely of Scots fans as England had declined to take any tickets.

At half-time Stein abandoned the sweeper system. 'Stein must surely realise now that Scottish players do not understand the system,' wrote Patrick Barclay in *The Guardian*. Alex Cameron wrote similarly in the *Record*. Barclay noted that the libero role had failed in Valencia, despite Hansen's standout performance, and it hadn't worked to any great degree of success with Souness there against Wales. The problem, Barclay noted, was no matter how good the player in that role was, the defenders around him had to perform close man-to-man marking. Burley in particular was caught out, allowing Trevor Francis freedom to roam while Burley found himself in midfield.

Hartford was withdrawn for John Robertson, Narey was pushed into midfield and the defence established an orthodox back four. The changes allowed Scotland to find more space in midfield, but still they couldn't create a scoring chance. Even Souness and Dalglish were off the pace. The best save Peter Shilton made all day was from a header back from his own defender Phil Thompson. Sat in the Hampden stand, Tommy Burns turned to Davie Provan and suggested that Scotland's performance was so bad it could be a blessing in disguise for the pair of them, as they awaited Stein's final squad selection for Spain. The crowd chanted for Gordon Strachan to enter the fray, but were left disappointed when the final Scotland substitution saw Sturrock replace Jordan on 63 minutes. The Dundee United man joined up well with Brazil up front, but an equaliser just wouldn't come. England held on for the 1-0 win that would secure them the Home International Championship.

'Gordon Strachan ran himself into the ground in the 120 minutes of the [Scottish] Cup Final,' Jock Stein said, defending his decision not to play him. 'For a player of his size and build I considered it too much, too unfair to ask him to do it again seven days later against England.' Strachan himself felt he was in the form of his life and was eager to get on the pitch. Wark and Miller weren't considered either with Stein stressing he wanted them completely fit for Spain. The boss said, 'Despite the result, I still believe this was the right decision. Of course I wanted to win. Of course I'm disappointed we lost 1-0 but as manager, I have to consider more than just one game. Performing well in the World Cup has been our objective for four years and continues to be my priority.' To the *Sunday Mail*, Stein commented, 'For the first time we put the World Cup before winning against England. Having players ready for the World Cup is more important than this game.'

The man who guided England to World Cup glory in 1966, Sir Alf Ramsey, gave his thoughts on the Scotland performance in his *Sunday Mail* column. 'It seems incredible that in their last competitive match before the World Cup finals and just seven days before they leave to prepare in Portugal the Scots should adopt a set up which clearly they'd never tried before,' he wrote. 'Not only did it cost them the game against England, it raises serious questions about their squad at a time when their confidence should be sky high. To be fair, Scotland did get it right when they moved Narey into midfield and allowed Hansen and Evans to find an understanding.'

Some good news came in the form of the under-18 side lifting the European Youth Championship, defeating Czechoslovakia 3-1 in the final at Helsinki's Olympic Stadium. Stein said, 'I am absolutely delighted. This is a great tonic for everyone in the Scottish game.'

* * *

In the dressing room at Hampden, once Stein had got the post-mortem out of the way he began outlining to the players details of the travelling arrangements for Spain. 'Obviously, not everybody is going,' Stein said. 'Tommy Burns and Ray Stewart will be staying behind.' Burns looked over to Stewart. 'By the look on his face, he was as stunned and disturbed by what had happened as I was, only he was trying not to let it show,' Burns said in his book *Twists and Turns*.

'I just felt empty,' Burns said in the days afterwards. 'I just sat and stared at the ceiling. Even though deep down, I felt I would be out, it was still hard to take. I didn't think I'd be going, no matter how well I played against Wales. I didn't get a lot of encouragement while I was with the squad. I think the manager knew the players he'd be taking by then. I always had the impression I was making up the numbers. But I still believe I am as good as any midfield players Scotland are taking to Spain.' Burns was happy, however, that his colleague was selected, 'Thank God Davie Provan is going. At one point we were a bit worried that it was the two of us.' Provan recalled the moment for Archie Macpherson that they heard Burns would be left out, 'I looked across to Tommy. I thought I saw the red mist coming over his eyes. He had a violent temper. When he lost it he lost it big time. For a moment I thought he was going to attack Stein. I went right across to him and gripped him.'

Burns felt he had never played in a meaningful international up to that point, noting that he had won two titles with Celtic in recent years, yet hadn't experienced competitive internationals at the top level. 'Why the final squad had to be named that day while we were all gathered at Hampden, I do not know, but the way the news was broken to us turned out to be deeply embarrassing for me,' Burns wrote in his book. 'A severe disappointment that would have been hard enough to take if we had been spoken to in private or even written to by the SFA was turned into a public broadcast.' Burns walked out of Hampden leaving his tailor-made suit hanging in the team bus. As he drove home he considered making it clear, publicly, that he would not be interested in playing for his country again.

Burns was of the opinion that he never got a fair deal from Stein, who had signed him for Celtic as a youngster. He said, 'I think that part of my problem always revolved around the fact that Jock Stein went through his life thinking of me only as "Wee Tommy", the ground staff boy who came from down the road in the Calton and used to look after the towels in the laundry at Celtic Park after the first team had finished training. I never felt I got the full respect I was due from Scotland for the efforts I had made to improve myself at Celtic Park while Jock was there, or after he had been succeeded by Billy McNeill.'

Burns was only 25 at the time, so his dream of playing in a World Cup was still available to him. As it was, he would gain only three more caps, two in friendlies under Stein in 1983 and his last at Wembley under Andy Roxburgh in 1988. The lack of either explanation or sympathy, and the public manner in which he was told, exacerbated the natural disappointment Burns felt. Speaking to Archie

Macpherson in 2004, Burns hadn't mellowed his opinion, 'I have to admit the passing years have made me angrier about that since I felt I was denied getting on to the greatest footballing platform in the world. I know he was a great manager, but why could he not have had a word about it with me? I'm 47 now and I still feel bitter about it.' Tommy was more reflective when speaking to Hugh Keevins in 2007. 'I won eight caps for my country and every one of them was cherished,' Burns said after quitting his national team backroom role, having learned he wouldn't be a candidate for the vacant manager's job. 'It was my misfortune to play in an era of so many talented players that I couldn't get any more international honours. My only regret is that I was overlooked for the squad that went to Spain for the World Cup finals in 1982 because I always felt I could have learned so much from that experience, both as a player and as a man.'

Ray Stewart was also disappointed. 'I'm absolutely sick,' he told the *Daily Record*. 'But even when we assembled ten days ago I had a feeling that I would be left out. Even being picked to play against Wales last week didn't alter that feeling, for I thought it was too late.' To compound the situation for Stewart, his wife was going to Spain while he stayed at home. He had booked a holiday for her in case he made the final 22, so she would go while he resolved to do some decorating.

'It was harder to tell them they wouldn't be going than to accept the defeat from England,' Stein said of his decision.

On stage at the Glasgow Pavilion that night was Christian with *The Official Scottish World Cup Touring Show*, which had been playing at venues around Scotland all month. Tickets ranged from £1.50 to £3.50, with special guest Andy Cameron. For the 6.20pm and 8.40pm shows on the Saturday, the World Cup squad were advertised as to be making a personal appearance at the show. Only, no one showed up. At a performance at the Edinburgh Playhouse, around 200 audience members walked out when they realised no players were appearing. The promoters and the footballers' agents argued over who was at fault. Frank Taylor, the show's promoter, said to the *Sunday Mail*, 'The squad's agent ProScot gave a verbal agreement that the players would attend.' ProScot spokesman Alan Ferguson said it was impossible for the players to attend because it was too close to their departure to Spain, 'We did have an agreement but we warned about the pitfalls of getting players there in their own time.'

In the *Sunday Mail*, John Fairgrieve was furious that Jock Stein treated an England match at Hampden as a World Cup warm-up and not the centrepiece of the international calendar as it usually was. 'Jock Stein was not only wrong to experiment against England, he was not entitled to do so,' Fairgrieve began. 'He forgot who pays his wages. The fans pay his wages and I mean fans who pay hundreds of thousands of pounds year after year to watch the annual confrontation with England. What the fans think counts for much, much more than what Jock Stein thinks. The hierarchy of the SFA are mere custodians of our game. I am sick to the back teeth of an attitude which amounts almost to contempt for the customers. Certainly, we want to perform with honour in Spain and the lingering trauma of 1978 in Argentina will be difficult to eradicate. But that cannot excuse the fact that the greatest single fixture in our international calendar should have been turned into what was virtually a practice match.'

Ticket prices for the game ran from £3 for a place on the terracing to £12 for a seat in the stand. Fairgrieve wrote, 'Each match for which full prices are charged is an event in itself. The stepping stone mentality, which permeates cup and league matches, never mind World Cup matches, is tantamount to fraud on the public. It always seems to be the next match that counts, doesn't it?'

The England game would soon be forgotten, however, as the now confirmed squad set out for their training camp in Portugal.

8

The 22: A warm-up in the Algarve

'Stein went bananas and came on the
pitch to slaughter me as he stood in
the six-yard box, leaving me cringing
with embarrassment because everyone
– including some of the Scottish press –
could hear his tirade.'

Jim Leighton

OF THE 22 heading for Portugal to prepare for the World
Cup, George Wood, Jim Leighton, Allan Evans and Alan
Brazil hadn't played in any of the qualifying games. This
was about par for the course as history attested. The squad
for the 1974 World Cup contained five players who hadn't
played in any of the qualifiers – Jim Stewart, Thomson
Allan, Gordon McQueen, Erich Schaedler and, surprisingly
considering the fuss that is generally made about him not
playing in West Germany, Jimmy Johnstone. The squad for
Argentina in 1978 similarly included five players who hadn't

appeared in the qualifying campaign – Jim Blyth, Stuart Kennedy, Graeme Souness, John Robertson and Joe Harper.

As a piece of trivia, it's perhaps interesting to note that every player in the 22 was born in Scotland. Not that surprising perhaps, but every other Scotland World Cup squad (with the exception of 1954) including the three subsequent, and indeed the European Championship squads of 1992, 1996 and 2021, contained at least one player born outside of the country. The average age of Scotland's players was 27.4. The youngest squad in Spain would be El Salvador's with an average age of 24.2. The oldest squad belonged to England, who had an average age of 28.7. The average age of players at the tournament was 26.9.

'In many ways it was a better balanced squad in terms of the players and what they could do than the '78 team,' commentator Arthur Montford said in 2010. 'I think the '82 squad looked as if they could do something and there were high hopes for it.'

Leighton spoke with his local newspaper, the *Aberdeen Evening Express*, before he left, 'I don't really expect to get a game in these finals, but I'm here to work as hard as I can. I'm the only player in the pool without a cap, so I can benefit greatly from just taking part. My target has to be the next two World Cup finals. I'm only 23. So if I can maintain and improve my standard then I will be eligible for Colombia in 1986 [at the time of the interview, Colombia was scheduled to host the 1986 World Cup but withdrew and was replaced by Mexico] and again in 1990 when the World Cup returns to Europe.'

Leighton was delighted just to be going to Spain and recalled the moment in the dressing room after the England match when he learned he was in the squad, 'It was almost impossible for me to take it in that I would be going. We were all feeling down after the result and our hearts went out to Ray and Tommy. But I was honestly so pleased at being named as one of the three keepers that I could have jumped up and down.' Leighton wrote in his autobiography *In The Firing Line*, 'Stein had previously told me he would not take me to Spain as an uncapped player, so I thought my chance of being included in his plans had gone. While he had talked about the possibility of bringing me on as a second-half substitute for Arsenal's George Wood in the British [Home] Championship match against Northern Ireland in Belfast, that did not happen. My heart sank when Stein spoke to Wood and I at Windsor Park the day before the game. He said he had decided to field the Arsenal player because, as well as wanting to see what Wood could do, he was looking for a victory. "If we are winning 3-0 with ten minutes to go, I might bring you on," he told me. I was shattered by his words. You can imagine how pleased I was to find myself named in the squad of 22 players.'

Trainer Hugh Allan packed 25 kit hampers. They included 150 pairs of socks, 150 pairs of shorts, 150 training jerseys, 14 sets of full match squad kits and 200 tracksuits. There were 66 balls, along with sweatbands, captain's armbands, substitute boards, 100 towels, 72 training bibs, scales, medical hampers, pumps and 50 wetsuits. Assistant secretary Bill Richardson said, 'It is a major operation, and we have to make sure we get it right. Nothing can be left out and we have to remember to include 100 jock straps.' Kilmarnock coach Allan played with Dunipace, becoming a trainer at Kilsyth Rangers in 1963. Three years later came a move to Stirling Albion. When Walter McCrae was promoted from trainer to manager at Kilmarnock in 1968,

Allan stepped into the vacant position. He was brought into the Scotland setup by Willie Ormond in 1973.

'Morale is good and it will soar even more once we get to Spain,' Jock Stein said as the players departed from Glasgow Airport. 'It's eight months since Scotland actually qualified. We have virtually had to wait a whole season for the finals.' Stein was confident the players would do the country proud, 'We're not going off with tumultuous cheers ringing in our ears. Maybe this isn't a bad thing. We were all unhappy about the England result and even more so because of the manner of it. However, that is behind us now and we intend to do a job in Spain.' In addition to not leaving with a win, Stein was perhaps referring to the departure for Argentina four years previously when the SFA, in a fit of ill-conceived hubris, decided to stage a victory lap before a ball was kicked and had the party leave from Hampden Park waving from an open-topped bus to the 25,000 crowd.

Captain Danny McGrain was still aware of Scotland's last appearance at the World Cup finals when he said, 'The past is past. We're all looking ahead and what can be more exciting for a footballer than the World Cup. The players are confident without being too sure of themselves. We feel we can do well and certainly, everyone is aware of the responsibilities to our fans at home and those who come out to see us.'

Old Firm managers Billy McNeill and John Greig were asked by the *Evening Times* what they thought about Scotland's chances in Spain. 'I think our greatest asset in these finals will be that we are not going to Spain expecting miracles this time,' said Celtic's McNeill. 'Argentina brought us back to earth with a bump and the low key approach to the finals by Jock Stein is just right.' Rangers boss Greig said,

'It's important that we go to Spain with the ambition to go all the way. That's the only way to approach football. Quite honestly, I don't think that England expected to win in 1966 even with home advantage, but they were determined and at the end of the day, they got the trophy. This time we are much better prepared off the pitch – and I say that with no disrespect to the men behind the previous squads. We have knowledge now of all the outside interests that affect a squad going to the World Cup finals and if we haven't learned from past experiences we don't deserve to do well.'

Despite what Ernie Walker had said previously regarding the national anthem, Scotland were now intending to make a permanent change. The SFA felt that it would be in Scotland's interest for them to have their own tune before their matches, as both England and Northern Ireland would have 'God Save the Queen' played. They wanted to demonstrate that, in a footballing sense, Scotland was a separate nation. For this reason, the SFA decided that 'Scotland the Brave' would be played before their matches in Spain. 'It was quite impossible to get unanimous agreement amongst Scots as to the most appropriate Scottish tune to meet football's requirements,' Walker said. 'But "Scotland the Brave" appeared to be the choice of the majority.' David Letham of Queen's Park, and chairman of the Scottish Football League, told the *Glasgow Herald*, 'It is a tune, not an anthem. It's been associated with the Scottish football team and is a stirring tune. The words are not so important but they differentiate Scotland from the rest.'

The song originated when lyricist Cliff Hanley wrote lyrics for use by Robert Wilson in a review show at the Glasgow Empire in 1951. It became popular among Glasgow audiences during the Alhambra Theatre pantomime of

1952/53 when the first act of *Jack and the Beanstalk* ended with a rousing version of the song. 'It took me a very long Saturday,' Hanley said to the *Herald*. 'I was asked by the late Robert Wilson to pen words to an old pipe tune for a pantomime. My initial cheque was £20. Since then, royalties have never been less than £200 a year.' It would transpire that the SFA's decision upset a few people, none more so than Scottish sports minister Alex Fletcher. A Scottish Office memo to the Department of the Environment read, 'When a team from the UK play abroad it does not seem appropriate for anything to be played but "God Save the Queen". To play the national anthem for one team but not another could lead some countries to think that the separate tune is indicative of a national breakaway movement. This is an aspect on which the Foreign and Commonwealth Office might well have views. Presentationally, for the outside world, it might be best if the main flag seen at all the games was the Union Flag.'

There was significant disappointment when they learned that 'Scotland the Brave' would be played and the Scots team would walk out under the St Andrew's Cross. Despite their concern, both the Department of the Environment and Fletcher were powerless to act, the minister writing, 'The question of which tune is to be played is left to the sport's governing body. As such, the secretary of state has no formal locus and there is no case for intervening.' Ernie Walker spoke to the *Sunday Times* on the issue in 2010. 'At that time the Conservative government took serious notice about what they regarded as the threat of a Scottish breakaway,' he said. 'Anything that was seen as predominantly or exclusively Scottish was deliberately played down. This was not just in football but on a whole host of fronts. Ultimately, this was a decision for the SFA, not the government. As it turned out those in government rightly decided not to become publicly embroiled in such an emotive subject.'

The other Scot heading to Spain was referee Bob Valentine. The 43-year-old from Dundee was 22 years into his refereeing career. He officiated at the Moscow 1980 Olympics, taking charge of Russia's 8-0 win over Cuba in the group stage as well as the bronze medal match where Russia defeated Yugoslavia 2-0 in front of a 45,000 crowd. Valentine had also refereed games in 1981's World Under-20 Championship in Australia, including the semi-final where West Germany beat Romania in extra time. Valentine would be spending a week in Spain in advance of the tournament doing the Cooper Test, a physical fitness test devised by Keith Cooper for the US Air Force in the 1960s, then used commonly to test referees' fitness for matches. A 12-minute run, it was first adopted in football by Cláudio Coutinho, the physical fitness coach for the Brazil team preparing for the 1970 World Cup. In addition to this, the referees would be timed over four ten-metre runs, a 50-metre run and a 400-metre run. The referees would also be going over the rules and working out signals to help with the language barrier.

* * *

As Scotland's players began their training sessions in Portimão in Portugal's Algarve, the press and Stein were focusing on how his team were going to score goals. Since Stein took over in October 1978, Scotland had scored 35 goals in 33 internationals. Only four games had seen Scotland score more than two goals: against Norway in both October 1978 and June 1979, Portugal in March 1980 and Israel in April of 1981. 'Our failure to score goals has always been a problem and we are trying to sort it out,' Stein said to the *Evening Times*. His first training session, watched by around 100 locals, had focused on quick, first-time shooting, both in drills and in the practice match. 'In World Cup finals, defences don't give people a lot of time to act, so it is important to get fast, accurate shots. The natural tendency of our players is to elaborate when they are close to goal, so we are working on that,' he said.

As well as Jim McLean, Jimmy Steele and Hugh Allan, the backroom staff was completed by Tom McNiven and Donnie McKinnon. McNiven was a player with Stonehouse Violet, becoming trainer with Third Lanark in 1958. He joined Hibs in 1963 and had been part of the Scotland setup for many years. McKinnon signed for Partick Thistle in December 1959 from Rutherglen Glencairn. The twin brother of Ronnie, who played with Rangers from 1960 to 1972, Donnie played with Thistle until 1973, making over 200 league appearances. After finishing playing he took on the position of physiotherapist at the club. McKinnon had a behind-the-scenes role on the Bill Forsyth film *Gregory's Girl*, credited as 'Football Coach' on the production.

The SFA knew that the heat in both Portugal and Spain would present problems, so they came up with one way to combat it. They turned to a lime-coloured West German drink called Power Back. 'Heat will be a very important factor in our games in Spain,' Stein said. 'So it was essential for us to discover an approved anti-heat stimulant. It is in powder form and is simply added to water. The players don't particularly like the taste, but the results seem excellent. It was used by some athletes at the Olympics. It quickly replaces everything the body loses when working in the heat.

It used to be that the players were given salt tablets, but only the best is good enough for this squad. It is very expensive, but it will be worth it.'

Stein was keen to make clear that this time there were no squabbles about money within the camp. 'Money matters have been sorted out beforehand,' he said. 'Leaving the players to get on with the important job. Money has not been discussed here and won't be. The players all know what they are getting and we've had no complaints.' The players would be getting £600 a game if they played in all three group matches, with £1,500 on top if they qualified and £6,300 to the players chosen in total. Players on the bench would receive £400. If Scotland actually won the World Cup the players in the final would earn £5,000. They had earned a split of £80,000 for qualifying. 'I assume the players are happy as no one has raised the subject of money with me,' said Stein.

While in the Algarve the players were staying at the Penina Hotel, a golf resort, where the SFA were paying £50 per head per day. What Stein liked was that the other guests there were rich and successful, and therefore had no interest in crowding around footballers. 'They chat away pleasantly on equal terms,' he said. Golf, swimming and tennis were all available to the players, although they were supervised by the backroom staff. 'Once the players do their training it can be a problem keeping them occupied,' Ernie Walker said, 'but we are laying on a variety of games and recreation for their spare-time activities.' The hotel was set in 360 acres, with an 18-hole championship golf course and two nine-hole courses designed by Henry Cotton, three times an Open champion. It was set to host the 1982 Portuguese Open in November. The hotel also had an Olympic-sized swimming pool, tennis courts, table tennis, a driving range, and *Space Invaders* machines.

'Stein made it immediately clear that it was a working trip and there was to be no messing around,' Graeme Souness recalled in his autobiography. 'He said we could indulge in a few beers during the evening but even this was said in such a way that few took him up on his offer, everyone wanting to impress and no one wanting the finger pointed at them at training the next morning.'

'We worked hard but also had some relaxation,' Alex McLeish told the *Sunday Mail* in 2002. 'Jock warned me to stay out of the sun with my fair skin as he didn't want me getting sunburn. He kept an eye out for me and after a wee while he'd be telling you to get back to the room and rest away from the heat. Jock was wonderful to work for. He was a very clever man and left nothing to chance, even things like looking out for the players and their welfare. He was also a very funny person and very subtle with his humour but a lot of the time his jokes would just go over some guys' heads. I suppose I'd class him as having the humour of a Chic Murray type if that is the right description. He could cut you down in an instant and sometimes you would walk away not realising he had been winding you up but it would hit you later on when you thought back to his comments.'

Alan Rough was training with a sweatsuit under his jersey even though the temperature was into the 80s. 'He's always conscious of his weight,' Stein explained. 'Not surprisingly his team-mates had been ribbing him about his weight, although the training staff say he is lighter than usual.' The *Daily Record*'s Jim Blair asked the goalkeeper if he was overweight. 'No way,' Rough snapped back. 'I'm 13st 7lb and that's what I've been all season. I've actually complained to Umbro about the jerseys because they make me look huge. Even George Wood, and he's a big fella, agrees. The jerseys are extra large, and when you tuck them inside your shorts, suddenly you look bigger than you are.'

The squad were readying themselves for the first of two practice matches against Portuguese side G.D. Torralta, who played in the Algarve District Association. The media were being told that the club had just been promoted to the Portuguese Second Division, but Patrick Barclay was one journalist in Portugal who couldn't be fooled. 'Far from being a Second Division club,' he wrote in *The Guardian*, 'Torralta players are accustomed to playing in Algarvean regional football. They were promoted to the Third Division only last month. Their team is made up of staff from the local holiday complex.' The kick-off times had been brought forward from 9pm to 7pm. Stein had wanted the kick-off time to match that of the group games, but when he realised Torralta's floodlights weren't suitable he decided to bring the start forward. The proceeds from the two matches would go to charity. 'We want competitive games and the Portuguese will give us this,' Stein said. 'Their players will be trying to show they are as good as ours, so they could push us hard. We would like to score a lot of goals, but since I've never seen the opposition there's no good saying too much in advance. Three or four goals might be as vital for us against this particular opposition as 15 were for the Argentinians the other night.' An Argentina side had taken on a local team in Alicante.

Stein said, 'My team is significant with the New Zealand game coming up next Tuesday. I'm not saying it will be exactly the same, but this is the basis. Our style of play will be the one we will use against the Kiwis. The first half will last 40 minutes and after that, I reserve the right to stop the game if I think our lads have done enough.' Stein stipulated that Scotland would supply the balls used in order that the players get used to playing with the official World Cup ball. In training they had been adjusting the pressure, as they were unsure if the balls would be hard or a little soft in the finals themselves. 'I will not be asking the Portuguese players to stand back in tackles,' Stein said to the *Record*. 'Players can be injured in routine practice games amongst themselves. These things can happen at any time and we simply have to take the risk. I want a fairly hard trial game for the players and the team I select for the first of these will be close to my choice for the New Zealand game. We must beat the Kiwis, so for the moment, I am not thinking at all about Brazil or Russia. Bringing the games forward to start at seven o'clock means we will not need the floodlights which are very poor anyway. It also means it will be very hot as it will be in Malaga and Seville. We are leaving all the arrangements about locals seeing the games to the Portuguese officials.'

Stein had no idea of the quality of the local players, or indeed of their fitness. He was counting on the sense of occasion playing against a World Cup side that would provide them with. 'Scotland will be a bad team if they cannot score 20 goals,' one amused local was quoted as saying. 'If they want a match why do they not play the boys on the beach at Praia da Rocha? It would be better for them.' Brazil had also played a club side in Portugal – Belenenses – where they won 13-3. West Germany had also racked up the goals when beating Baden 9-0. 'The opposition may not amount to much but a few goals from the strikers can only help their confidence,' Stein said to the *Mirror*. 'It was a ploy which worked perfectly for the Hungarians in the 50s. They used to go out and send a barrel-load of goals past insignificant college sides and such like to build up morale and confidence.'

For the first game, Stein picked a side lining up in a 4-3-3 formation: Leighton; McGrain, Gray, Hansen, Evans; Souness, Strachan, Wark; Dalglish, Archibald, Robertson. Brazil had originally been named in the team but after he felt a slight strain he was replaced in the starting line-up by Archibald. Joe Jordan aggravated a knee strain in training, so Stein thought it best not to chance him. One look at the pitch at the Estadio Bois Iruahos would suggest the Scotland boss made the correct decision. There was hardly any grass through the middle, or in the goal areas. It was hard, rutted, bumpy and there was even the odd pothole to be found in it. The pitch was, as measured by the backroom team, 80 yards wide, which, at least, suited the way Stein wanted his side to play, 'There is plenty of grass down the wings and there is also plenty of width.' Stein laid out what he wanted to achieve by the exercise. 'A cricket score would be meaningless,' he told Alastair MacDonald of the *Aberdeen Evening Express*. 'What is more important is our players have a chance to overcome the difficulties likely to be presented by a big pitch and controlling the ball on a hard surface.'

The team wore the previous season's shirt with the new-look shorts. A crowd of around 800 turned out to see what was a training session for the Scots as they won 9-1 with hat-tricks for Souness and Archibald. All of Souness's goals came from outside of the box. Evans, Dalglish and Sturrock scored the others, with Sergio Gomez notching the consolation past substitute keeper George Wood. Archibald and Dalglish missed a dozen more chances between them. Fifteen players were used with George Burley, Davie Provan and Paul Sturrock all, like Wood, coming on from the bench. Stein intended that all the players in the squad would get some game time across the two matches. 'Scoring goals against anybody is good for a side,' Stein said. 'I was very happy with the game overall and it was just the right type of match.' The *Evening Express*'s Alistair Guthrie commented that the game was played in a lighter mood than the training match between the squad the night before.

One thing in the match stood out for Jim Leighton. 'I'll never forget my first blast from Stein during Scotland's preparations for Spain '82 in the Portuguese Algarve,' he told the *Sunday Mail* in 2000. 'It was a bounce game against a local team and my first touch came via a pass-back I should have eaten for breakfast. But the pitch was poor and the ball struck a divot two yards in front of me, [and] bounced off my shoulder. Stein went bananas and came on the pitch to slaughter me as he stood in the six-yard box, leaving me cringing with embarrassment because everyone – including some of the Scottish press – could hear his tirade. But for all that Jock was a superb manager, exceptional motivator and a great man.'

* * *

Staying at the Don Carlose Hotel in Marbella, New Zealand played their own bounce game, beating Spanish Third Division side Atlético Benamiel in an encounter played over 35 minutes each way. Grant Turner picked up an ankle injury when he caught his foot in a pothole on the pitch. Turner played in all but one of New Zealand's matches in qualifying, scoring eight times along the way.

Manager John Adshead said, 'Grant is a vital player for us. We shall miss him if he is out. We wanted to give the lads a run-out in the heat. Okay, it wasn't too impressive perhaps, but it served its purpose.' The injury would rule Turner out of the World Cup.

At a news conference at La Rosaleda, Malaga, Adshead talked up Brazil and Russia but made scant mention of Scotland. 'From what we know of Scotland,' he began when asked why he hadn't mentioned his first opponents, 'we feel we'll be more at home playing against them than we would be if we were playing against Russia or Brazil. We play the game in a similar way and I am damned sure that Jock Stein would be happier if his team played against Brazil in the opening match.' Adshead didn't fancy Scotland's chances much, suggesting they would be third or fourth in the group. 'I can't see them beating Russia or Brazil,' he said. He did admit that Scotland should win their game comfortably. 'We are just a tiny nation with 22 amateur players,' he added, 'but David did beat Goliath.'

Brazil had now moved from their training camp in Portugal to Carmona, 33km north-east of Seville. Zico was confined to his room after taking ill, with what was being termed as summer flu, following training. Brazilian radio, TV and the 700-strong press corps had now ruled him out of the opening game with Russia. Manager Telê Santana lost his patience with them, saying, 'Bastards, they are all bastards. I was very happy to have everyone watch us train – but no longer. This is the last straw. No one will be allowed in, in future. Everything will remain private. I was willing to co-operate beforehand but not any more. People are disturbing our preparations. That cannot be tolerated. Zico will be all right. He felt dizzy at training and we sent him back to the hotel. It is a mild flu. Nothing more. The other stories are rumours and no more than that.'

The next day, Thursday, 10 June, Scotland would play their second match against Torralta. There were some changes in the team, with Brazil and Jordan leading the line. 'It's not the reserve side that's playing tonight, not by any manner of means,' Stein stressed. Gordon Strachan was left out, Stein saying that the midfielder didn't need to prove anything to him. Andy Roxburgh wouldn't be at that match as he set off by car for Sotogrande. It was a drive of around 500 miles, but Stein insisted that someone had to go on ahead of the party. 'I thought it was going to be a straightforward drive into Spain,' Roxburgh said to the *Evening Express*, 'but I have been told I will have to make a crossing by boat.' Roxburgh would ensure the training pitches and other facilities were as had been promised.

Roxburgh began his playing career in the 1961/62 season with Queen's Park. A centre-forward, he moved on to East Stirlingshire, then Partick Thistle. Seventeen league goals in the 1964/65 season was his best return, but he went out of favour at Firhill. A move to Falkirk reignited his career. His 17 goals from 24 league games, along with strike partner Alex Ferguson's 15, helped Falkirk to the 1969/70 Second Division title. In 1972 Roxburgh moved again, this time to join his uncles Jack and Charlie Steedman who were in charge at Clydebank. It was at New Kilbowie Park where he devoted more time to coaching, which he juggled with his full-time job as a headteacher. In 1975 he left the Bankies to move into the SFA's coaching system.

In the second game against Torralta, Scotland had no problems as they swept to a 7-0 win. Three players – Brazil, Jordan and Robertson – all scored braces with Hartford netting the other. Jordan crossed for Brazil to score after nine minutes, and added the second himself after killing the ball with his right foot then lobbing it with his left from 25 yards five minutes later. Brazil made it three when the keeper blocked but couldn't hold a Sturrock shot. Dalglish came on for Brazil at half-time and Robertson took over from Provan. The second half was about playing the ball around, for the Scots, instead of going all out to add to the goals total, but ten minutes in Dalglish was pulled down and Robertson got his first with the resultant penalty. A minute later Hartford made it 5-0, and with 72 minutes on the clock, Robertson netted the sixth. A powerful header from Jordan with five minutes of the 80 remaining finished the scoring. After the game, the Scottish team presented their jerseys to the club.

Someone who had watched both matches was Manuel Fernandes, the Sporting player who had scored twice against Scotland in the final qualifier. 'They seem to be reaching their peak at just the right time,' he said to the *Aberdeen Evening News*, 'and I would expect them to do well in Spain.' Fernandes was on holiday in Portimão. 'It does not matter how strong the team were – these goals will still be in the Scotland players' minds in Spain. I think I preferred the first team that played, as they had more movement,' he added. Fernandes highlighted Souness, Strachan and Robertson and rated them all as 'exceptional'. 'Scotland knocked us out of the World Cup, although they did not beat us in our two games, so I know Portugal will be on Scotland's side to qualify,' he said.

Before his squad left at dawn to catch a flight from Faro to Malaga, Stein was happy to chat to the press about a couple of the successes he had seen over the week. John

Robertson and Gordon Strachan were two players he had considered leaving behind in Scotland, Strachan due to the serious stomach injury he had suffered and Robertson due to his weight and his general form. 'They are both in top form,' Stein told the *Daily Record*. 'We know what Robbo can do, but I doubt if New Zealand, Brazil and Russia realise Strachan's full potential. You know, Robbo does everything we ask of him in training. But if there's a slovenly way to do something he'll find it. He doesn't do himself any favours in this way. Strachan is different. He's flat out all the time. Robbo is one of those marvellous players who can hold the ball and go past opponents before passing it accurately. Strachan does the same thing on the other side of the pitch. Robbo is fit now and Strachan is rested after a tough run-up to his season.'

Stein explained why he had left Robertson out of the England game, 'If I'd played Robertson at the start at Hampden he would have been unfit and people would have said he would be no good in the World Cup. I've had to shame him into getting back to his best. He's done this to my satisfaction. He's really worked.' Stein had spoken to Robertson after the Northern Ireland game in April. 'The John Robertson who played against Northern Ireland was no use to anyone, but he was really too good a player for us to sit back and watch him wasting away. We couldn't hide what was happening, so we had to shame him into sorting himself out,' he explained. Robertson was now sitting at just under 12 stone in weight. 'After Belfast, I told him that he had very little time in which to prove himself willing to get into shape,' said Stein. The winger had also been involved in a transfer wrangle with Nottingham Forest. 'Robertson is going on to the world soccer stage. If he wants a transfer, then this is the place to earn it. He will be seen all around the world,' he continued. Stein suggested to the *Glasgow Herald* that an on-form Robertson was good for Frank Gray – 'Not an outstanding defender, but is so good at going forward,' – and Asa Hartford, who, Stein said, suffers if Robertson is off form; 'It knocks that whole left triangle out.'

'Not being a first choice really hurt me,' Robertson told the *Record*. 'I'm at my best weight and playing in the World Cup will be the pinnacle of my career.'

Of Strachan, Stein said, 'For a long time he seemed he would never shake off his injury, and although he kept playing away he was not the same player. Now he is sharp and eager. He could be a real ace for us in Spain, putting people under pressure. I think he is going to have a good World Cup.' Growing up in Edinburgh, Strachan was a Hibs fan. He had two heroes in the Easter Road side: Pat Stanton and Peter Cormack. The young Strachan began playing with Craigroyston Boys Club, joining Dundee on an 'S' form in October 1971. The Dens Park side were in the second tier of Scottish football at the time, and Strachan was one of their star performers as they pushed for promotion to the Premier League in 1976/77. They missed out by finishing third, but in November of 1977 Billy McNeill brought him to Aberdeen in a swap deal for Jim Shirra, plus £50,000. He became a regular starter throughout the 1978/79 season and played 33 league games as the Dons won the 1979/80 Premier Division title. Strachan made his international debut in Belfast in May 1980 as Scotland lost the Home International match 1-0 to Northern Ireland. Strachan was much admired in Scottish football. Rangers boss John Greig said of him, 'He's great at taking players on and if I had him in my team I'd give him a free role, letting him go after the ball and making things happen.'

At the previous World Cup in Argentina, Scotland had been rocked by Willie Johnstone testing positive for a banned substance and being sent home. Jim Reynolds asked Stein what steps had been taken to ensure that Spain wouldn't provide a repeat of that. 'I'm positive there will be nothing like that this time,' Stein said. 'Every player has been warned. They have all been asked to declare what they have been taking with their clubs, and everything has been checked out by the doctor.'

'Discipline is different this time,' Robertson said. 'The lads know they can't step out of line. Really, that's what went wrong in Argentina, but it won't happen in Spain. The big man has things going the right way and everybody is happy. There's no actual "dos" and "don'ts". We're all men and are expected to act like adults. Every one of us wants to be in the New Zealand game because we know how important it is.'

The trip had the effect Stein wanted. The players had relaxed, become used to the heat, and built up their confidence in those bounce games. 'It's all been so relaxing on the Algarve I've almost forgotten about the World Cup,' Danny McGrain said to the *Belfast Telegraph*.

It was now on to Spain, to look at La Rosaleda Stadium, make their way to their base at Sotogrande and prepare for their first match against New Zealand.

* * *

Scots fans were now beginning to arrive in Spain, many of them without tickets. The ticketing situation for the 1982 World Cup would prove to be notorious. The Spanish Football Federation decided to sell all tickets for the visiting nations to Mundiespana, a consortium formed jointly by the four biggest Spanish travel agencies – Ecuador, Marsans, Melia and Wagon Lits – and the country's four major hotel chains – Entursa, Husa, Hotasa and Melia. Julio Abrau, the director-general of Mundiespana, told the *Evening Times*, 'What we did was to take a gamble. We bought up the whole allocation of tickets assigned to foreign countries – 40 per cent of the total.' This would be around one million tickets. As it turned out, Mundiespana's operation was something of a national disaster. Or, as David Yallop put it in his book *How They Stole the Game*, 'This group were destined to make an art form out of incompetence.'

The SFA had been told in June 1981 that in the event of qualifying they would only be able to access 250 tickets for officials. At the time, Ernie Walker refused to accept the situation, saying he had assurances that Scotland would receive a direct allocation. As qualification became apparent, Walker entered into negotiations with Mundiespana, only to have to admit defeat. The Scottish Football Association would not be allowed to sell tickets to their own matches directly to their fans.

'The different associations could never guarantee that kind of deal,' Abrau said, 'and I really don't see why some of them are complaining. Why the Spanish organising committee took up our offer to purchase all the tickets to be allocated abroad is perfectly simple. It was a very convenient operation for them to handle.' Of course, the British agents for tickets were Sportsworld, and it was proving hard for Scottish fans and organisations to wrench free of their grip. SFA assistant secretary Peter Donald told the *Glasgow Herald*, 'We are awaiting confirmation from the Spanish

FA, but it seems we have come to the end of the road. Our 1,200 members of the SFA Travel Club will have to look after themselves.'

It wasn't only the various football associations who were complaining – travel agents and supporters associations were too. John Reilly of Universal Travel told the *Evening Times*, 'This whole contract with Sportsworld sabotages the whole principle of the Scotland Travel Club, which was set up specifically with the World Cup in mind.' Sportsworld's cheapest package was now quoted at £450. 'Scottish travel agents could certainly undercut that deal if we were allowed to have tickets,' Reilly said.

The National Federation of Football Supporters' Clubs urged a boycott of Sportsworld. Chairman Charles Bent said to the *Glasgow Herald*, 'We feel this offers poor value compared with standard package holidays to Spain and have recommended our members do not use this company. Our experience shows that early matches are not likely to be attended, and we believe there will be no shortage of tickets available in Spain.' The SFA initially didn't back the Sportsworld deal either. 'We are not interested in promoting Sportsworld Travel, a company based in London,' Ernie Walker said. 'We want to control our own fans, but the Spanish organisers will not let us do that.' A FIFA spokesman said to the *Evening Times*, 'We agreed to this form of ticket distribution, which we felt would save everyone a lot of trouble. Although some associations have complained about it we are not going back on our decision.' In a letter from the Royal Organising Committee to Mundiespana, the organisers expressed their 'regret at the attitude of the SFA' and denied there was any possibility of Scots obtaining tickets directly.

As the tournament drew closer, the relationship between the SFA and Sportsworld thawed, and a partnership between the company and the SFA's Travel Club was established. Walker had emerged from bartering with Mundiespana and Geoffrey Phillips at Sportsworld with a ticket-only deal for Scots fans, albeit with considerable strings attached. The SFA came to a special deal on tickets for long-serving members of the SFA Travel Club. Those members would have to buy tickets for all six games in Scotland's section. The deal would not be available to new members, and fans would need private accommodation for the first ties. 'We have agreed to supply a number of tickets to members of the SFA's Travel Club,' Phillips said, 'with the proviso that they go to members who can show they already have accommodation booked in Spain.' The fans would need confirmation of a booking at a hotel, apartment or campsite. Travel bookings would have to be made with Sportsworld. A booking with any other company than Sportsworld would not be accepted. A spokesman said Sportsworld considered package holiday companies to be in opposition. The ticket prices were £3 for the terracing and £6 to £10 for seating. Phillips wasn't prepared to announce the number of tickets supplied to the Travel Club. The SFA would issue members who qualified with a letter they would have to provide in their application to Sportsworld.

In the lead up to the finals, the *Financial Times* wrote, 'Mundiespana's sales policy has proved little short of disastrous.' Having initially indicated that up to 200,000 packages could be sold for the first phase, Mundiespana had sold only 25,000. The Spanish press levelled criticism at the company for grossly overpricing at a time of national recession. Mundiespana had to make major cancellations of hotel bookings – up to 100 per cent in some areas of Spain. Mundiespana were also now awash with tickets. One official said they had 'trunkfulls'.

As the initial plans for package deals fell apart, this led to confusion over how the tickets were being sold. The relationship between Mundiespana and Sportsworld, too, had begun to break down. Juan Garcia, the Costa del Sol delegate for Mundiespana, told the *Evening Times*, 'We are not happy at all. I'm fed up with all the problems.' Tickets were now on the black market and Garcia wanted to know where the touts were getting the tickets from. 'I have been quoted huge black market prices of up to 3,000 pesetas [around £16] for tickets.' Garcia claimed Sportsworld appeared to be selling tickets on their own as demand for their hotel package deals slumped. But Sportsworld executive director Hamish Ogston categorically denied Garcia's claims, 'We have not issued tickets or vouchers to anybody in Britain, except those who own properties in Spain.' Scottish fans who bought their tickets through Sportsworld would have to call at a hotel in Torremolinos to collect their tickets. 'We are paying good money for our holiday,' a Scots fan told the *Glasgow Herald*. 'The least the travel agents can do is deliver the tickets to us.'

In all the chaos, Hermann Neuberger, vice-president of FIFA, criticised the Spanish organisers for their foreign ticket sales policies and a decision to spread the games around 17 stadiums in 14 cities. He told the *New York Times*, 'The Spaniards have recognised that they have failed in some ways with regard to ticket sales.' There were now fears that grounds would only be one-third full. 'Football should not be commercial,' Neuberger said. 'Enthusiasm is waning, and that is not the best atmosphere for football.'

WE MADE THEM ANGRY

Raimundo Saporta, head of the Spanish organising committee, began to worry publicly about the likelihood of low attendance at some of the games and modified earlier predictions that the World Cup would be an embarrassment of riches for Spain. 'If I make one peseta for the King, I will have done my job,' Saporta said to the *New York Times*, which suggested that Saporta was known to have irritated Juan Carlos I by giving visitors photocopies of the royal decree naming him to the World Cup post.

The *Financial Times* would report in December of 1982 that Mundiespana only managed to sell 30 per cent of the package deals it had organised, and 16 of the 24 teams participating in the World Cup, as well as all the members of FIFA, simply refused to pay the prices that Mundiespana was asking.

An unlikely alternative to Sportsworld emerged in June. Offering competition to Sportsworld's official package was Brian Doran. He took delivery of 5,000 tickets for all three Scotland games. 'People only have to come into my office to buy them,' he told the *Daily Record*. Doran came by the tickets in an unusual manner. He put up funds to help CD Malaga finish the extension to their stadium. 'They ran out of money. I said I would guarantee £200,000 for the final stages and I was given the tickets. I negotiated direct with Malaga Football Club and agreed to pay a fixed price for tickets in four new stands being built at the corners of the stadium.' Tickets for these new stands were to have no face value and, therefore, the club could charge what they liked. However, the first tickets to become available for Scotland were for other similar areas in the stadium and they did carry a face value of £5. 'This does not mean that I get these tickets for any cheaper. They are still the best seats in the ground and I have to pay the price agreed with Malaga Football Club,' Doran said.

Doran was based at Albaco Holidays in Berkeley Street Glasgow. It was suggested that he had 12,000 tickets. 'They are all very good seats. For a four-game package involving all Group Six games played in Malaga plus the Scotland–Brazil game in Seville we are charging £55. But with all the trouble I have gone to, they have cost me £48,' he said. A former schoolteacher, Doran had previously run the Scottish end of holiday company Blue Sky. A fluent Spanish speaker, he had now struck out on his own. Doran, it would turn out later, would have his own problems to contend with in Spain.

* * *

Bobby Jamieson and Kevin Donnelly were among the supporters who bought the bundle of match tickets from the SFA. Chic Brogan from Clydebank bought tickets from Brian Doran. He said, 'They were £50, which was a lot. He was charging £50 for a block of four. Our three games plus the Russia–New Zealand game. You had to take the four. Okay, we're fine with that. Four of us paid for the block of tickets. One of my mates, Greg, he wouldn't. He's a miserable sod. "I'm not paying that. No way." So, we're flying out early so Greg can find tickets over there. We're going on the Wednesday but now it's Tuesday and our tickets still haven't arrived. Suddenly, our mate comes into the pub, "I've got them." The reason there was no tickets was because they didn't put them out until the last minute to stop forgeries.'

The party made a bus journey to London before getting a flight to Malaga. Chic continued, 'At the time you had to have one year passports and you'd go to the Post Office.

Greg wouldn't get a passport. We're all going, "You need to get a passport." The Post Office is next to the pub. He's going, "Aye, I'll get one." He's in the pub every day, the Post Office is two doors along, someone even went in and got him the forms. We're thinking something's not right here. The day before we went he got the passport, he's sorted. Before we get off the plane in Malaga, Greg says to me, "I'm barred from Spain." I say, "You're what?" "Aye, I got banned." He got the jail in Spain twice. First time in Barcelona after the Rangers European Cup Winners' Cup win. The second time made it to the front page of the *Herald*. He stole a donkey and a cart with bricks in it. He went about ten yards and the polis pulled him off it. So he got the jail for stealing that and that was him banned. "That's how I didn't get my passport until the last second so no one knows I'm here."'

The father of Stuart Russell from Cumbernauld was a former player. Frank Russell played in senior football with Clyde, Morton and Clydebank, winning the Scottish Junior Cup with Johnstone Burgh. 'It was the first time the *Daily Record* had ever been sold *in day* in Spain,' Stuart told me. British newspapers sold in Spain would typically be a day or two old. 'My dad was at a boxing group and he got introduced to a guy called Liam Kane who was the editor of the *Daily Record*. They hit it off right away. Liam mentioned they were looking for someone to distribute the paper. Pick it up from Malaga Airport, then distribute it round the vendors. My dad was an antiques dealer so always had an eye for opportunities, so he said, "Aye I'll dae it."

'We drove from Cumbernauld all the way to Puerto Banús. We got the ferry at Portsmouth into Santander and drove all the way right into the heart of Spain. The boat to Santander was full of English fans. There were a few English managers on it: Malcolm Allison, Dave Sexton, a couple of older players. An England fan jumped into the water. They were all steaming. The ship had to turn. These big ferries, it takes a while for them to turn. I could see the guy [in the water] but I thought everybody else could see him so I didn't say anything. Then my mum started screaming, "There, he's there! There, he's there!" They went in and got him and the guy survived. I always remember my dad saying, "Oh, that was great Cathy, you've saved that boy's life." I went, "Well, I actually saw him first, but I thought everybody could see him."'

With his original plan of hoodwinking the AA scuppered, Kevin Donnelly came up with a much better idea to get to Spain. 'I had a friend whose wife was teaching in Madrid,' Kevin told me. 'So he had got a hotel sorted out for him and anyone who wanted to join him. So I had a hotel for two weeks in Torremolinos. My dad was a train driver and I used to get really cheap train travel around Europe that helped me start to support Scotland. I went from Dumfries to Torremolinos by train. Left Dumfries at midnight and got to France really easy. It was all right, you met a lot of other guys who were doing the same thing. One of them was a complete arsehole. He was one of those guys who thought if he added an "o" to the end of every word he was speaking Spanish. "Beero". "Vodkao". "Cokeo". All that sort of stuff. Then some people hadn't realised that the train was splitting and they ended up in Barcelona.'

Iain McAuley's group left Dunfermline in their van on the Friday night. He said, 'The van broke down in a place just outside Paris called Poix. Nobody would fix the van because it was a Sunday. So we ended up going to a village fete in Poix and booking a hotel. We were just in about the fete enjoying ourselves. There was bumper cars, the local lassies are jumping into the bumper cars with you and we won prizes at this fete. We had a game of football with these French guys and we were asking them about our van because nobody works on a Sunday in France. The next day we went to the garage at six o'clock in the morning to get the van fixed and turns out the guys we were playing football against were the mechanics.'

Stuart Russell says one of his regrets now as an older man is not stopping to enjoy Spain as they travelled through the country, so focused were they on getting to their destination. But, as Iain found out, stopping to smell the roses wasn't always possible, 'We had "Malvinas" getting shouted at us on the way down. Because the Spanish were in favour of Argentina in the Falklands. And we're like, "What does that mean? What does that even mean?" We didn't know. We're Scottish, we're going to watch the football. We're not involved in politics, but we've got a lorry driver wanting to run us off the road at one point.'

'Another group of us were out there, and they'd went in the van,' Chic Brogan said. 'Split new transit van, they'd put a mattress in it. Sounded good at the time. They had a nightmare of a journey. The polis kept stopping them and fining them. Malky the driver said, "We didn't even know what we were doing wrong." Sometimes they got fined for having their lights on and sometimes they got fined for having their lights off. When you're filling up in a petrol station if they're not on or off. Things like that. They argued once, "But I need petrol," so the polis looked at the petrol gauge and he went, "That's enough to get you out of France," and reduced the fine, but they were just putting it in their pockets.'

Bobby Jamieson's party flew out from Manchester, 'Clad in kilts, tammies and assorted tartans, complete with Saltire borrowed from my younger brother. His gang were notorious for not keeping themselves in the most hygienic of conditions on trips to Wembley, unlike the more mature members on our bus, and they became known as the "Leper Colony". So, that moniker was proudly emblazoned on the flag.' To their great delight, they found that their villa was up in the mountain above the coastal resort, complete with a communal swimming pool, shops, bar and restaurants for the residents. Once in their residence, the group took the decision to divide tasks for the weeks ahead amongst themselves.

Bobby said, 'We sorted out the rooms and had to share of course, but nobody cared. I assumed the role of commanding officer, Alan Campbell (RIP) was appointed quartermaster, Drew McManus was placed in charge of beer procurement, which in hindsight was a mistake as he fell in love with San Miguel and failed spectacularly to fulfil his role. Ginger-bearded Danny Curley was given responsibility for the flag as standard bearer.' They set out looking for a bar owned by a friend who had taken early retirement and set up shop in the Costa del Sol. Bobby continued, 'The first bar we hit was owned by former Dundee goalkeeper Bert Slater, who was famously remembered for his outstanding performance in the Scottish Cup Final of 1964 when Dundee lost to Rangers. We asked him if he knew where our friend's place was located but old Bert tried his best to keep our business in his own establishment, by telling us his bar was the best in town.'

Slater's bar in Fuengirola was called Las Almendras. He had been in Spain for three years without once returning to

Scotland, and although he was 46 he still played in goal for a local team. Slater was confident he'd see many more Scots fans through the doors, telling the *Record*, 'I'm hoping to see as many of them as possible. Already a bundle of them are staying nearby, but I'm ready for an invasion. They will be made very welcome by the people here. The Spaniards were very impressed when they saw some of the Scottish games on television. They are convinced that Scotland will go through along with Brazil.'

Kevin Donnelly was also settling into his accommodation. He said, 'We were with a big crowd of Scots in this hotel. Some real characters. Old school, what you would call Bears, just complete bevvy merchants. One of them was this guy called "Whisky Davie" who these Scots guys had actually found in an underpass in Madrid begging. You're going to have to take my word on this. He had actually played in the Spanish equivalent of The Beatles called Mizque de la Tones in the 1960s. They'd been playing five-a-sides and this guy was basically a jakey and he was begging, going, "Boys, boys could you help a Scot out?" Basically he'd been on the rock 'n' roll path of drugs, drink, oblivion and he was living on the streets of Madrid. So they took him in, helped get him sorted and got him back on his feet. Years later he was living in a caravan site in Helensburgh. I knew this guy called "Ronnie the Reaper"; he was called that because every time you met him at a Scotland game he told you that someone else had died. He told me that when Whisky Davie died there was an obituary for him in *El País*, because he had been in Mizque de la Tones. Possibly the only person in a Helensburgh caravan site to have his obituary in *El País*.'

For the boys from Clydebank there was still the matter of procuring tickets for one of their party. 'We got off the plane in Malaga,' Chic says, 'we're walking through and there's a guy trying to sell tickets for the Brazil game, which was the hardest to get. So Greg's like that, "I'm your man." It was maybe £8. Sorted. The New Zealand game, we went up to the ground. There's ticket touts everywhere. We went to the ticket office. Shut. It was siesta time. The touts are going, "We've got tickets." It worked out at maybe 50 pence extra. So he paid that.' That left only one ticket to get, and it was left until the day of the final match with Russia. Chic said, 'At the hotel we had met up with Willie Miller's mum, his stepdad and his sister. They ended up coming to the game with us. So she's on the phone to her son. He says, "I'll get tickets for him at the main gate." So we go up and it's Kenny Dalglish [handing out the players' complimentary tickets] and he gives Greg the ticket. Greg's over the moon.' But then Greg noticed that there were also uncollected tickets there. Chic continued, 'Greg says, "Somebody would want them," and Kenny flung them away. Greg went nuts, shouting and bawling at him, "You ya basturt," and Kenny Dalglish is looking at him going, "Right I'm out of here," and he's through the doors. Greg's half scooped, "You're throwing tickets like that away? People are desperate for them." Everybody's out to see what's going on, the polis are coming out. So Greg got all his tickets for a couple of quid and he's laughing at us for paying 50.'

9

The Scare: New Zealand

*'They were terrible goals to give away at
this level. We are the greatest nation in the
world for punishing ourselves at every turn.'*

Jock Stein

'WELL, THE holiday is over,' Danny McGrain said as
he looked around the gallery of press and television men in
CD Malaga's La Rosaleda Stadium. Having made their way
into the ground passing through armed guards, the Scots
gave a press conference. 'This is where the real work lies,'
McGrain continued. 'This sort of reception is the best way
of illustrating to players involved in their first World Cup
just how much the pressure can build up.'

Brought up in Drumchapel, the son of Robert, who
had a brief career with Hearts during the Second World
War, McGrain began his playing days with Queen's Park
Strollers. He was a Rangers supporter in his early years. 'As
a youngster, my dad used to take me to watch great players

like Eric Caldow, Jim Baxter, Ian McMillan and Davy Wilson,' he told *Shoot!* in 1985. 'I dreamed of playing for them and heard a whisper that they were interested in me. In the end, nothing happened and I'm told it was because they thought I was a Catholic. I'm not, but if that was the reason then I am glad I didn't sign for them.'

Celtic's Sean Fallon spotted McGrain playing for Scotland in a schoolboy international against England at Ibrox. McGrain signed for Celtic in May 1967, just weeks before Jock Stein led the club to that European Cup in Lisbon. It was customary in those days to farm out the young players at Parkhead to toughen them up, and in McGrain's case he was off to Maryhill Juniors. At Lochburn Park, McGrain claimed he learned to look after himself and improve his awareness of the game.

Although McGrain was originally a midfielder, Stein moved him to full-back. Despite his own initial uncertainty about his attributes for the position, McGrain quickly found he was comfortable in the role. Throughout the 1970s McGrain had a few ups and downs. He made his Celtic debut against Dundee United in a League Cup tie in August 1970, following that with more appearances across that season and the next. Just when it looked like he was beginning to establish himself at right-back, Danny was hit with a major setback. In a match against Falkirk in March 1972 he fractured his skull after clashing with Doug Somner. McGrain actually played on after the collision, with the *Evening Times* noting, 'McGrain and Somner went down after a clash of heads. Both were OK after treatment.'

McGrain was substituted at half-time, and it was later found that the fracture was between three and four inches on the right side of his skull. He was taken to the Falkirk

Royal Infirmary and placed in intensive care. The injury put him out of football for five months, before he returned for the Drybrough Cup semi-final against Aberdeen in July. In the 1972/73 season, he firmly established himself as the first choice at Celtic Park. Willie Ormond awarded McGrain his first Scotland cap in a Home International match against Wales in May 1973. He became a mainstay of the Scotland team, and by the time the year was out he had earned eight caps.

At the 1974 World Cup in West Germany McGrain played in all three of Scotland's games. It was at that tournament he began to worry something wasn't right with him physically. 'It was during our game against Zaire that I began to worry,' McGrain told *Match* in 1984. 'At half-time, I was really thirsty and I remember one of my team-mates telling me to steady on with my drinking otherwise I'd empty the water tap. I just put it down to the weather and playing in the finals, but when I arrived back at Glasgow my wife persuaded me to see a doctor. I was glad I did.' When McGrain went for tests he was diagnosed with diabetes. He later referred to it as 'much ado about nothing', saying it didn't affect his game.

When Kenny Dalglish left Celtic for Liverpool in August of 1977, McGrain was handed the Celtic captaincy. He was named the Scottish Football Writers' Association Player of the Year at the end of the 1976/77 season. In October 1977 an ankle injury while playing against Hibs kept him out of the game for over a year. It meant he missed out on going to the World Cup in Argentina. McGrain's playing return came against Montrose in November 1978, and he made his first Scotland appearance for over two years when Stein named him in the team for the European Championship qualifier against Belgium in December 1979. 'I have no hesitation in naming him as the biggest influence on my career,' McGrain said of Stein in 1981.

In Spain, Stein intended to make training sessions later in the day, to ensure that the players gained experience of playing in the same kind of heat and humidity the 9pm kick-offs would give them. 'The atmosphere has come alive,' was Willie Miller's view. 'We can all sense how important it is to put on a good show in the World Cup.'

The players had time to have a look at the pitch. 'It really looks tight,' McGrain said. 'It's a defender's pitch all right. The pitch looks good, but the playing surface is small. It's narrow, much narrower than the park on which we played in Portugal, and it should suit defenders rather than forwards.'

The stadium was still in the process of being built. 'We are slightly behind schedule,' a spokesman for the World Cup organising committee said, 'but everything will be completed by Tuesday without any problems.' The playing surface was being re-laid, the four corners of the stadium were being filled in, and a moat was being built around the perimeter. The capacity of the ground would swell to 45,000 and a new electronic scoreboard was also being installed. 'We get to the first game and it's not a word of a lie when I say they were still painting the doors as we were going in,' said Kevin Donnelly.

La Rosaleda was the work of architects Enrique Atencia Molina and Fernando Guerrero-Strachan Rosado. The first stone was laid on 21 June 1936, but the outbreak of the Spanish Civil War the following month caused work to stop. It resumed at the beginning of 1940, with some modifications made to the original design. Originally planned to house 16,000 spectators, this was amended to an 8,000 capacity. The first game was played there in April 1941, with the official inauguration match between CD Malaga and Sevilla taking place on 14 September of that year.

Former Scotland striker Denis Law was in Spain to work as co-commentator for the BBC. 'I was impressed by the professional manner in which they went about their business in the two warm-up friendlies in Portugal and the discipline looks better than ever,' he told the *Evening Express*. 'In the 1974 and 1978 finals, we were expected to reach the second stage but failed. This time, Brazil and Russia are favourites to qualify and I reckon that sort of challenge plays right into Scotland's hands. They are never more dangerous than with their backs to the wall and I am certain they will reach the next round.'

Law was a hero to many of the Scotland squad, not least Kenny Dalglish. 'To me, he stood for everything that was just right in football. He ... showed great pride and passion for the game,' Dalglish said in 1980. 'That man was amazing,' Steve Archibald added. 'His reflexes were breathtaking, and, although he wasn't particularly well built, he never shirked a tackle.' Graeme Souness admired Law for 'the traditional fighting spirit which turned the tide for so many Scotland teams'.

'Everything stands or falls on the first game,' Souness told journalist Patrick Barclay. 'If we get off to a good start, anything can happen. But it won't be easy. There has been talk about it being a matter of how many goals we score, but that's ridiculous. Winning is the most important thing.'

As Scotland made their way the 60 miles to Sotogrande there were heavily armed Guardia Civil policemen posted at every junction and every bridge. Before the party arrived, the Brazilian press were outside the hotel in Sotogrande filming. They insisted they would be back to spy on the Scots training. The complex manager told them, 'Do that and you will be banned from the whole area.' Alan Rough recalled what Stein said when the Scotland party arrived at Sotogrande, 'He told us, "Look, we're just off a flight, so I want you all to get up to your rooms, unpack, and grab a couple of hours' sleep." His instructions could hardly have been clearer. Jock rammed home the message he didn't want us lying out in the sun and risk being burned. Footballers being footballers, we all splashed on the suntan oil and dashed out to our verandas as rapidly as we could. Naturally, Jock fathomed that we would do this, and within ten minutes he walked along the outside of the hotel apartments, nailed absolutely everybody; asked us what the hell we were doing, and, much as a parent might react to a naughty five-year-old, sent us to our beds. From then on we obeyed his orders explicitly.'

Stein was very much aware of his players staying out of the sun. In the summer of 1966, on a tour of America with Celtic, several of his players, including Jimmy Johnstone, missed games having come down with sunstroke. Before the European Cup finals in Lisbon in 1967 and Milan in 1970, Stein warned his players to stay out of the sun. Gordon Strachan was well aware, as a redhead, he had to keep out of the sun, playing tennis in a long-sleeved shirt and tracksuit bottoms. 'I just hope the hotel has a dark room,' he told the *Evening Express*. 'I think I will be keeping indoors or well covered up when I go outside.'

Speaking with Gordon Waddell of BBC Scotland in 2020, Strachan said, 'It wasn't easy being away in those days. We got one phone call home a week from the SFA. There was no internet, no social media to keep up, the only telly was Spanish telly, and Willie Miller was the room-mate who just wanted to sleep 24/7. The room was the first I'd ever been in that had the harling [rough plaster] on the inside. And Jock used to berate me every time he saw me outside because he thought the sun would kill the wee ginger guy – never mind the fact I might have to acclimatise to play three games in it!'

Also arriving in Spain was a contingent of Scottish managers led by Rangers' John Greig and Aberdeen's Alex Ferguson. St Mirren's Ricky McFarlane, Benny Rooney of Morton, Ayr United's Willie McLean, Kilmarnock's Jim Clunie, Clyde's Craig Brown and Alex Smith of Stirling Albion were all in Spain, along with Morton's chairman Hal Stewart. Ferguson spoke with Allan Herron of the *Sunday Mail*. 'I'm looking forward to going to the finals and watching and meeting the top players and managers in world football,' he said. 'But I would be less than human if I did not admit to being a wee bit disappointed at not being more intimately involved. Don't get me wrong. There's no way I'd criticise Jock Stein, who is something of a father figure for us all in Scottish football. He has done more than anyone I know for the game at domestic level. I'm just a bit surprised and disappointed he had not used the likes of Billy McNeill, John Greig and myself, who have all been involved at European level, to help in preparations. I often send people to scout out what opponents are up to. It doesn't necessarily mean I take their advice. But there is no question that I can pick up a lot of useful information and I believe any of us would have been only too happy to do that on behalf of Scotland.'

Ferguson suggested that were he in charge he would play the strongest team from the start, and not think about saving players for later games, 'The fans are entitled to know what our strongest side is and the players have to be made to believe it. It's as simple as that.' Ferguson expressed some concerns around two of his own players: McLeish and Strachan. 'I think both had something of a raw deal. This season McLeish has played as well as he has ever done and played a significant part in taking Scotland to the finals. His current replacement is Allan Evans and he worries me a lot. He has arrived late on the scene and, while his club, Aston Villa, have won the European Cup, they have been very inconsistent in the league. As far as Strachan is concerned it's a straight choice between him and Kenny Dalglish. If Jock persists in playing Kenny in a deep-lying role I don't think he can play them both. Naturally, I'm a Strachan man and I think Jock favours Dalglish. In that role both play off the front. While Dalglish is one of the top club players in Britain he does not measure up at world level. For one thing, he lacks genuine pace. It's a straight choice and I know the one I would make.'

Ferguson suggested Paul Sturrock start up front with either Archibald or Brazil alongside.

* * *

New Zealand's manager was John Adshead, a 40-year-old from Lancashire who had spent his playing career in the Combination League there. Adshead had gone to Australia to be sports director at Perth in 1970. He arrived in New Zealand in 1976, joining Manurewa. Having won the Northern League, Chatham Cup and the Adidas Challenge Trophy in 1978, he moved on to take on the NZFA regional coaching job but returned to Manurewa in 1981 before being appointed to lead the national team.

'Back home with their club they get a few dollars for expenses – a fiver or, at most, a tenner in British money,' he told the *Record* of his players. 'But playing for their country they don't get paid at all. If at the end of the day our association makes money from being here in Spain then they will be paid something. Right now, though, they are here to play for their country, and for the prestige. They have achieved something just by getting here. Now they want to show they can do better than people would imagine – but they don't ask for money to do it. They'll probably just get on with the job. We travelled something like 78,000 miles in our qualifying games. We went to Peking, Kuwait and Saudi Arabia. It was a marathon journey for us and we succeeded where everyone thought we would fail. It's a dream come true for all of us. This is the summit, isn't it?'

Adshead was held in high regard by his players. 'John Adshead, a brilliant motivator, great man,' Wynton Rufer told me in 2021. His colleague Sam Malcolmson spoke similarly of his boss, but had different thoughts on assistant Kevin Fallon, 'Adshead was the equivalent of a man manager, but Kevin Fallon, they were the good and the bad, Kevin Fallon was an absolute arsehole. He ran us – train, train, train. Nobody liked him much to be honest, but in all honesty we wouldn't have got to Spain without him. Then Adshead was the guy who just sort of calms things and put his arm around you and said, "Come on, big man." They were just good cop bad cop. I had no problems accepting their decisions. I always remember that when we were raising money to play the second phase [of qualifying matches] he [Adshead] came in and he said, "Listen, a wee boy's just given me a dollar, his pocket money, he said can you put that towards the savings for the players?" and

Adshead said, "If you can't play for that then take your boots off and go out." He was just that sort of bloke, you know.'

* * *

Adrian Elrick of Hanimex North Shore United was a 33-year-old brewery representative who had spent 20 years in New Zealand after leaving his native Aberdeen. He made his debut for the Kiwis in 1975 against China and now had 71 caps. 'I'd like to see Scotland going through but I am a New Zealander and I think like a New Zealander and I'll be doing my best against the Scots. That's the way it has to be,' he said.

'I am still a Scotsman at heart,' Sam Malcolmson said. 'Obviously, I'm torn in two. But for 90 minutes I'll be doing my best for New Zealand. My mum and dad will feel terrible that I'm playing against Scotland. But I just hope that no matter what happens in our game Scotland go through. Kenny Dalglish for me is the complete professional. Graeme Souness is all class, with a bit of stick added, and Alan Hansen is the best thing since Franz Beckenbauer. I worry about their full-backs though. Our players might cause them problems. But I want Scotland to go through. I really do.'

Malcolmson played with Kenwood East Coast Bays, making his debut for his adopted country against Burma in 1976. He said, 'A lot of people think we can beat Scotland and if we approach the game properly then we could surprise them. The first 20 or 25 minutes could decide it for them. We'll be tuned up, we want to play well and if Scotland haven't scored in that time our confidence could rise.' He had one request for the *Record*'s Ken Gallacher, 'Can you do me a favour? Ask Joe Jordan if I can get his jersey after the game.'

New Zealand were staying in the five-star Don Carlos Hotel in Marbella. While Stein hammered it into his players to stay out of the sun the Kiwis were enjoying the weather. 'People have seen us on the beach at seven in the morning,' Adshead said, 'but we are out for a 12-kilometre run and we follow this up with a stiff training stint at Marbella's municipal ground.' Adshead said he was putting no restrictions on players, but as he was treating them like adults he expected them to behave like adults, 'They all know that if one steps out of line they will be on the first plane home.' The players' wives were staying in a hotel 500 yards away and were free to visit their husbands at any time they liked. 'We are really only an amateur side. In fact, the players are only being reimbursed the cost of time off work, but in many ways, I believe we are reacting more professionally than some of the professionals,' Adshead said.

The Kiwis' accommodation was sorted out for them by Roger Mahan, a one-time loose forward for Christchurch rugby club, who moved to Spain in 1976. 'The Don Carlos is the only place to stay in this area,' he said to the *Aberdeen Evening Express*. 'I knew that and immediately booked it for the squad. When they arrived the security was extremely tight, but we asked them to be a bit more unobtrusive. There are 36 guards inside the grounds and six specials inside the hotel, and we even have a helicopter patrolling overhead.' Archie Macpherson was one of the journalists who visited their base, to find the players 'lying around the pool and wolfing down chips like any average holidaymaker from the UK'. Macpherson remembers speaking to Charlie Dempsey as the players lay exposed to the sun. Dempsey told him that New Zealand had one of the highest rates of skin cancer in

242

the world, and Dempsey himself had three operations to defeat it.

While the Kiwis were sharing their hotel with a congress of dentists, the 40 heavily armed guards around Scotland's camp were ensuring no unauthorised personnel could gain access. The hotel manager and Willie Harkness were both refused entry because they didn't have their passes with them, while a visiting Denis Law was also turned away. Even Jock Stein found himself in trouble. Alan Rough recollected, 'Stein left in a World Cup vehicle with his backroom staff, but without warning the guards in Sotogrande, who thought the vehicle had been stolen. Jock had a hard time convincing the throng of officers he had made an honest error.'

Jim McLean recalled the incident for the *Daily Record* in 2005. 'One day Jock and I, along with a couple of the backroom boys, went into town for a change of scenery. There were several people carriers at our disposal so we jumped in one and headed from our base. Within minutes we were being chased by a car and eventually pulled over as a couple of stern characters approached. I remembered Jock was the manager and I slipped into the shadows but the men were actually policemen attached to the hotel who noticed a car had gone missing. It turns out we actually needed permission to leave the base, such was the security, but we still had to wait an age while they went through their checks before they eventually left us to go on our way.'

One visitor who was allowed into the camp, though, was Sean Connery, who snuck through the security cordon one evening. 'We were in the sitting room watching another World Cup match on television,' Gordon Strachan recalled, 'when I was conscious of this man beside me, with smoke belching from his cigarette. It was annoying me and I was on the point of asking him to put out the cigarette when I suddenly realised the smoker was none other than James Bond.'

Careca left Brazil's squad, having torn a muscle in his right leg. Vasco da Gama's Roberto Dinamite would be his replacement. Telê Santana had made his peace with the Brazilian press corps. 'The pressure has been too much for us,' Santana said. 'Everyone is saying we are going to win the trophy and, psychologically, that has not been the best way for the team to prepare. In Brazil, one newspaper has even used a headline which said "God is a Brazilian – nothing can stop us". We do have a chance, but I believe Argentina are a better team now than they were four years ago when they won the competition. And West Germany are powerful, as we have seen ourselves in Rio.' In contrast to the New Zealand players and their lack of any kind of bonus, the Brazilians were on a promise of £35,000 a man if they won the World Cup.

The Scottish fans were still being warned not to cause any trouble in Spain. 'It terrifies me,' Ernie Walker said to the *Mirror*, 'because it is the one thing which can bring genuine disgrace to a country. There is no disgrace in losing a football match. Mad delinquency is another matter.' John Little, the former chief constable of Tayside, was in the country as the SFA's troubleshooter. 'There is bound to be trouble,' he told the *Record*, suggesting young Scots fans sleeping rough and swigging cheap spirits would clash with police. There was also a fear of domestic terrorism. Little said, 'Police are really concerned about Basque terrorists staging some atrocity well away from their own area in the north to get maximum world press coverage. They are really edgy with their fingers on their submachine guns all the time.' The Basque separatist movement ETA said it had no intention of disrupting the World Cup.

Of the Scots fans, Little added, 'Some have virtually no money and are sleeping on the beach, drinking out of large flagons of gin. These are the types who are bound to cause trouble. When they do there is nothing I can do to help them. They will be on their own.' Little had made headlines five years earlier when he freed a woman held hostage at gunpoint for seven hours, taking her place himself in an incident known as the Claypotts Siege. He was later awarded the Queen's Gallantry Medal.

Around 5,000 Scots fans were already in Malaga, with thousands more expected in the days leading up to the New Zealand game. The British Consulate in Malaga had doubled their staff for the tournament. Thomas Tuite, the British consul, said of the Scottish supporters, 'We can only hope for the best. We cannot get them out of jail. We are here to serve people who have problems like lost passports and air tickets.' Tuite, originally from Dublin, had been the consul for 20 years, previously working for the Foreign Office.

Arriving from London, heading for his villa in Estepona, near Marbella, was Rod Stewart. He said, 'I am confident that the Scottish fans will not misbehave or cause trouble. I know if they have a few too many they can be a nuisance, but I am certain that's all they will be. I think the English fans will cause all the problems. They are the big troublemakers. We have seen what they can do.' Although born and brought up in London, Stewart was famously a fan of the Scottish national team.

After Scotland's win over England at Wembley in 1977 Stewart invaded the pitch along with hundreds of other visiting supporters. Several chaired him around the pitch, although one of them was later fined £150 after they were convicted of stealing Stewart's gold Cartier watch from his wrist.

* * *

Both managers named their sides just over 48 hours before the match. Adshead was first to get his teamsheet out. The New Zealanders would line up as: Frank van Hattum (Manurewa), John Hill (Gisborne City), Bobby Almond (Invercargill Thistle), Adrian Elrick (Hanimex United), Sam Malcolmson (East Coast Bays), Keith Mackay (Gisborne City), Allan Boath (West Adelaide Hellas), Kenny Cresswell (Gisborne City), Steve Sumner (West Adelaide Hellas), Wynton Rufer (Miramar Rangers), Steve Wooddin (South Melbourne).

There were only four New Zealand-born players in the 11. There were three Scots, three Englishmen and one Irishman. The inclusion of Van Hattum in goal was a surprise. He had sat on the bench for all 15 of the Kiwis' qualifiers, with Richard Wilson of Preston Macedonia making the number one shirt his own. 'I've made the change because Van Hattum is the form keeper. All the players have been picked on the form they are showing,' Adshead said. 'I have every respect for Jock Stein who will ensure Scotland don't make the same mistakes they did in Argentina four years ago. He is a very astute man.' The three Scots-born players – Elrick, Malcolmson and Boath – were all selected. 'Stein said a lot of nice things to our face,' Boath said, 'but he forgets we get the papers from the old country. And we were far from happy when he said we were rough and tough. I owe Scotland nothing. And one or two others who came from Scotland will have more than a passing interest in putting one over on the Scots.'

Speaking at a press conference at their hotel. Adshead said, 'I haven't picked them because they are Scots and because they might want to prove themselves against their own country. They have been chosen because they are the best players for the job. Sam Malcolmson is good in the air – the best we have – and he will be there to handle [Joe] Jordan. I'm here to learn things and I've learned something from Jock Stein already. He isn't naming any substitutes until the day of the game because he wants to keep an eye on all the players. I've thought about it and I'm doing the same.'

Adshead was about to learn more from Stein when the Scottish team was announced a few hours later, and Jordan was omitted. 'If they thought Joe would play it may be because of something they heard while I was in New Zealand seeing them playing recently,' Stein said. Sam Malcolmson recalled for me the news of the team, 'Jock Stein was talking about playing Joe Jordan. Of course, Jordan's a big guy and I was the strongest, the biggest, the oldest so when they thought Joe Jordan would be playing I was a shoo-in and, of course, Jordan didn't play so I had to mark Kenny Dalglish.' Sam was just happy to be in the team at all though, 'To be honest, when that draw came out I was fourth choice at centre-back. When the League of Ireland and Watford came over I trained and I worked my bollocks off.'

The Scotland team was: Alan Rough, Danny McGrain (captain), Frank Gray, Alan Hansen, Allan Evans, Graeme Souness, Gordon Strachan, John Wark, Kenny Dalglish, Alan Brazil, John Robertson. The outfield players were the same as originally selected for the first game against Torralta before Brazil picked up his knock and was replaced. Stein was confident he had chosen enough proven goalscorers while not leaving the side open to being run through at the back. 'This will not be a team for the whole of the World Cup competition,' he said. 'It has been picked solely for the first game and we believe we can beat New Zealand if we apply ourselves properly. It would be nice to score a few goals – but the most important thing of all is to win.'

Stein said he was not worried about the opposition. 'I'm worrying about ourselves. We can be our biggest enemies. The players know this. However, don't think there is any apprehension in the camp because of what might have happened in the past. This team doesn't have an apprehensive look about it, does it? There are players who are in there to get goals against New Zealand and I think they will do that. Alan Brazil is the sort of player the New Zealanders will not have faced before. They expected Joe Jordan, but, of course, Joe isn't in the team. I didn't pick this team just to confuse them; Brazil is in the line-up because at the moment he looks the best man for the job. Gordon Strachan is in because I think he can be a revelation here. If he gets off to a good start then the people will take to him.'

David Begg would go on to become one of Scottish football's best-loved voices behind a microphone, but Spain '82 was his first World Cup and it was one where he would learn a few lessons. 'I shouldn't have been there,' he told me. 'In those days BBC Scotland didn't have their own place at the table if you like, so they had to share facilities with Radio Two, and Radio Two somehow or other had decided that David Francey, who should have been there, that his voice was unacceptable. That was just awful. I mean, I was just a beginner and David was a legend. Still is a legend. He should have been the man to have been there, but anyway, they made that decision and I was given the gig. I'd hardly done a handful of games, at international level certainly. I was making progress but really I felt at the time, gosh this is too much of a privilege. Really David Francey should be here.'

Ahead of the match, one of Begg's tasks was to find out the team and file a report for broadcast. 'Jock Stein was a wily old fox and he didn't really know me. He was under a lot of pressure from various football writers of that era and they wanted the team. The radio guys saw him separately from the writers; there was no question of just an all in press conference in those days, there was definitely a pecking order and it was kind of adhered to by a very complicit SFA, and John Blair, who was their press officer at that time. I said to Jock at 12 o'clock before I went back to watch the opening game on TV at the hotel, "When will we get the team for the first game?" And he said, "The players will be available tomorrow at 12.30." Now, he wasn't telling me a lie. But he wasn't telling me the truth either. And the BBC had weighed in very heavily to get into the co-operation of Stein.

'Peter Lorenzo was the kind of head honcho of the BBC's coverage of the World Cup. So I was back at the hotel and the phone eventually goes, "Where's your piece on the team?" I said, "Well, the team won't be out until tomorrow." "No, we've already got a piece filed by PA." Gordon Simpson was the PA guy and he was again kind of kept to the sidelines by the writers because he would be stealing their thunder as he had the pieces in before they had. So, it was quite a complicated situation. Then the following day I said to Stein, "Don't you ever do that to me again. I'm a young guy, trying to make my way in this business; I may not be well known to you but that was unfair." I think that Alex Cameron of the *Daily Record* had lent on Jock and demanded that he give him the team the day before. I don't think he necessarily wanted to do that, but I think Alex and he had previous. So, the writers had been given the team, Gordon Simpson had filed the piece on the team and I was left looking like an idiot. I then had to get hold of Gordon somehow or other and get the team. Then file a piece. That was me not off to a very good start. Made to look a complete idiot.'

Having landed a place in the starting 11, Alan Brazil was out to make sure people knew he was worthy of the role. 'When you go through a season in the English First Division you come up against hard men and dirty players and there's no problem; I can handle it,' Brazil said. 'I'll be playing the same game as I play with Ipswich. I'm very conscious of the fact that I haven't scored for Scotland yet and this is my eighth international but I don't worry about it. In club football, you can get away with a few misses, but at this level, you have to score to succeed. In my first few international matches, I was a bit nervous but now I'm beginning to enjoy it. If I can get my first goal for Scotland in my first game in the World Cup finals and on my birthday I suppose it will be a bit like something out of a fairy tale.' Dalglish was Brazil's idol growing up as a Celtic supporter. He said to the Ipswich Town match programme in 1979, 'Kenny is the player I most admire. I doubt if there's a more lethal finisher in the country and he's also terrific at holding the game up and laying the ball off.'

Brought up not far from Ibrox Stadium, Dalglish followed Rangers as a boy. He had trials at West Ham United and Liverpool when he was a teenager but it would be Celtic who would sign him in May 1967. A Scottish schoolboy international, he was farmed out to Cumbernauld United for the 1967/68 season. When he returned to Parkhead he signed professional terms. He made his debut in the first team in September of 1968 but went back to the reserves where his impressive performances led to him being selected for a May 1971 testimonial for Kilmarnock's Frank Beattie. Kenny scored six in a 7-2 win and never looked back after that day. 'He made an instant impact on every senior player,' team-mate Billy McNeill said in 1984. 'In the football sense, Kenny has never been a boy. He has an uncanny instinct for the game. He is a playmaker and a player maker.'

In November 1971, Dalglish made his Scotland debut at Pittodrie in a 1-0 win over Bulgaria. With Celtic, he won four Scottish First Division titles, four Scottish Cups and one League Cup before moving to Liverpool in August 1977 for £440,000. He played in every league game for his first three seasons at Anfield, scoring 57 goals along the way. He had played all 42 league matches in 1981/82, scoring 13 times. Liverpool's league title was Dalglish's third. He had also lifted the European Cup on two occasions. His club manager Bob Paisley once said of him, 'He always gives his utmost to the team, he always wants to contribute, and yet he has remained so modest about his ability I have often been tempted to remind him of his own individual skill.'

Gordon Strachan was delighted to be in the starting 11. He told the *Daily Record*, 'I have had a good upbringing playing in the Premier League. You have to remember that they will be playing in front of a worldwide audience of millions and they won't get away with anything really rough. The referee won't allow that to happen.' Asked if he had worries over his own temperament, Strachan said, 'Maybe a year ago I would have worried. But not now. I ran out of money paying Fergie fines at Aberdeen. This season I think I have been able to control myself well.'

The temperature the game would be played in was one thing on Strachan's mind, 'I am feeling good. I have stayed out of the sun – apart from training – because it can weaken you. My one worry is the heat. Graeme Souness can slow things down a bit and push the ball around, but I am a player who has to be buzzing and you wonder how long you can do that when it's as hot as it is here.' Stein said he had never seen Strachan as fit as he was in Portugal, 'He is in great shape. I think he and Graeme Souness could be our outstanding players.'

Souness would be renewing a relationship with an old acquaintance – Kiwi sweeper Bobby Almond, who had played alongside him for Tottenham Hotspur's youth team in the 1969/70 season. 'I have vivid memories of the marathon that was the FA Youth Cup Final with Coventry,' Almond told superhotspur.com. 'We had cleaned up all before us in all other competitions but this was the big one. Two specific memories come to mind though. One was Johnny Oliver scoring the equalising goal in the 2-2 draw at Highfield Road to get us back to our home ground for what was to be the final game. Two was Graeme Souness scoring the only goal at White Hart Lane to win the cup. Magic.'

'He was a very good player,' Souness said of Almond to Allan Herron in the *Sunday Mail*. 'He knows he should be playing in the English First Division and there will be four or five other players in the side with the same attitude.' It was fair to say that Souness was not looking forward to the Scots' opening match. He explained, 'I wish to hell the game was over. Everyone seems to be telling us that we have got to knock in a bundle of goals in this match. That's all very well but first of all, we've got to beat them. You can't go out and throw yourself at this team with seven forwards and leave yourself open. That could be suicidal. This will be their World Cup Final. They'll be desperate to prove to everyone that they can beat the best in Britain.

'There are no guarantees in football. The big boys do fall to the wee boys occasionally. Players cannot go out and play for themselves at this level. We'll only succeed if we play for each other. It is the only system that brings success. Not one of us in the pool of 22 have come out here to sit on our backsides. Those who are left out of any game are going to be angry men. This is the greatest platform that football can offer any player and we all want to be a part of it. We have a chance that many of the great players never had. Just to play in the World Cup finals is special.'

The central defensive partnership was Hansen and Evans, with Willie Miller missing out. 'There is nothing between them,' Stein said of Evans and Miller. 'They are probably equal in our penalty area, but Allan is more dangerous in the opponents' box, and against a team like New Zealand that gives him the edge over Miller.'

Not naming his substitutes until late on was not gamesmanship by Stein. He had sound reasoning. He felt that it kept everyone on their toes, and gave those not named in the 11 something to play for, 'The fact that you leave naming the other five to the last minute keeps them all on edge and everybody hopes they might be one of the five.' It was also to keep morale up in the camp and to ensure that players sharing a room didn't have different needs, with one player selected wanting to nap before the game and the other, knowing he had no chance of playing, feeling he didn't have to. With every man in the squad still thinking they could play a part, everyone would be getting the same rest. Of the players omitted from the 11, Davie Provan was one who was most unhappy. 'Before we left Scotland Jock took me aside and told me that he would play me in the first game,' he said to journalist Archie Macpherson. 'He was also very frank in telling me that he wouldn't pick me for the other two matches.' Provan was expecting to be part of a Scotland team that made use of his pace and skill by attacking down the wings. 'To say I was angry is an understatement. When I arrived in Rosaleda that night to watch the game, I had made up my mind that I would go back to Sotogrande, pack my bags and get a flight home right away. I knew I wouldn't be playing in the other games, what was the point of hanging about? However, I slept on it and reluctantly decided to stay.'

The man in the middle was an American: David Socha from Ludlow, Massachusetts. He would be the first American to referee at a World Cup finals. A former player, he had been on the books of Portsmouth in the mid-1950s, although there's no record of him making a first-team appearance for them. He also played in America's semi-professional leagues. 'When I stopped playing I was out of the game for seven years. I only returned when a friend persuaded me to become a referee,' Socha said. He had been on the FIFA list for four years, handling 18 internationals, mostly in South America. He continued, 'My last international was in front of 100,000 in Mexico City when Honduras forced a draw to put Mexico out of the World Cup. If I can handle that I can handle anything.' The 43-year-old came third in the FIFA referees' Cooper Test, behind Scotland's Bob Valentine. He was rated the number one referee in the NASL.

Stein spoke to Radio Clyde ahead of the game, 'We are not going to have a cavalry charge at the New Zealanders by any way. We'll want to settle down. We are hoping, though, that Strachan and Robertson will play their normal game of attacking people, taking people out of the game, pulling another man out of defence, getting in enough crosses for Brazil and Dalglish with John Wark following in.' Graham Taylor's Watford had taken on the Kiwis three times as part of their build-up. He said, 'Their fitness is not in question and they will give Scotland a rough ride for 20 minutes. Afterwards, the Scots should go on to win comfortably.'

* * *

Before Scotland took on New Zealand though, there was Group Six's opening match. 'I will be going to Seville to watch Brazil play Russia,' said Stein, 'and I want a Brazilian win. Then, if we can do our job, we will go into the last section game with the Russians knowing that we are 90 minutes away from the second phase. That will be the game which counts – and we won't be frightened by it.' The team trained on the adapted polo park in Sotogrande in the morning before settling down in front of the television to watch Italy's goalless draw with Poland and then the game from Seville. Stein and Jim McLean set off in a chauffeur-driven limousine.

In the match which kicked off at 9pm in a temperature of 90°F, Russia took the lead on 34 minutes. Dynamo Kyiv's Andriy Bal hit a speculative shot from around 30 yards which squirmed under the body of Waldir Peres in the Brazilian goal. At half-time the Scottish players were joined by Jimmy Hill who chatted with them for the BBC's live coverage of the match. Alan Rough expressed sympathy for his Brazilian counterpart, 'I think he expected the ball to bounce up a lot higher than what it did.' Of the players Hill asked for opinions, Rough, Hansen, Souness, Brazil and McGrain all thought Brazil would win through in the end, but McGrain was confident the USSR would hang on to their lead. The Soviets remained in front until the 78th minute when Sócrates smashed the ball in off the post from 35 yards to equalise. With 89 minutes on the clock, Éder stepped up and hit a bending drive that flew past Rinat Dasayev to win the game.

The result was the one Stein had wanted, although he could have done with Brazil scoring a few more goals. 'So far it has all gone the way we wanted it to and other teams have done their part for us,' he said on his return to base. 'But it is no use relying on others if we cannot go out and do the business ourselves. A win for us would put all the more pressure on Russia, particularly if we can come out of the New Zealand game better than they can. It would even give us the opportunity to exclude the Brazilian match, as we would need only a draw from our final game against Russia to qualify.' Stein was spot on in his thinking, but it was down to the players to accomplish the task on the pitch.

While the game was in progress, a ceasefire was agreed upon in the Falklands. 'The biggest round of applause came here when that news of the possible ceasefire came through,' Jimmy Hill said of the Scotland players who heard the news while watching the game. Hostilities officially ceased on 20 June. The war cost the lives of 655 Argentine and 255 British servicemen.

'I'd gone up to see the Brazilians play the USSR,' David Begg told me. 'Stein had seen me there and he said, "Oh, you're doing your homework." I said, "Yeah you'd expect me to do that." I sat beside Eusébio, which was amazing. He didn't speak any English, and I had no Portuguese. I was kind of a starstruck youngster; I'd seen this hero of the '66 World Cup and I'd got something signed by him, which was good. It gave me great preparation to see the two teams that Scotland were going to play and it helped me identify who was in the teams. But then I also got a good break with the New Zealand manager John Adshead. I phoned John and said, "Can I come to your training?" He said, "Yeah, you can." So, we went to see them train. Then he said, "Come on to my hotel and I'll tell you exactly how we're going to play. On the basis that it doesn't go any further." I said, "Yeah. It won't go any further." And he told me exactly how they would play. It didn't do them much good as they were a bit overcome early on against Scotland but I'd caught a real break there. I'd seen New Zealand very, very briefly and he told me who would play where. So I wasn't guessing at the formation. I was maybe more guessing at the Scotland formation.'

The New Zealand game was screened live on ITV in Britain with BBC One showing *Killer Fish*, a 1979 film starring Lee Majors and Karen Black battling piranhas. Before kick-off, Adshead highlighted what he saw were the dangers his team would face, 'In John Wark, Graeme Souness and Kenny Dalglish, Scotland have three world-class players and I only wish I had men of their ability at my disposal. Wark, in particular, must be every coach's dream player. He is the man who causes us most problems. He makes runs into the penalty box my players don't really know about. But we intend going home with respect on our side and right now that means scoring against Scotland tonight. You know there are bulls and bullfighters in Spain and we are not here to be the bull. Anyway, a few bullfighters go down as well.'

'New Zealand don't really know what to expect of us as they have only watched us on TV, and I would imagine they would sit back a bit,' said Stein. 'All I want is for my players to go out and play their natural club game. That should be sufficient.'

Sam Malcolmson explained for me what the Kiwi thoughts were going into the match. 'We knew there was a difference in class,' Sam begins, 'Kenny Dalglish, Graeme Souness, all these players. The plan, first of all, was to go out and enjoy it, then play our own game. Because we'd played a lot of warm-up games. We'd played well against Watford, and we'd believed we could keep it within the realms of not being embarrassed. That was the thing, to go out and play our normal game and not be embarrassed.'

For Wynton Rufer the game was a massive occasion, 'We're the total underdogs. For us it was just a dream come true to be in that group. We had nothing to lose. We're travelling in this amazing bus and staying in this amazing hotel and there's all this big fuss. We had all the Kiwi supporters who also came. There's probably only a few hundred but it seemed like thousands to us. I had my family over there. It was all happening, it was just brilliant.' Playing against Scotland was a special thrill for a teenager brought up on a diet of British football, 'I knew all about British football because of the influence of our team, Sam Malcolmson he was Scottish, Allan Boath was Scottish. But I was a football fanatic.'

Wynton became hooked watching the 1970 World Cup and in particular the triumphant Brazilian team. He said, 'So 1974 Scotland are in the same group as Brazil and I wanted Brazil to smash Scotland, so I was gutted that Scotland drew 0-0, so that's how the connection was there with Scotland because of my beloved Brazil. By 1978 we're watching *The Big Match* every Sunday in New Zealand; Brian Moore was the commentator and you've got Graeme Souness and Kenny Dalglish, John Wark and Joe Jordan – they're all my childhood heroes.' Wynton goes through Scotland's results from the 1978 World Cup for me, listing the scorers with the enthusiasm of the most fervent Scottish supporter, 'I was just a football encyclopaedia. That Netherlands game was amazing. So all that was a big influence on me.' Wynton rhymes off almost the entire 1982 Scotland squad, remarking how brilliant he found it to be on the same field as players he had admired watching for years. 'These were household names for me personally. You remember the *Shoot!* magazine? I had pictures on my wall from the *Shoot!* magazine of all those players I've mentioned. They were all my heroes. Getting to play as a 19-year-old at the World Cup was just a dream come true. Scotland, Brazil, Russia, and Scotland had that phenomenal team.'

They weren't the only household names in town that night, as Bobby Jamieson remembers, 'Prior to the match I was people watching, and saw a famous face being interviewed by TV. I went over to shake his hand and to say hello. It was Eusébio. This was in the days before iPhones and selfies so I have nothing to show for meeting one of the most famous footballers ever.'

* * *

Although not as hot as the previous night, the temperature in Malaga, as the game kicked off at 9pm local time, was in the 80s. It didn't help that the Scottish players were out on the pitch for just over ten minutes before the match actually kicked off. Leaflets dropped from the air before the game were still lying all over the grass. Around 15,000 Scots were in attendance, with the ground covered in flags and banners. 'I had never been so inspired by a stadium full of fans,' Brazil wrote in his book. 'Most of them were bare-chested, but they had smuggled bagpipes and drums into the ground and the atmosphere was intoxicating.'

'That was the first time I'd ever heard that song "Here We Go",' says Iain McAuley. Chic Brogan recalls similarly, 'I always say it was us that started that chant "Here We Go", because I'd never heard it before at any game ever, not at Parkhead or Hampden or any Scotland game. I mind we were standing there and the teams were starting to come out. "Oh, here we go", "Right, here we go, here we go …" and it just built up. It always amazed me how chants just start up. And it went all the way round within seconds. I mean nobody believes you, but I'm pretty sure that's where that started from.'

In his book *In Sunshine or in Shadow*, Danny McGrain recalled, 'When they came out on the park against us, the Kiwis, I have to say, looked to me for all the world like a pub team.'

It's perhaps worth noting that the Scotland starting line-up contained six European Cup winners – Hansen, Souness and Dalglish with Liverpool; Gray and Robertson with Nottingham Forest; and Evans the latest winner with Aston Villa. No other starting line-up in the 1982 World Cup featured more winners of Europe's premier trophy; England managing only four against Kuwait, starting with Peter Shilton and Trevor Francis, who had winners' medals with Nottingham Forest, and Liverpool duo Phil Neal and

Phil Thompson. Co-commentating for ITV, Denis Law emphasised the need to get goals in this opening fixture, citing the Zaire game he played in eight years previously, where Scotland's 2-0 win was ultimately not enough, contributing to their exit on goal difference.

'Scotland the Brave' played, but despite the talk previously about how this change of anthem might instil some national pride into the players and fans, it wasn't having the desired effect. 'Either on the stadium sound system or the actual recording, the throbbing, discordant screeches made you want to hide under a seat,' Archie Macpherson wrote. Scotland started well, but the first shot on goal came from the Kiwis when Cresswell fired past the post after four minutes. Strachan burst through the defence a moment later but his shot was blocked by Malcolmson. 'First touch, you could tell these guys were different class,' Malcolmson said. 'John Robertson, he looked like he wasn't interested, then he got the ball and he was magic.'

Scotland moved forward frequently in the early stages with Strachan, Brazil, Dalglish and Robertson all passing and moving to test the New Zealand defence. Strachan's stealth and skill were obvious as he picked the ball up on the halfway line then weaved and bobbed his way into the box. He beat three men, one of them twice, before sliding the ball into Dalglish who took a touch, created space, and put a right-foot shot across Van Hattum to make it 1-0 to Scotland after 18 minutes. Malcolmson was the defender who slid in with a vain challenge. 'In Kenny's book he's got me in the middle pages. There's him scoring the first goal and there's me on my bum,' he said.

'I got it badly wrong,' David Begg says of Scotland's opening strike of the tournament. 'Kenny Dalglish scored the first goal, and I always remember this, I went over the top like a Brazilian commentator, because I thought this was how you did it. I'd no idea. You just did it your normal way. Behave sensibly.'

Scotland's second goal came on the half-hour mark with Strachan again at the heart of the move. He played the ball into Brazil, who turned, then hit a half volley which Van Hattum parried, and John Wark was on hand to stick in the rebound. Two minutes later it was 3-0. Strachan crossed as Wark made one of those runs Adshead said his players wouldn't see coming. Wark sneaked into the six-yard box and from his back-post position headed into the net for his fifth goal for his country. By Wark's own admission, the game was his best in a Scotland shirt, although he kicked himself for missing a good chance to complete his hat-trick late on. Scotland were flying and it now seemed just a matter of how many they could score, with defenders flooding forward in support of the attack. Danny McGrain charged down the flank, knocking the ball past Almond and running past him to collect it. 'I had now played 12 times for Scotland,' Strachan wrote in his 1984 autobiography, 'and I felt myself getting right into this game. I knew I was on song that night. We looked unstoppable.'

As the teams trooped off to the dressing rooms for the interval, it was certainly the Scots who were the happier. 'Unsurprisingly, Stein was purring with pleasure throughout his half-time talk,' Alan Rough wrote in *The Rough and the Smooth*. 'On the surface, the hard work had been achieved, and now all that remained, in his estimation, was for us to capitalise on our superiority by completing a 5-0 or 6-0 victory, which would ensure that goal difference didn't become a factor.'

New Zealand had not given Scotland anything to worry about during the first 45 minutes. The Scots had looked stronger, faster and more tactically astute. At this point, there was no reason not to think Scotland would bury the fears of the past and begin their campaign with a comfortable win that provided a healthy goals for column balance. After Stein's talk, McGrain remembers John Robertson sneaking into the toilet to smoke a cigarette. Stein turned to Alan Brazil. 'Are you sure you're all right, son?' he asked his striker. Brazil nodded, but he wasn't. 'I was seeing two of him,' Brazil said to Hugh Keevins in 2006. 'I couldn't answer him back because my tongue was so dry it had stuck to my palate.' He had become dehydrated in the heat and was suffering from double vision. 'There was no way I was being taken off in this game,' he wrote in his autobiography *There's An Awful Lot of Bubbly in Brazil*. 'There was a hatful more goals in this game and I was determined to be among the scorers.' To alleviate his dryness, Brazil poured water down his throat and all over his head. He felt his shorts were slipping from his waist. He would realise later that during the match he had lost ten pounds in weight.

Steve Sumner recalled the mood in the Kiwi dressing room for the *Lancashire Post* in 2008, 'At the break, the coach said, "You deserve the chance to be at the World Cup finals, don't let yourselves down."' Sam Malcolmson told me, 'Adshead said at half-time we had to get the midfielders – we were getting destroyed that night by Gordon Strachan – to stop the delivery of the ball to Gordon Strachan. If he's not got the ball he can't do anything. Keep marking tightly and push forward ourselves. Because we'd had a couple of attacks out wide.' Adshead also employed a little psychology. Malcolmson said, 'He would say things like, "Danny McGrain's having a bad game, let's get on him." Danny McGrain's not having a bad game but that would get you thinking, "Oh, here I wonder if we can play in there." That's who he was, you know.'

'I just told them the second half was going to be all about legs,' Adshead said later.

Out on the terracing, there were other matters at hand. 'I went down to get a Coke,' Chic Brogan recalled, 'and the guy selling the Coke goes, "You want rum?" Aye. He brings out a bottle of Bacardi and tops it up. I'm trying to carry half a dozen of them back up. I says, "It's Bacardi and Coke." "You're kidding." Suddenly word got about and everybody started piling down. That wee guy suddenly made a fortune, nobody was caring what the price was.'

New Zealand were much more attacking in the second half, but the first shot in the half came from Scotland when Alan Brazil wasted a great chance by putting the ball over the bar from six yards. His deteriorating physical condition had manifested itself in his poor finishing. 'The problem was that he didn't turn his body square to the goal,' Davie Provan said. 'He was always side on to it, which made it difficult to keep the shot down. If he had scored then we wouldn't have had that scare.' Next, Frank Gray fired a shot across goal which was turned back to the goalkeeper by his defender. Brazil came off for Steve Archibald on 53 minutes. By this time the heat had made the Ipswich striker practically delusional, as he recalled, 'I didn't even understand the instruction to come off. One of the coaches had to run on to the pitch and guide me to the dugout. I got such a fantastic ovation from the fans that I thought we had scored again. We hadn't.'

Nine minutes into the half, McGrain made an uncharacteristic mistake. Rufer, out on the right, put a simple cross in front of the Celtic captain who didn't get much on his back pass as Rough remained rooted to his six-yard line. Steve Sumner nipped in to bundle home his ninth World Cup goal. 'I remember Wynton Rufer beat Frankie Gray on their left-hand flank,' Sumner said to fifamuseum.com in 2016. 'When he got down there it was my role to get forward and try to put pressure on. Wynton bent the ball in behind their back line and that's what I did, just put pressure on and see if there's a mistake. I seemed to be chasing a lost cause because McGrain had eight yards on me. But when he played the ball back to Alan Rough, McGrain dropped his pass short. Before Rough could get to it, I was in. Rough had committed himself but I got there first and managed to get a toe at it, poked it underneath him and as I'm stumbling over the top of him I manage to stick it away. In that split-second, I remember just trying to keep it down and tuck it under him. I couldn't miss that from there. It gave us a lift, knowing we could score. '

The Scotland fans responded to the setback with a chorus of 'We'll Support You Evermore'.

Rufer had to leave the field for several minutes with a foot injury, but it didn't slow the Kiwis' momentum, and on 64 minutes they had another goal back. Dalglish lost the ball up front through poor control before Hill sent a pass forward fully 50 yards. Evans didn't pick up his man as he waved frantically for offside. But Gray was playing Steve Wooddin on and he charged forward on his own to fire past Rough from the edge of the box.

Wooddin was originally from Birkenhead. He began his career at local club Tranmere Rovers where he was managed by a Scottish international in Ron Yeats. 'When he was with us he could have gone right to the top,' Yeats told the *Liverpool Echo*. 'He had a wonderful left foot and natural ability, but he wasn't too keen on the training. If there was a way to skive then Steve would find it. I thought that if I put him in the team he would respond, but he only had a couple of first-team games.'

'I gave away the first goal through a combination of weariness and the ball sticking to the studs on the sole of my boot,' McGrain wrote, 'and when New Zealand scored again the possibility of the ultimate humiliation did cross my mind.'

'You would think at times that Scotland like to see how many silly goals they can give away while still winning the game,' Strachan wrote.

'When the second goal went in,' Sam Malcolmson recalled, 'which I thought was a mistake by Alan Rough, I was standing next to Kenny Dalglish and I said, "Oh, don't say it's happening again for Scotland. That was the keeper's fault," and he said, "I cannae say anything bad about my team-mates, son."'

Archibald was fouled a minute later on the corner of the box but Souness saw his shot from the free kick tipped around the corner by Van Hattum. 'When Steve Wooddin got our second, suddenly it felt like we had the edge over Scotland,' Sumner recalled. 'The momentum of the game shifted because they started having a go at each other as if what had happened wasn't part of the script. Then John Robertson fired in a ferocious free kick, spinning into the top corner, and the Scots fans went mad.'

A handball just outside the penalty box gave Scotland a free kick on 73 minutes. Gordon Strachan recalled, 'During training we were working out some set pieces when Jim McLean said, "You boys at Aberdeen have some good ideas for free kicks. What about trying them out for Scotland?" So we told him the one where two players seem to argue in front of the ball then suddenly they separate and a third player chips it over the defensive wall towards the corner of the net. We practised that one and were delighted that the opportunity arose when we were struggling to regain command of a game which had slipped away from us.'

As Gray, Souness and Robertson crowded around the ball, Gray and Souness appeared to bump into each other. As everyone in the ground sniggered at the schoolboy error and waited for the players to reset, Robertson calmly lifted the ball into the back of the net. He turned arms aloft to acknowledge the perfect execution of the training-ground routine. Then, on 79 minutes, Archibald headed in Strachan's corner to make the scoreline 5-2. Stein had told Strachan not to spare himself as he would be replaced once the heat took its toll. With seven minutes remaining Strachan came off to rousing applause, Stein rising from his seat in the dugout to acclaim him. David Narey came on and cracked a shot at goal with his first touch, and Frank Gray had the final attempt late on.

In the commentary booth, David Begg had survived his first World Cup game. He said, 'I was sharing commentary with George Hamilton. George was an experienced broadcaster, very talented. At the end of it I still had my cans on, this was a thing that Arthur Montford had said to me, "Never talk about anybody when you're doing any broadcast, even if you think the microphone's dead, because they may be listening and they may be recording and it may be played back to them and you could find yourself in trouble." So when Peter Lorenzo came on to [talk to] George Hamilton, he said, "Thank goodness, George, you were there with that mad Scotsman," 'cos I'd gone over the top with the Dalglish goal, way over the top. I think the other goals were OK. I did Scotland's first goal and New Zealand's two goals, the other goals were George Hamilton because he was broadcasting by that point. So I then said to Lorenzo, "Peter, if you've something to say, say it to me, I'm here to learn as well." "Oh, I didn't know you were there." I said, "Well, I am here." Then when it got to the next game I was much more measured.'

'After the New Zealand game I went out to phone home,' said Chic Brogan, 'and there were three American couples standing outside the phone box. They obviously know you're a Scotland fan, you've got a Scotland top on and your kilt. "Oh, you did well today." I'm going, "Oh, you're joking! They scored two goals, the goal difference will be …" They're looking at me as if I'm speaking Martian. This animated Scotsman going, "Aaah! They two goals will put us out."'

* * *

Scotland had flown, had their wings clipped, then rose again, or as Ian Archer would put it, 'A night of high drama and low farce.' The win was their biggest at a World Cup finals and remains so to this day. The last time Scotland had scored more than four goals in an international had been on 8 September 1976 when Finland were beaten 6-0 at Hampden Park in a friendly. Dalglish was also on the scoresheet that night, along with Don Masson, Bruce Rioch, Eddie Gray and two from Andy Gray.

The 5-2 win was good, but the feeling was it may not have been enough. New Zealand had been there for the taking and the goal difference could and should have been much greater. 'There was little celebration at the whistle,' Rough wrote, 'and the glowering displeasure from Stein was indicative of our general disappointment. It might have been different if we had struggled to break the deadlock, or wilted in the heat. Instead, bolstered by Strachan, who ran himself into the ground for 84 minutes ... we had established a magnificent position for success and then done our best to undermine with sloppy mistakes. That was what rankled with Stein, and he let us know it.' Stein's team talks had all centred on the fact that this was the game where they could establish a goal difference that would put them in the driving seat for the final match. That the team had self-sabotaged that aim was what really incensed Stein.

'We lost goals because of self-inflicted wounds,' the manager said in his post-match press conference. 'They were terrible goals to give away at this level. We are the greatest nation in the world for punishing ourselves at every turn. We began well and did everything right in the first half. I think there will be changes for the next two games against Brazil and Russia. We cannot play like that against them. If we had played with someone at sweeper, which we tried before, then we would not have lost these goals. Almost every other team in this tournament plays with a sweeper. But we did attack from the start, we did win, and the players will be the better for that. But it could have been better. In the second half, we lost our way a wee bit but we came back well in the second part of the half. All in all, being the first game you'd be reasonably satisfied but the team was picked for one game and there will be changes for the next. They didn't come back so much as we let them come back with defensive errors we should have sorted out ourselves.'

'The crowd was fantastic, absolutely brilliant and that helped us too,' Sam Malcolmson recalled. 'It was a colossal moment for us. And, of course, for me, when they played the national anthems I was able to sing both of them. My late dad, when I got substituted in the 78th minute he was delighted because then he could support Scotland. He didn't want New Zealand to get beat by much but he's a Scottish nationalist. My mum said he was always very reserved because he had his son playing against Scotland so he was supporting me. Mum said after I was substituted he was delighted and he started cheering and he started shouting. I was the only player in the World Cup whose dad wanted him substituted.'

'Through a lack of concentration, the clearly superior Scots missed a suitable opportunity for them to reach the second group position,' read FIFA's official match report. 'The pleasant New Zealand team were appreciated for their open, honest attitude.'

'For ten minutes I thought we did reasonably well,' manager Adshead said. 'We had Scotland worried. It's a credit to us that our players didn't let their heads go down, even when they were three behind at half-time. I don't feel we will be pressured as much as that by Russia or Brazil. We were under enormous pressure out there.' Adshead was full of praise for Wark, 'John isn't a showy lad, but by God, can he play. The man is world-class and that's not a phrase I use lightly.'

Wark felt his performance was down to being asked to play the same way he did at his club. 'In the past, I've had a different kind of role,' he said, 'but before Tuesday's game I was given instructions to make my runs, get into scoring position, and it worked.'

Born in Glasgow in 1957, Wark grew up a Rangers fan, never missing a home game in the 1971/72 season as the Ibrox club won the European Cup Winners' Cup. Wark started his playing career with Drumchapel Amateurs. He was spotted by Ipswich scout George Findlay and signed straight from Victoria Drive Secondary School. 'I came down to Ipswich when I was 15 not even knowing where Ipswich was,' he recalled. Wark made his debut for Ipswich in an FA Cup quarter-final third replay against Leeds United at Elland Road. 'I was a bag of nerves, but we won and it was a great experience.' He established himself in the first team in the 1976/77 season, playing 33 times in the league and scoring ten goals. In the summer he joined the Scotland under-21s to play in the Toulon Tournament, scoring twice in the fifth and sixth-place play-off match as Scotland lost to Italy on penalties. In 1978 he was part of the Ipswich team that shocked Arsenal in the FA Cup Final with a 1-0 win.

Wark was first called into the Scotland squad under Ally MacLeod, but had to pull out of the squad for the 1977 game against East Germany through injury. His second chance of a cap was scuppered when the February 1979 European Championship match with Belgium at Hampden fell victim to the freezing weather. Wark was handed his first Scotland cap in the spring of 1979 in the Home International Championship as Scotland travelled to Cardiff to take on Wales. It wasn't one of the best days to be a Scotland fan as John Toshack scored a perfect hat-trick and Wales won 3-0.

Alan Brazil, John Robertson, Sam Malcolmson and Adrian Elrick were the players chosen at random for drug samples. 'All I had to do was urinate into a glass bottle,'

Brazil wrote. 'I couldn't.' Brazil watched his team-mates get showered, dressed and climb on to the team bus. Still, he couldn't pass water. 'We all had trouble because all of us had felt the heat out there,' Elrick said. 'But after an hour or so, or maybe just a little more, we were OK and Alan was left on his own.' After being substituted, Brazil had been drinking water by the pint, but he still couldn't produce. 'Alan even asked the doctor if he could give him a blood sample but that was not acceptable,' Elrick said. 'They tried everything. They had water running, had him standing on packs of ice, but nothing worked. We weren't allowed to take a drink or even a shower until the test was done. I felt sorry for Alan. Here he was, still in the ground, five hours after the game.'

Brazil was allowed to leave, just after three o'clock in the morning, and return the next day at lunchtime. At that point he provided a sample, which proved negative. However, the authorities declared the test invalid. A spokesman explained, 'The Scottish player, Alan Brazil, should have been kept at the stadium until the sample was given. Or a FIFA official should have remained with him if he went back to the hotel. He should not have been allowed to rejoin the team on his own. These are the rules of the tournament. A mistake was made and the people in Madrid are angry. No blame at all attaches itself in any way to Scotland or to the player. This is the mistake of the organisers.' The medical team in Malaga would carry the can for the error. 'Alan had run himself out for us in the heat and I suppose that explains what happened,' Stein said. 'He seems fine for now. But it was an ordeal for him.' The rules stated that players chosen to give a sample should be kept at the ground for up to 16 hours. 'It was a complete misunderstanding,' Stein said, eager to avoid any suggestions of impropriety given the situation with Willie Johnstone in 1978. 'Purely an organisational mix-up outwith our control.'

Of the match, Brazilian manager Telê Santana said, 'The Scots were impressive. It was a hard game for them to begin with but they scored goals.' Commentating for Brazilian television, Portugal legend Eusébio remarked, 'The Scottish team can beat Russia. Maybe they lost bad goals – but they scored five and they made many more chances. I liked them.' The one Scots player who stood out for the Black Pearl was Gordon Strachan. Eusébio said, 'He is one of the finest players I have seen in years and I have never before been so impressed with anyone playing their first game in the World Cup finals. I have heard Strachan's name before, but I did not know he was that good. He is the best player in the Scottish team. I would say that he is as good as the Brazilian players – and better than some of them.' The Spanish fans had picked the red-haired Strachan out too, christening him Naranjito after the little orange who was the World Cup mascot.

John Adshead spoke to *FourFourTwo* in 2014. 'Ian St John said he thought it was a pity that FIFA had allowed such small teams to play at the World Cup and predicted New Zealand could lose some matches by a cricket score,' he said. 'We scored two goals early in the second half and then we hit the post. Suddenly the Scots were rattled and players like Souness and Strachan were arguing amongst themselves. It was great to watch from the sidelines. We gave the Scots a good game. People said the only way we would be able to compete was to kick our opponents, but we were the only team in 1982 not to get a single booking. Afterwards, Jock Stein was full of praise for the way we played and he said we had done our country proud.'

'To have Scotland in the group, that was outstanding,' Sam Malcolmson said. 'Once I'd played against Scotland I didn't care. I didn't want to play anymore. It was a dream come true as far as I'm concerned.' That World Cup had a lasting impact for the country. Malcolmson said, 'It was the start of international football in New Zealand and people taking an interest. It was great for touring clubs because we started to get teams come out. England came out. We're called The People's Team for the simple reason that people remember the '82 team. We came from nothing. It's 40 years now and the squad all keep in touch. We've had a couple of deaths Steve and Dunky Cole, but we try to get together every six months or so.'

In the *Lancashire Post*, Steve Sumner recalled, 'I played directly opposite Souness. He was a class player but in that match, I didn't think he played well. We'd come from poles apart. He was playing for probably the greatest club side in the world at that time, Liverpool, and I was a part-time footballer in New Zealand. But I came away from the Scotland match disappointed because I didn't think I'd got to grips with it. I didn't watch any of our three World Cup ties on film for eight years afterwards. I passionately wanted something more. But when I did view the film I thought I was hard on myself. It was a tough, physical game against the Scots. Souness caught me hard in the throat with an elbow, and John Robertson got me too. The Scots were hardly shrinking violets, but New Zealand were hard, tough competitors and that physical aspect never worried us one bit.'

Sumner gained 105 caps for the All Whites and is generally credited as being the player who made the greatest impact on New Zealand football. He passed away with prostate cancer aged 61 in 2017. 'He wasn't born a great player, but he wanted to be the best, he had the desire,' Sam Malcolmson said. 'He was single-minded, self-driven. He demanded from the players what he demanded from himself. Stevie was special. He stood up for the team when anything was unfair. When he played the game he was 100 per cent. He was straight to the point. He was tough. We all followed him and it broke my heart when he died. His death was so sad. He was a great leader.'

'After the New Zealand game my abiding recollection of that night was the people of Malaga coming out to the streets afterwards and cheering the Scottish bus through the streets,' Archie Macpherson wrote in *Action Replays*. 'Every village and cottage on the route from Malaga to Sotogrande had locals out waving to the Scottish players.' The Scots fans were happy enough with their team's performance. As Jim Reynolds wrote in the *Glasgow Herald*, 'The Costa del Sol was treated to Scottish celebrations of Hogmanay proportions.' The fans drank and celebrated long into the night. SFA troubleshooter John Little said, 'I cannot praise the fans enough. The police are delighted with the behaviour and I must compliment the police on their attitude.' 'The behaviour of our supporters at the match with New Zealand in Malaga was excellent,' Ernie Walker added. 'There was no trouble at all and the Spaniards are speaking very highly of them.'

In the other game played that night, Hungary defeated El Salvador 10-1, before the post-mortem began the next day into how Scotland had let a three-goal lead slip. 'Don't blame Alan Rough,' Danny McGrain said to Alex Cameron in the *Daily Record*. 'The goal was my fault. Some will blame Roughie. But the simple fact is I should have cleared the ball. A player of my experience shouldn't have been caught in that way. I could have put the ball out for a corner ... or just hit it away. Roughie came out as I ran to get the ball. I was too casual and too clever. When I tried to pass back I didn't strike the ball properly and Sumner got a shot in. Alan took the sting out of it but Sumner followed up to bang it home. I thought the second New Zealand goal was offside, but the situation shouldn't have arisen.' The manager was more critical of his goalkeeper than the captain was. 'I felt Rough should have come out and commanded the situation even if he risked hitting both players to win the ball,' Stein said. 'McGrain had to run a long way and it was the kind of game which sapped players' energy.'

'It was the old story,' Souness wrote in his first autobiography, 'sloppy defence, two gift goals and the familiar black feeling that we had put ourselves under undue pressure, when a five-goal victory, as it could so easily have been, had been there for the taking.'

'It's easy in hindsight,' Joe Jordan said in 2020, 'but I felt it at the time on the bench as well, 100 per cent. If you're being professional, you just don't give these goals away. That was a regret. I instantly felt it could come back and bite us. And that's borne from experience. I go back to Zaire in '74 and the fact we never scored enough goals. We settled, and it cost us. This was the same.'

The loss of those two goals and the team selection was something that rankled with substitute Willie Miller. 'I did not play in that game and was very angry that I was not picked,' he wrote in his 2007 book *The Don*. 'The reason I was furious was because I had played in most of the qualification and build-up matches. Indeed, Stein's decision to select Allan Evans instead of me in the opening game still riles me. I could not understand the logic of such a choice. Allan had been in the Aston Villa side that had lifted the European Cup, but he occupied a peripheral position in the Scotland setup. I had helped Scotland reach the finals and had played out of position, against my better judgement against Sweden, and also looked on when an unfit Kenny Burns took my place in a game against Israel during qualification.'

Miller was convinced that he could have prevented both goals had he been playing. His normal position, he felt, would have seen him lying deeper than either of the central defenders, where he would have been confident of making successful challenges. Evans taking his place in the team seemed to rankle with the Aberdeen captain, 'I'm assuming big Jock gave him the nod to complement his European Cup winners' medal.'

Miller's Aberdeen team-mate Alex McLeish also thought he could have made a difference on the pitch. 'I'd appeared in 13 consecutive internationals after making my breakthrough into the Scotland team,' he said to Hugh Keevins in the *Daily Record* in 2012. 'But then I got injured prior to the tournament and big Jock Stein decided to leave me and Willie Miller, my Aberdeen team-mate, out of the side to play New Zealand in our opening match. I just remember the side being read out and not hearing my name. I immediately thought to myself, "I've been bombed out," and I was still staring straight ahead into the distance until the moment the match changed with far-reaching consequences for us. I'm a great believer in partnerships. I believe Willie was the most consistent player I ever had the pleasure of calling a team-mate. I don't think he and I would have conceded the goals Scotland lost that night.'

The players would have a day off on the Wednesday, but, by the evening, preparations began for the Brazil match.

10

The Toe-poke: Brazil

*'I don't wish to be rude to David Narey, but
I think he might have caught that on the end
of his toe. I don't know, he was stretching
for it anyway. But it certainly didn't lack
for acceleration.'*

Jimmy Hill

JOCK STEIN was eager to put the focus on the positives of beating New Zealand. 'A load is off our minds,' he said. 'The first game is over and now we must meet two of the best teams in the competition. Anyway, would we not have settled before the game for a three-goal win? After Tuesday's game I said that if we played the same way against Brazil and Russia we'd be assassinated. We won't even attempt to run at them as we did New Zealand. Our approach will be more controlled. We'll be taking no chances about leaving the back uncovered. You have seen for yourself how all the top teams such as Argentina, Brazil, Russia and Italy have played in their opening games. They have all used a spare defender at the back and yet we want to play it differently from the rest of the world. We have stood a lot of criticism because we played with a man behind the defence in certain games, but all the best teams play in that manner and I don't think we should be the exception.'

'Scotland may get a goal against us, perhaps even a couple,' Brazil boss Telê Santana said. 'But a team who are determined to attack and entertain as we are must accept this.'

After the defensive display against the Kiwis, Willie Miller was optimistic that he would be in the starting line-up this time. 'The next two games are the ones that everyone would want to play in,' he told the *Record*. 'New Zealand doesn't do much to lift you. Now it's different. It would be all right if I was asked to mark Zico. I wouldn't mind. It's a challenge that you have to rise to. On their day Brazil are quite frightening. After watching them beat Russia it just confirmed in my mind that they are deserved favourites. I liked that big striker Serginho. He managed half a dozen good scoring chances. He's quick and he's good in the air. Zico was maybe marked out of the Russia game, but they have so many others. The main danger doesn't come from them getting behind you, it comes from them playing the ball around on the edge of your box. We have to stifle them further forward. It's the only way to play them, I think.'

Born in Glasgow in 1955, Willie started out with Eastercraigs Amateurs. He signed for Aberdeen initially on an 'S' form in June 1969, being called up to the club in June 1971 and loaned out to Peterhead for the 1971/72 season. A centre-forward in those days, Miller's 23 goals made him Peterhead's top scorer and the second-highest scorer in the Highland League. He also helped Peterhead to the Aberdeenshire Cup. In the Dons' reserves for the 1972/73 season, he found Teddy Scott and George Murray both big influences on him as he developed as a player. Just before Christmas, an injury crisis necessitated his move into defence. 'Mark tight and try to win the ball early,' Scott told him before he went out for that first game against Rangers. The Dons won 2-0 and Miller had found his rightful position. He excelled in the centre of defence as the reserves won the League and League Cup.

Miller was called into the first team for the final game of the season against Morton at Cappielow, coming on as a second-half substitute for Arthur Graham, then he played 31 league games in his breakthrough season in 1973/74. He made at least as many league appearances every season after that. Manager Ally MacLeod appointed Miller as captain when he was only 21 years old. ' I think once I settled in my natural position, I had everything in front of me,' Miller told Ally Begg in 2018. 'The responsibility of being the captain became more apparent; having to organise the guys playing either side of me and in front of me.' Miller's international debut came in a European Championship qualifier in Bucharest as Scotland drew 1-1 with Romania in June 1975. He had to wait almost three years for his second cap, in a friendly against Bulgaria in February 1978. Miller picked up the League Cup with Aberdeen under MacLeod, then when Alex Ferguson took over Miller scored the goal which sealed the 1980 Premier Division title. Rangers manager John Greig was one of Miller's admirers, saying of him, 'A magnificent reader of the game and an inspiration to those around him.'

'We have to tighten things a lot more,' Stein said, 'and we need a player like Miller who is a deeper defender. He knew before that he was being kept for these two games that are coming. It's always been in our minds.' Stein was also aware that some of the Russian players had to receive oxygen after the match in Seville. 'It is the humidity we have to guard against,' he said. 'You can feel a different atmosphere in the air once you travel those 160 miles or so inland.'

Stein knew that the win against New Zealand had ensured at the very least a winner-takes-all match against Russia, and while he felt that was the most important tie he was still looking to come away with something against the Brazilians, 'We will not be using tomorrow's game as an exercise. We have got to be on our toes all the time and I think we will set them problems they didn't see before. Brazil can't ignore any international side which scored five goals in their opening game.' Stein was also aware that Scotland could beat Brazil and still not qualify if they then lost to Russia. 'That's why the Russian game is key,' he said. 'We have got to ensure that we don't endanger our chances by trying to beat Brazil. We don't want to win and, in doing so, take so much out of our players that we can't beat the Russians.'

Brazil had played 30 matches under Santana, losing only two. They had ten consecutive victories from February 1981, a draw with Czechoslovakia in March of 1982 stopping a run that had seen them beat England, France, West Germany and Spain on a European summer tour. They arrived in Spain unbeaten in 19 matches. 'Coaching Brazil is not like coaching the other big teams,' Pelé said in 1980 as his country looked for a replacement for previous coach Cláudio Coutinho. 'You don't have one target at a

World Cup but two demands. Not just to win it, but to play beautiful football.'

Coutinho's football was anything but that, attracting derisory descriptions such as 'robotic' as Brazil made their way to third place in Argentina 1978. The style would now change as Santana took charge in February 1980. He was the Brazilian Football Confederation's first full-time appointment. All his predecessors held club posts simultaneously. 'As soon as he came in things changed drastically,' Falcão told fifa.com in 2016. 'Playing for a Seleção [team] became a lot more fun. He understood that he had intelligent players – he wanted us to play intuitively and not systematically. He urged the full-backs to attack. He didn't want central midfielders who only knew how to stop the opposition – he wanted ones who knew what to do with the ball. He gave us freedom to try what we wanted. He always wanted us to put on a spectacular show.'

'It was such a pleasure to play for Telê,' Zico said to *FourFourTwo* in 2020. 'He had a game plan, but he gave us freedom to be creative. He aimed for perfection. If someone had ten shots during training, scored nine and hit a post, he'd ask, "Why didn't you score all of them?"' Michael Serra, the historian of São Paulo, where Santana would end his managerial career, wrote of him, 'Idol wherever he went, he consecrated soccer art in the Brazilian national team, showing that being champion was not enough, it was necessary to make each match an unforgettable moment.'

Born in the mining town of Itabirito, in south-east Brazil, on 26 July 1931, as a boy Telê Santana started out as a goalkeeper, but began to show promise as a centre-forward. In 1945 he started out at Itapirense, then moved to America Recreativo de São João Del Rey, where his father was coach and president. At the age of 20 he signed professionally for Fluminense, in February 1951. There the coach, Zeze Moreira, moved him to the right wing. He played for Fluminense from 1951 to 1960, becoming Rio de Janeiro champion in 1951 and 1959 and Rio–São Paulo champion in 1957 and 1960. Despite his accomplishments, the abilities of Garrincha and Julinho would keep him from making an appearance for the national side. He was called up for a friendly against Portugal in 1957, but a heel injury during a training session ruled him out of selection. Moving into coaching, Santana took Fluminense to the regional title in 1970, the first of eight league championships he would win in Brazil. The following season he led Atlético Mineiro to the country's first national league title, the Brasileiro. He would have spells in charge of São Paulo, Botafogo, Grêmio and Palmeiras, before taking over the Seleção.

With an average age of 26.5, Brazil's squad had experience throughout. Zico was the most capped player with 56, making his debut in 1976 and playing in the 1978 tournament. Two players featured, not only in 1978 but also in West Germany in 1974: goalkeeper Waldir Peres and midfielder Dirceu. Players in the squad came from all over Brazil. São Paulo contributed four, with Atlético Mineiro and Flamengo providing three each. Two players played their club football abroad: Falcão at Roma in Italy and Dirceu in Spain with Atlético Madrid.

The flair in the side was expected to come from Zico, Falcão and Atlético Mineiro's Éder, but the biggest presence in their squad was 6ft 3½in defender and captain Sócrates. A qualified medical doctor, he completed his degree while playing part-time for Botafogo, only turning professional in 1978 at the age of 24. He then joined Corinthians, based in

São Paulo. In his midfield role he often seemed to operate at a walking pace, so comfortable was he on the ball. He could deliver piercing through passes with either foot as he orchestrated attacks. Pelé would say that Sócrates played better backwards than most footballers did forwards.

'Scotland and Brazil games have always been close in past years,' Santana said, 'and we know we are in for a hard game again this time. In the 1974 tournament, Scotland fought well and our team could not beat them. This time I think there will be goals.'

* * *

The mood in the Scottish camp was good. They had got off to a winning start and despite the loss of those two goals it was still by a comfortable margin. 'Stein was at his best in the next few days,' Rough told Archie Macpherson. 'There was a lot of humour about him. He was good to be about. The banter between him and the players was great. I think it was because winning the game made it so different from our start in Argentina and because the place we were in was superb compared to the shithole in Alta Gracia.' Stein also made sure the players knew that Brazil wasn't the most significant match for them. He impressed upon the players the general feeling that the 1982 vintage was the best Brazil side since the 1970 World Cup winners and that they shouldn't worry about getting a result against them. Russia was the important match and had to be won.

Scotland would travel to Jerez on Thursday, staying there at night, leaving only a 50-minute journey to Seville on Friday morning. When they got there, Rough was told he was in for some extra training. 'On the morning of the match, I suffered one of the worst hours of my life on a training pitch,' he wrote in his book *The Rough and the Smooth*. 'The manager had identified the fabled South Americans' strength at corners, which they could swerve in every direction, and decided to put me through the wringer by testing me at set pieces. "They are going to be targeting you, so we had better get ready for that and build your confidence."' Stein gave John Robertson a ball and ordered him to fire crosses in at his keeper. The manager then assembled some players to go in and challenge Rough for the high balls. 'For 60 minutes John Robertson did nothing but dispatch corners for these three to attack, and they weren't too particular about snaffling a bit of me as well. In fact, I was battered to pieces in the process as they hurled themselves at me with the same ferocity as if I had been Peter Shilton. As a psychological preparation, it was scarcely ideal,' Rough said. In his 1988 book *Rough at the Top*, he added, 'I confess to missing every ball in a howling gale and the manager refused to halt the work-out until I gripped one confidently. It took another half hour.'

'He hated goalies,' Rough said of Stein to Hugh MacDonald in 2015. 'He took the goalie in training as there were no goalkeeping coaches then. He worked us hard, put us through it. We always thought he had something against goalies.' Rough, though, always thought highly of Stein, 'He was the best. He commanded respect, there was an aura about him. Team talks were very, very thorough. He knew the opposition inside out. He had that something that people respond to. He was the kind of manager that when we went on a trip the players got off the bus before the SFA officials. It was not unknown for him to go into the hotel and book all the best rooms for the players and let the SFA take what was left. He was always for the players, the players always came first.'

When Stein announced his starting 11 at lunchtime on the day of the game, there were some surprises. Out went Danny McGrain, Allan Evans, Alan Brazil and Kenny Dalglish. In their places came David Narey, Willie Miller, Asa Hartford and Steve Archibald. In his 1997 book, *My Autobiography*, Dalglish recalled, 'In training a day or two before, Big Jock told us he wanted to play one up front. When Jock used Steve Archibald in training I knew I wouldn't be playing against Brazil. My team, the lads who weren't now in the first team, were ordered to play like Brazil. The "mugs" team, as I called us, didn't have enough players, so we played Roughie up front. Off we went, with me and four others in midfield, and just Roughie in attack. Embarrassingly for the first team and Big Jock, Roughie scored twice and we won 2-0. When Jock's team had the ball at the back, I shouted to Roughie, "Just leave them and drop back." Big Jock stopped the game, came over, and asked me, "Kenny, what are you doing?" "Well," I replied, "you said play like Brazil. I thought that was what you wanted us to do. They always drop off." Big Jock said, "You've always got to be clever, Kenny." But I wasn't. It was true. Brazil did use that tactic.'

Jim McLean recalled the team announcement, and McGrain's reaction, when speaking to the *Daily Record* in 2006. 'A lot of players at international level do have big egos but Danny's reaction that day was the act of a true professional. He must have been shattered when Jock announced the starting 11 in a team meeting a few hours before the game. But as soon as Jock finished listing the team and addressing the squad Danny was the first player on his feet to roar encouragement to the others. I'd never seen

that side of Danny. He was not an out-and-out motivator because he preferred to set his examples quietly and was enormously respected by the rest of the players as a result. Football is a team game but we're still all selfish at times and in that situation every player was sitting nervously, hoping he'd be picked. Danny was a fixture in the side and must have been so disappointed not to be listed. But his first thought was for the team and I will never forget his reaction.'

The humidity certainly played a part in Stein's thinking with McGrain, Brazil and Dalglish all suffering from dehydration in Malaga. After his less-than-convincing performance against the Kiwis, Evans could hardly have been surprised at his omission. Narey had never played right-back before for Scotland but he was in ahead of George Burley, who had suffered an ankle knock in training.

Narey was born and brought up in Dundee, attending St John's RC High School. He joined Dundee United from St Columba's Boys Club on an 'S' form in 1972, signing professionally the following year. He made his full debut at Tannadice in a league match against Falkirk on 21 November 1973, playing as an attacking midfielder. By the 1974/75 season he was a first-team regular. Narey's international debut came as a substitute for John Blackley in a 3-1 friendly win over Sweden in April 1977. He was the first Dundee United player to receive a full international cap. Ally MacLeod selected Narey in the initial squad of 40 for the Argentina World Cup but cut him from the final 22. Of where he was best utilised – in midfield or in defence – Narey told *Shoot!* in 1982, 'I still prefer playing at the back. I believe I am a better player there because it is where I feel most comfortable and most confident. That's where I played at school and through all United's teams into the Premier

League side. Naturally, I play where the manager selects me, but my opinion has not changed.'

Miller's return to the team was no real surprise. 'Willie was told before the England [Home International Championship] match that he would probably be needed for the games against Brazil and Russia,' said Stein. 'I'll be happy to mark Zico or anybody else,' Miller said. 'Against the Brazilians, you must defend against their midfield men, because that is where they like to shoot from.' Miller called his inclusion in the team 'the biggest thing to happen to me yet'.

'Whatever happens tonight we won't qualify with this 90 minutes, so I've got to have everybody ready for Tuesday against the Russians,' Stein said. Strachan had recovered well from the game with New Zealand and Stein felt he would play for at least an hour against Brazil. 'If he does run out of steam then the men chasing him won't be feeling too clever either.'

Archibald's goal against New Zealand had now landed him a starting place. Born in Glasgow, the son of a merchant seaman, Archibald started out with Rutherglen sides Croftfoot United and Fernhill Amateurs. In the summer of 1974 he was signed by Stan Anderson for Clyde, then also based in Rutherglen. In a 2021 interview with *The Guardian*, Archibald claimed that the only time he ever felt pressure in his career was his debut for Clyde against Ayr United. By 1976, Archibald was a regular in the Clyde team as a part-timer – he worked as a Rolls-Royce mechanic, with a sideline in buying cars, doing them up and selling them to his team-mates.

When Craig Brown took over in 1977 he converted Archibald, then playing in midfield, to a striker. Aberdeen boss Billy McNeill, who had been in charge at Clyde for two months in 1977, came in to sign Steve in January 1978 for £20,000. Although he made an early impact, scoring twice against his boyhood favourites Rangers at Ibrox in a March 1978 3-0 win, it was when Alex Ferguson took over at Pittodrie that Archibald's career really flourished. He scored 13 goals from 32 league games as the Dons finished fourth in the 1978/79 Premier League. The following season he netted 12 in 34 as Aberdeen became the first non-Old Firm team since 1965 to win the title. 'I found him an aggressive, quick, resilient type,' Ferguson wrote of Archibald in *A Light in the North*. 'He had two good feet, was good in the air and seemed to have a spring about him. He was like Denis Law in terms of a shot coming off a goalkeeper – Archibald was always first in.'

Archibald made a scoring debut for Scotland coming on as a 49th-minute substitute for Kenny Dalglish at Hampden in March 1980 against Portugal, notching the third goal in a 4-1 win. An £800,000 transfer to Tottenham Hotspur followed in the summer of 1980, making Archibald the most expensive cross-border transfer at that time.

Brazil's team had only one change from the one that beat Russia. Falcão had come in due to Cerezo's suspension, but his performance against the Russians had been so good that it was Dirceu who made way for Cerezo's return.

* * *

The Estadio Benito Villamarín was initially designed in 1912 with the construction beginning in 1923, completed in 1928. Then named Estadio de la Exposición, it was officially inaugurated on 17 March 1929 when Spain beat Portugal 5-0. Real Betis began playing there in the early

1930s, obtaining the lease and becoming sole tenant in 1936. Seville's city council requisitioned the stadium during the Spanish Civil War handing it over to the military command. After the war, the stadium underwent reconstruction to repair the damage it had suffered. The stadium was reopened on 12 March 1939, bearing the name of Estadio Municipal Heliopolis. Real Betis became owners in 1961, renaming the stadium after Benito Villamarín who served as the club president between 1955 and 1965. While improvements were made to the stadium throughout the 1970s, major renovation works were carried out between 1979 and 1982 for the World Cup and the capacity was increased to 50,253.

In FIFA's official film of the tournament, *G'olé!*, Sean Connery's narration describes the match as 'a confrontation between the nation who thinks it's the best at football and the one that knows it's the best'.

After starting the tournament with a victory, the Scottish fans headed for Seville from their various bases around the Costa del Sol in a hopeful mood that perhaps, with a bit of luck, their team could get a better result against Brazil than the goalless draw the 1974 side achieved. Stuart Russell was facing a journey of around 180km from the coast. He recalled, 'There was a guy called James Mortimer. He owns the Rogano, he used to own Vicky's [nightclub]. He organised a couple of buses from Puerto Banús to take us to the games. One of the buses had Rod Stewart and Sean Connery on it, our bus was just full of nutcases from Glasgow. Well, a few football players were on it. Dom Sullivan was on it.' Sullivan, from Garngad, was part of the Celtic team that had just won the Premier Division. Russell continued, 'It went from Puerto Banús right through the Andalucian mountains, I would imagine, into Seville.

We stopped off at one of these mountainous cafes. There was a couple of old Spanish guys probably sitting in the same chairs for 30 or 40 years and they're playing, it wasn't draughts, it was something like that, and that Dom Sullivan was always a bit of a joker and he had a 50 peseta note attached to an invisible wire and he dropped it down beside the auld yins. Everybody's just sitting watching them ready to take the bait. Of course they did and he pulled it back. They were all having photographs and laughing and all that so it was a good atmosphere.'

Lifelong Arbroath supporter David Dewar had travelled to Spain with eight friends. He said, 'We were staying in a hotel in Benalmádena about 150 miles away from Seville. I think the bus left about 11 o'clock, we got off in Seville about 4pm.' However, not all of their party would make the trip. 'Malcolm had been left on his own the night before when some Spaniards set a fierce dog on him. He was running back to the hotel when he decided to jump over a low wall. However, there was a drop on the other side of ten feet or so and he busted his knee. Malcolm like myself had been to a few of the away qualifying games in Sweden and Israel so I felt sorry for him missing the game.'

'The second match against Brazil was the one which everyone was waiting for,' said Bobby Jamieson, 'and it involved a three-hour drive to Seville. We hired two cars and drove down to Marbella, then veered north over the mountains, through the walled city of Rhonda before reaching our destination. Different place this as hardly anyone spoke English. We stopped at a restaurant for some grub, and with my limited knowledge of Spanish, I opted for the safe option and chose chilli con carne. My pal Drew, the one in charge of beer procurement, didn't fancy the menu and piped up, "Ah, look here – safe as houses. Esparragos! I bet that's asparagus soup. I'll have that," he proclaimed defiantly. So, as the rest of us tucked into our hearty lunch, Drew was served six strips of cold asparagus and a knob of butter. Glorious – you had to be there.'

'The journey to Seville took forever,' said Chic Brogan, 'because they didn't use the main road because it's all tolls so they used the wee roads.'

Once in Seville, there was only one thing slowing the Scots fans down. 'God, the heat nearly floored me,' said Dewar. 'It was so humid I could hardly breathe. I think it was the same for everybody.'

'Seville was the warmest place I'd ever been to in my life,' said Russell. 'Unbelievable heat. It must have been 45 degrees it was so warm. It was a case of walking 20 yards and you had to stop for a drink. I was slim and fit but even I found it difficult.'

'We were chapping at doors for water it was that hot,' Iain McAuley said. 'Just various doors along the road. "Can we get water?" We were taking oranges off the trees. As long as you took just one everybody was fine but when you started shaking the tree I remember the locals getting quite angry 'cos we were shaking the tree to get about 20 oranges at a time.'

As kick-off drew nearer, swelling numbers of Scottish and Brazilian fans took over the streets around the ground. 'The atmosphere was intoxicating,' said Jamieson. 'I didn't touch a drop all day, as I wanted to savour every moment. The sound of pipes and drums was accompanied by the rhythm of the samba beat as both sets of fans mingled in a display of friendship. I'll never forget the arrival of a Brazilian band in uniform – about 20 of them alighted from a coach, assembled in the street and started to play their instruments – drums, timbales, maracas, trumpets, the lot. Absolutely fantastic.'

'Outside, before the game, they're all marching with their Sambas,' Brogan said. 'The Scottish fans got in front and joined in. All singing and dancing with them. The fans were all intertwined, there was no "their end" and "our end".'

'I remember swapping my number ten Kenny Dalglish Scotland top that my girlfriend had bought me for a Brazilian top from this Brazilian babe,' said McAuley, 'and the top still had her boob shapes in it when I was wearing it. So I didn't have a Scotland top after that; the game against Russia I had to wear a Brazil top.'

The atmosphere only intensified when the supporters got inside the stadium. Russell recalled, 'The Brazilians have got their big samba drums and we're right behind them so the noise was incredible for the full game. They just battered them all the time.'

'The Brazilian fans were playing a samba,' said Brogan. 'They had lots of drums and maracas in the ground. The Scottish fans are all standing and you could hear it starting, "Mmm, hmm, mmm," and we started to make up words to their tune. I can't remember what, just nonsense, but the Scottish fans are all singing their own words and that really annoyed them. So they stopped and played another tune. The Scottish fans took a minute "Mmm, mmm" and started singing again, just stupid words but we were singing and dancing to their songs.'

'The Brazilians were marching round the stadium,' McAuley said. 'We're standing at the bar and every time they came round we'd cheer them for doing another lap.'

'We wandered up to the stadium which was swarming with fans from both sides,' Jamieson recalled. 'The Brazilians were cheering, as one of their fans had climbed up the stairs to the top of the stadium and was waving a Brazilian flag. I thought, "I'm not having that," and grabbed the Saltire from our standard bearer and walked up the steps to confront my Brazilian counterpart. He smiled, stepped aside, and allowed me to introduce the crowd below to the Leper Colony flag. That's the way it should be – mutual respect. When I came down, I noticed a man wearing a Scottish jersey – 1962 model with the huge badge and white V-neck. It was Dave Mackay.' Mackay won 22 Scotland caps between 1957 and 1965, so Jamieson couldn't resist striking up a conversation, 'I asked him his thoughts on the game and he replied, "I wish I was still playing, son." A true Scottish football legend if ever there was one.'

Scotland's line-up was: Alan Rough, David Narey, Frank Gray, Willie Miller, Alan Hansen, Graeme Souness (captain), Gordon Strachan, Asa Hartford, Steve Archibald, John Wark, John Robertson.

Brazil, for their part, went with: Waldir Peres (São Paulo), Leandro (Flamengo), Oscar (São Paulo), Luizinho (Atlético Mineiro), Júnior (Flamengo), Falcão (Roma), Toninho Cerezo (Atlético Mineiro), Sócrates (captain, Corinthians), Serginho (São Paulo), Zico (Flamengo), Éder (Atlético Mineiro).

Brazil set up in a 4-2-2-2 formation with Éder playing off centre-forward Serginho, a player many people remarked as being 'un-Brazilian'. With Leandro and Júnior moving forward from the wing-back positions and the midfield, anchored by trequartistas Zico and Sócrates, all moving around the pitch, it was a system destined to keep the

Scottish players on their toes. The exact formation Brazil used is up for debate. Observers of the match speak of certain players taking up five or six different positions on the field as play dictated. Stuart Horsfield, in his book *1982 Brazil The Glorious Failure*, contends that along with 4-2-2-2 there are at least three other formations the Brazilians could have been playing that night: 2-7-1, highlighting the tendency for the midfield to move all around the pitch; 4-5-1 with Éder as a wide left midfield player; 4-4-1-1 with Cerezo, Falcão, Sócrates and Zico in midfield.

The Scottish players became concerned about the conditions they would play in as soon as they arrived at the ground. Stein encouraged his players to get out on to the pitch and sample the heat and the conditions underfoot. Alan Rough recalled that, while he was undergoing a gentle session in his goalmouth, some of his team-mates were sweating through their training gear, and he began to wonder how long they were all going to last in the heat. After their warm-up, the players returned to the dressing room and put their heads under the shower before donning their kits. Stein's team talk centred on the necessity of retaining possession and striving to set the tempo. He knew the Brazilians would adapt far better to the conditions than his players so slowing the game down was a must.

As the Scots got back on to the pitch and lined up for the national anthems, they began to see the contrast between the two teams. Both Wark and Souness recalled looking across to the Brazil side with not a bead of sweat forming on their collective brows, while the Scottish players were already perspiring. 'The stadium was tight and compact, generating a tremendous atmosphere rather like that in an English stadium,' Souness said, 'but there the similarity ended, the grass was long, the air was hot and humid.'

Willie Miller remembers, 'The heat got to us as it hit 48°C before kick-off.' 'I was gasping for breath while the Brazilians were casually wandering all over the park.' Davie Provan had an explanation, telling Archie Macpherson, 'I still have a Brazilian jersey from that game that I was presented with afterwards. It was of the finest material; you could hardly feel it when you held it. Our jerseys? You wouldn't believe it. Ours had a lining. A lining. You couldn't make it up.'

As Souness remarked, the pitch was also a problem. 'We never had a clue what studs to wear because the grass was so long, which was the way the Brazilians liked it,' recalled Gordon Strachan in 2020. 'There was actually a lot of physical engagement to their play, it wasn't as much about moving the ball quickly as it is now. In the end, it didn't matter too much – we never saw the ball when they got going anyway.'

There were around 15,000 Scots in the crowd, officially recorded at 47,379. 'At a Scotland game, it was like a tartan Halloween with all the weird and wonderful costumes people had on,' said Chic Brogan. Brazil attacked from kick-off, winning a corner in the first minute as Narey blocked a cross from Éder. Referee Luis Paulino Siles Calderon came over to help the police attempt to move the crowd of photographers out the way so Júnior could take the kick. Cerezo flashed in a shot after four minutes that whistled past the post. Souness did the same at the other end a minute later. Scotland certainly looked in no way overawed and were happy to take the game to their more illustrious opponents. In the TV studio, co-commentator Jimmy Hill remarked of

Brazil, 'They do look like they can be beaten with a quick pass or a dribble, so that's encouraging.'

It was perhaps telling, however, that striker Archibald's first touch was on the edge of his own penalty box. He continually found himself retreating into his own half in search of the ball throughout the first half. There were no serious attempts to segregate the two sets of supporters and Scots fans happily mixed with the samba bands and dancing girls who came to cheer Brazil, the respective supporters attempting to out-shout each other. Rough recalled, 'The atmosphere was wonderful, with so-called rival fans mingling together, dancing sambas and shaking maracas. Mercifully, there was not the slightest hint of trouble between the supporters in Seville – on the contrary, they forged this immediate bond and the camaraderie was tremendous.' The Brazilians had a couple of free kicks early on, Éder whipping a shot over Rough's crossbar from 30 yards after 12 minutes, while two minutes later Zico chipped across the face of goal only for Sócrates to head narrowly wide.

In the right-back position, Narey found himself up against Éder at outside-left, but 18 minutes into the game the Dundee United man was much further up the park. Souness sent a raking crossfield ball to the edge of the penalty box on the right-hand side. Wark climbed and headed the ball down for Narey to run on to. Narey's first touch took the ball between the two defenders; as he caught up to it all he could do was hit it firmly with his right foot. The ball flew into the net. To the astonishment of everyone, including the scorer, Scotland were 1-0 up.

Back in the BBC TV studio, Jimmy Hill uttered words that would haunt him the rest of his days. 'I don't wish to be rude to David Narey,' he began, 'but I think he might have caught that on the end of his toe. I don't know, he was stretching for it anyway. But it certainly didn't lack for acceleration.' Hill would be forever associated with the phrase 'toe-poke', and it sealed his fate as a pantomime villain for Scots fans. In the 1998 documentary *Are You Watching Jimmy Hill?* he said, 'David Narey will be one of the words on my grave, I think, on my tombstone. Someone who the whole nation thought I was insulting. I was very pleased he scored.'

'Poor Jimmy Hill,' Patrick Barclay said. 'It was a great goal for everyone in the world except Jimmy Hill. Knowing Jim, I'm sure he wouldn't mean it disparagingly. To keep the ball down in those circumstances was a great skill. There are toe-pokes and *toe-pokes*. If you or I would have toe-poked it, it wouldn't have gone in the net. Narey was a terrific player actually.'

'Jimmy Hill I knew, though, as soon as I heard Jimmy Hill, sitting in his presentation seat on top of a block of flats outside the ground watching the game on a television monitor, describe Narey's strike as a "toe-poke" that it would not be taken lying down by our people,' wrote Archie Macpherson in *Action Replays*. 'It was to be construed as some monstrous cultural insult, like calling the Clyde-built *Queen Elizabeth* a paddle steamer.

'He [Hill] loved the attention of the Scottish supporters forever after. On matchdays that he attended or watched from the studio, that I can vouch for, no man could have been prouder of being singled out for mob abuse. The "Jimmy Hill's a Poof" banner frequently seen amongst Scottish fans was not only singularly inaccurate but was to Jimmy simply an eccentric sign of endearment.' Alan Hansen, who would go on to become Hill's colleague at the

BBC, recalled after Hill's death in 2015, 'He said, "When I go to Scotland they're always great." I said, "But that's the Scots people. If you go up there and you're on your own they'll be great to you, but try getting off a bus at Hampden and see how you're treated." It didn't matter if people hated him because he felt that was recognition. "Love me or hate me, but don't ignore me."'

'I can't believe Jimmy Hill called it a toe-poke. What a lot of rubbish!' Jim McLean would say years later. 'Garbage – it was a great strike from a guy who could genuinely have pulled on the yellow shirt of Brazil and not looked out of place. David was a class act, a guy who always played with his head and read the game magnificently. His goal came as no surprise to me because he turned out often for United in the centre of midfield, where he was clever enough to make runs off his man and find positions such as the one he did that night.'

When challenged over the years by Scots, Hill would contend that in his playing days a toe-poke was a skill. 'He persuaded them that toe poke was an old-fashioned view of how he actually hit the ball,' fellow commentator Barry Davies would say in the BBC documentary *Jimmy Hill: A Man For All Seasons*. In *Action Replays*, Macpherson wrote of the fallout the remark would cause, 'After that comment, the relationship between Stein and Hill was never the same. Stein, in fact, was looking for blood and became unusually anti-English, unusual in the sense that he never wished to be seen to be stupidly nationalistic and did value their football. But on this occasion, he told me that if Hill approached him he would chew him up and that had it been an English goal it would never have been interpreted in such a dismissive way. Hill himself complained of a gross overreaction and, in truth, there was something to that. He has always insisted that toe-pokes can be the product of great skill. I agree with him in the sense of his own definition and for the very fact that Dave Narey proved it. If it was one.' Several years later, in *Adventures in the Golden Age*, Archie Macpherson elaborated, 'It was the tone. It was one of belittlement. In short, he loved stoking the fires. What he hadn't bargained for was Stein's ultimate reaction.'

'It was a brilliant ball by Souness,' Wark said to the *Record* in 2012 when discussing the goal. 'I was out on the right but was more comfortable inside, so I'd move off the line and I just headed it into an area hoping someone would run on to it. When I saw it was big Narey, I was wishing it had been anybody else. But then he hit it. You could see when he scored that he couldn't believe it, he didn't know how to celebrate. He didn't have a clue what to do. He obviously hardly ever scored so he ended up running around like a wee boy who didn't know what day it was!'

In *The Football Years*, Andy Cameron remarked, 'That was the first time I ever heard the expression, "Aw naw, we've got them angry."' It's a reaction many of the players now consider to be accurate. 'I should have known that at that precise moment it wasn't the Brazilians who should have been worried – it was us,' wrote Alan Rough. 'We'd wounded the lion – now we were in for it.' Gordon Strachan presented similar recollections in his 2006 book *My Life in Football*, 'It was a wonderful moment for David, but I think the rest of us were thinking, "We could be in right trouble here – this is going to fire them up." We weren't wrong.'

In the Radio Scotland commentary box, David Begg, after his exuberance in the New Zealand game, had learned to control himself, 'I've heard back in the years since then the commentary on the David Narey goal; normally that would be the one you would go apeshit on but actually, I handled it really quite well. It was a very measured and controlled, informed, decent commentary and I happily learned my lesson. Thereafter I enjoyed the World Cup, there's no doubt about that. I always remember the feeling when Narey scored. I didn't ever class it as a toe-poke. I thought it was a wonderful finish. I can still picture that goal and the explosion of noise. The late Murdo Macpherson [former editor of *Sportsound*] said, "You always pause to let the crowd noise come in before you then recap the goal," which I did, and I think that worked quite well.'

After the restart, Scotland were still moving the ball about well. The short passes were all finding their man. Souness intercepted a Brazilian pass and slid a ball through for Archibald, only for the Tottenham man to be muscled off the ball. 'When big Dave Narey shot us into the lead,' Strachan wrote in his 1984 autobiography, 'I think we were all a bit stunned and trying to convince ourselves we were actually a goal ahead against the great Brazilians. We were then playing it tight, I suppose trying to hold on to what we had in the belief that we might never be in front of them again. Personally, I believe we should have been driving forward in search of a second goal.'

With 25 minutes gone, Éder had an attempt at chipping Rough from out on the left wing. Two minutes later Miller was in quickly to dispossess Zico at the edge of the Scotland box. It was then Asa Hartford's turn to stem a Brazilian attack when he took the ball from Falcão, just as the Roma man was moving into the penalty area. There was no question of Brazil panicking to find an equaliser. Their players were content to string passes together and look for the opening that would bring them level. 'It was all about searching for beauty and elegance on a football pitch,' said Rough.

Brazil always looked dangerous from outside the box, and everyone began to fear the worst when Cerezo went down easily under a Souness challenge on 33 minutes. Hartford stood with arms outstretched in a vain plea to the referee, as he suggested the 27-year-old midfielder had dived. In the BBC studio, John Motson commented, 'Sometimes when you give Brazil a free kick 20 yards out in a central position, it's almost like giving them a deferential penalty.' Éder, Zico and Sócrates gathered around the ball. Zico stepped up and casually placed it past Rough and into the top right-hand corner. He went off on a celebratory run, jumping for joy at levelling the scores. 'God gave me that ability, but I practised a lot,' Zico told *FourFourTwo*. 'At Flamengo I'd take 70 or 100 after training.'

'Questions must be asked about Alan Rough,' Jimmy Hill said.

'While I was frustrated that all our homework had come to nought,' recalled Rough, 'you can't really hope to joust with giants without sustaining injuries. Subsequently, I received a great deal of condemnation for conceding the goal. Both Jock and I had attempted to study their methods to the nth degree, but there is only so much planning you can undertake.' Rough would explain that in Scotland when you conceded a free kick, almost in the centre of your goal, you assembled your wall to one side and stood as cover at the other side. 'I had a tremendous wall up. I think there was about eight in it. I just kept saying, "Pack the wall, get as many as you like." When you're a goalkeeper, when you've got too many people in the wall, the first thing you can't see is the ball. I got confused.'

Éder made a run and Rough, convinced he was the kicker, followed him and made a minimal movement to one side. 'Just as I had done that, Zico had hit it. I never even seen the ball. It came over the wall so quick I just lost it completely,' he said. John Wark recalled, 'I was the end man in the wall and Roughie was giving it "Perfect, John" with the big thumbs up. Two seconds later it's round me and in the top corner. Two keepers couldn't have stopped it.'

'That Brazil team had some wonderful footballers like Sócrates, Falcão, Júnior and Éder, but Zico was the best of them by a country mile,' Souness wrote in his 2017 book *Football – My Life, My Passion*. 'He was untouchable. A big part of the game back then involved trying to mess your opponent around physically to see if they fancied it. The two players in my career who I never laid a finger on were Zico and Alan Ball. They just had this ability to sense where you were, where you were coming from, and would just pop the ball off before you got within a yard of them.' Willie Miller agreed, 'Zico ... was the most intelligent player that I ever came up against, and was difficult to mark as he pulled opponents all over the pitch and made optimum use of the space available. Indeed, all of the Brazilians that I encountered in the World Cup were tactically clever, and also most adept at working for each other, a quality that is sometimes overlooked because their individual skills are so outstanding.'

Brazil returned to attack as the game resumed, Serginho heading over the crossbar. Scotland came back, though, and on 41 minutes Wark's header almost put Archibald in, but Waldir Peres came out to smother the ball.

At half-time the sides went in all square. Scotland had started better than could have been expected but every indication was that the Brazilians would soon be in control. In the dressing room, Stein was calm. Patience was key, he said, to persevere and maintain possession as often as was possible. Rough felt that Stein's principal concern was that no one was lost to injury or dehydration ahead of the pivotal match with the Russians. In the Brazilian dressing room, there were discussions on why they weren't dominating the game. Zico told his midfield he wasn't happy with being isolated on the right side of the pitch. He let Santana know that if he was going to remain on the park then he needed more help. They agreed to rotate positions more and went out with renewed vigour.

Spotted in the crowd standing together were Sean Connery, Coventry City boss Dave Sexton and comedian Andy Cameron.

It didn't take Brazil long after the second half began, with the temperature still in the 80s, to edge in front. Hansen swept out a low Sócrates cross for a corner. Júnior whipped the ball in and Oscar beat Souness to the header, scoring at the near post on 48 minutes. Souness would admit culpability, 'I was guilty of letting Oscar get a yard on me for a near-post ball three minutes into the second half and, instead of settling down and holding things together, we went chasing goals.'

Minutes later, Zico fired past the post, while the sure passing of Scotland's midfield was soon becoming a thing of the past as Souness played the ball straight to the opposition in the centre circle. With 59 minutes on the clock, Zico shot over the bar, but six minutes later Brazil extended their lead in style. Sócrates broke out of defence and played the ball out to Serginho, who slipped it through to Éder. The Atlético Mineiro man took a touch as Rough moved off his line to narrow the angle. Éder moved into the box on the left-hand side then chipped Rough, who stood rooted to the six-yard line as he watched the ball sail over his head and into the net. 'You don't want to be beaten at your near post,' Rough told Macpherson, 'You have to defend that, and I was thinking there was no way he could put it across me. But then came the chip. There was nothing I could do about that.'

The Brazilians' pace, panache and flowing football were beginning to overwhelm Scotland and, although the first 45 minutes was as good as any Scotland team had played in a long time, they were now being left behind. Despite going that goal down, Brazil never flinched. They gave the impression they could speed up and slow down the game any time that suited them.

Beside David Begg and George Hamilton in the Radio Scotland commentary booth was summariser Frank McLintock, winner of nine caps for Scotland and the First Division and FA Cup double with Arsenal in 1971. 'Frank was one of the best summarisers I ever worked with,' Begg said. 'Because what he would do was, when George was commentating Frank would take the time to take me aside and say, "Look, see what's happening. Watch what they're doing here." And he talked about the wheel of the Brazilian team. "Look at them. They're running in a wheel." He explained the game to me in a way that very few summarisers have done even since then. He was absolutely brilliant. I could see why he was taken to that World Cup. His analysis of the game was spot on.'

Dalglish came on for Strachan, which left the Edinburgh-born midfielder disappointed. 'If only because it effectively ruined my chances of being in a position to swap shirts with one of the Brazilian stars like Zico, Falcão or Sócrates,' he wrote in 2006. 'It was just my luck that the only Brazil jersey I could get was that of their centre-forward, Serginho, who was widely considered to be by far the least impressive member of their team and who was being substituted at the same time as me. The other lads all wanted Zico's shirt. It must have been embarrassing for him because in the last five minutes of the match, he had about six Scottish stalkers.'

The other Scottish substitution saw McLeish replacing Hartford, as Hansen moved up into midfield. McLeish recalled in his autobiography, 'When I took the pitch first I could hardly breathe, such was the heat and humidity, and it took me some time to get my second wind.' To the *Sunday Mail* in 2012, he said, 'We were 3-1 down when Jock decided to unleash me. I ... planned to man-mark Zico to help keep the score down. But he already had five of the lads tight on him and they weren't even interested in stopping him scoring – they just wanted to get his jersey at time-up.'

Also on the bench that night was Paul Sturrock, as he recalled in his book *Forward Thinking*, 'A sense of anticipation filled me when I was asked to go down the track and warm up. I had started doing loosening exercises all the way down to the byline some 50 or 60 yards down the track. I will never forget stretching and at the same time looking back to the halfway line where a movement around our dugout caught my eye. Scotland were making a double substitution – my dream of playing in the World Cup on the same park as Brazil was ended.'

John Robertson offered Scotland's last attempt on goal as he fired a 20-yard shot over on 72 minutes. Brazil then made a substitution, bringing on Paulo Isidoro of Grêmio for Serginho. Hansen recalled the striker in his 1999 autobiography *A Matter of Opinion*, 'To me, the most extraordinary aspect of that Brazil team was that they played with virtually ten men,' he wrote. 'I say that because they had a centre-forward, Serginho, who was the most uncharacteristic Brazilian footballer I have ever seen. He appeared quite clumsy; compared to all the others he looked hopeless. Yet Brazil were still able to string countless passes together and force us to do a lot of chasing after the ball in the searing heat. That night Seville was like an oven and what Brazil did to us can be summed up by one word: "Torture."'

With three minutes remaining Falcão completed the scoring as he arrived to meet a cushioned pass from Sócrates around 20 yards out and hit a shot in off the post. Jim Leighton watched the match from the stand. 'It wasn't until the Brazil game that I woke up to the realisation that I was in a squad playing for the World Cup,' Leighton would later tell Alastair MacDonald in the *Press and Journal*. 'Up to then, I think everything was so new and there was so much to take in that I forgot about the World Cup. The tremendous atmosphere brought it all home to me. I have never experienced anything like that atmosphere and it's an occasion I shall never forget.' In his autobiography, Leighton elaborated, 'It was sometimes difficult to concentrate on the play. You could not hear yourself speak because of the throbbing samba drums that seemed to set the rhythm for our opponents and it was like being in the middle of a huge party. Brazil's fans sang and danced around me as they celebrated each of their team's goals, and you had to smile at their uninhibited joy. I felt I needed a souvenir of the occasion and I exchanged jerseys with Brazil's third goalkeeper [Carlos of Ponte Preta] after the game.'

* * *

Dejected as they were, the Scots fans still cheered the Brazilian side off the pitch. Scotland had lived with the World Cup favourites for 45 minutes but they had been outclassed individually and collectively. 'They have another degree of class. They come from a world we don't understand,' said Jimmy Hill.

'It was funny at the final whistle,' Wark recounted. 'Souness, Hansen and Dalglish all made a beeline for Zico to get his jersey – it was the closest Hansen got to him all day – but he walked past them all and pointed to me. You should have seen their faces when I walked into the dressing room wearing the Brazil number ten shirt.' Wark revealed that the reason Zico wanted to change with him was that he collected number ten shirts.

In the dressing room, the players sat in silence. Although the disappointment was palpable, the real reason they were lost for words was that after chasing the Brazilians in the stifling heat the energy had been sapped from them. Brazil made Scotland work harder without the ball than the Scots did in other matches with it. As they attempted to normalise their breathing the click-clack of studs could be heard from the corridor. 'The dressing room door opened,' recalled Gordon Strachan, 'and it was Alan Rough. Still clearly finding it difficult to get his head around the way that Éder had chipped the ball over him from the edge of the penalty area for the third Brazil goal, he said, "That chip – does anyone here think that he was going to do that?" At that, everybody just burst out laughing.'

'I can still remember the feeling of admiration of how Brazil played in the second half,' David Begg said to me in 2022. 'They were just a different class. The Éder chip, that was just amazing. Roughie just standing watching. You could only admire what they were doing.'

That the 1982 vintage of Brazilian players were technically gifted is well documented, but what surprised those who met them in close quarters was their strength and physicality. 'I thought I was pretty strong,' Strachan said, 'and I'm eyeing up wee Júnior for a challenge, maybe knock him over when I'm taking the ball off him, and bang, I went down like a cartoon character, I just crumpled.' It was also apparent from the terracing as Iain McAuley attested, 'What struck me that day was how dirty the Brazilians were. Brazil were like the gods of football for every one of us especially since 1970. I remember watching them in Seville thinking, "You dirty bastards." They really were strong on defence. I'm watching it, going, "That's not what I thought Brazil were." I thought they were all skilful. On the telly you see Brazil scoring goals, scoring absolute peaches, but you don't see all the pushing and shoving that went on off the ball that you could see from behind the goals.'

Willie Miller was selected for the random drug test, while Sócrates was the Brazilian representative. 'To help me along I asked for a Diet Coke,' Miller said, 'and Sócrates requested a couple of bottles of beer and 20 cigarettes.' In Andrew Downie's book *Doctor Sócrates: Footballer, Philosopher, Legend*, the Brazilian captain recalled the event, 'When the guy opened the fridge I tried to hide my smile. It was filled with all kinds of drinks. It was beautiful! I was drinking my second can of beer when I realised that the others had already completed their mission. And I didn't feel at all ready. To be honest, I didn't want it to end. I drank all the beer they had and then I moved on to champagne. And still nothing. Wine, nothing. Soft drinks, nothing. It was only almost three hours later that they got their sample. When I left the stadium the rest of the team had already gone but I was the happiest of men. It was one of the best days of my life.'

This wasn't just another football match, this was an occasion. It would be a defining moment in the lives of many Scottish football fans.

'It was in Seville where suddenly football spectating came of proper civilised age,' Archie Macpherson said. 'Where we became the Tartan Army in Spain on that wonderful carnival night.'

'The atmosphere was unbelievable,' recalled David Begg. 'After the Brazil game we stayed in Seville for a couple of hours. It was a party with about half a dozen Scotsmen and we were identified as Scots. These glamorous Brazilian women all decked out in the canary yellow. It was just unbelievable in the middle of Seville. The Scots that were there they were outnumbered hugely. It was just a party, an absolute ball.'

'This game was a bit of an epiphany for me because I didn't realise football could be played to that level,' Kevin Donnelly told me. 'But it also opened my eyes to what a shower of complete and utter wankers Brazil fans are. Everyone goes, "Oh, sexy samba soccer. We were sambaing with the Brazilians." No, I wasn't. When the fourth goal went in I was getting hit on the back by them saying, "Hey, this is how you play football." So that started a lifelong intense dislike of Brazilian fans.' Despite that, Kevin was still keen to obtain a souvenir of the night, 'After the game

I got a top which I still have from a Brazilian fan; I swapped a Scotland away top and a Travel Club kipper tie. I think it was the kipper tie that swung the deal.'

Stuart Russell and his dad Frank, sat behind the Brazilian fans and their samba drums, took the one opportunity they had to noise them up. Stuart said, 'When Dave Narey scored, my dad's rubbing their heads. Then they scored four past us and they returned the gesture, put it that way. So I think we just made them angry. I hadn't heard about this toe-poke comment until I got back. It was an amazing night really. Just a big party. Disappointing result, but hey-ho we're Scottish fans you know.'

The night also left a lasting impression on Patrick Barclay. He reflected, 'It's still a tournament we can fondly look back on. Mainly because, I would say, of the Brazil game, which is one of the greatest 24 hours I've spent around football in my life. I still love Seville because of it. The restaurant we went to after the game – I went on a holiday to Seville about two years ago and I went, "We've got to go to this restaurant, it's absolutely brilliant." I think it's seen better days now. It was called the Rio Grande, overlooking the Guadalquivir river. It wasn't that great but on that night, oh ... I was at the same table as Billy McNeill and it was just one of those nights where everybody was together and it was just a celebration of football. That's why I have such happy memories of it. I think it was a wonderful night for the Scotland fans. I don't think you'll find a single one there who was too bothered about the scoreline. It was a great game. Brazil unfurled the whole repertoire of majestic skills. Zico proving himself one of the best players even that Brazil ever produced. And of course the excitement of David Narey's goal.'

After sitting at the restaurant long into the night, Barclay made his way across the bridge to his hotel feeling a little the worse for wear. Approaching him he saw a group of fans also enjoying the occasion. He explained, 'Six of them were summed up by a bit of gingery hair and sunburn with tammies. Six of them had Scotland tops and six of them had Brazil tops. Six of them were swarthy, dark-eyed, skin took a good tan.' As the group got closer, Barclay began to sense something a little unusual, 'I realised that the swarthy ones with the dark eyes and the Scotland strips and the tammies were Brazilians and the ones with the freckles were wearing the Brazil tops. They had swapped their clothes. That was typical. And I promise you that's true. That was typical of the Scots, they had swapped their songs and they had swapped their friendship and swapped everything else. God knows whether those lads got home with Brazil strips on days later. To me, that just summed it up, the camaraderie and the love of football. It was as pure a football night as I've ever known in my life.'

Not all the Scottish support had as easy a journey home that night as simply walking over the other side of the bridge. 'The trip going there was okay,' said Kevin Donnelly, 'but the trip back was one of the worst trips of my life. A complete nightmare. It took forever.'

Of the journey through the mountain roads, Chic Brogan recalled, 'Coming back, all the wee old women in every village are sitting out with the flags and the bus is missing them by inches. It's roads that are made for horses and carts and the buses weren't even slowing down. Just zooming by. If you slowed down they tried to grab your scarf. Sometimes you just gave them it; if it was a young boy you'd give him your flag or something.'

'The journey home was a bit of an adventure,' said Bobby Jamieson. 'Driving at night over dodgy mountain roads, we managed to get lost. We found ourselves in a remote mountain village and stopped at the local bodega, which looked like a scene from a spaghetti western. Lanterns, corrugated metal roof, horse trough, the lot. We went inside to ask directions to Marbella, but had nae chance. We didn't speak Spanish, they didn't speak English. I offered to buy everyone in the house a drink, and that cut the ice. Soon we were being serenaded by the locals with a guitar, castanets and a tambourine. We reciprocated with a few Scottish songs. The place came alive. We were in full battledress, they were in standard issue black trousers and white shirts. Through a comical cocktail of mime and pidgin Spanish, we managed to get what we wanted and soon we were on our way, but not before we had given our new friends a chorus of "Viva España". I often wonder what they thought about that impromptu visit after we had disappeared into the night.'

The win for Brazil meant that Russia knew going into their game with New Zealand that a 2-0 win then a draw with Scotland would take them through. 'Scotland have missed the bus,' Telê Santana said afterwards. 'They and Russia are good teams. But Scotland lost more goals against us – and that could be crucial in the eventual qualification. We were very concerned in the first half because the Scots played well and caused us problems. But Zico's goal was the turning point of the game for us. It may be the most important goal we will score in this tournament.'

'It is never easy to face defeat,' said Jock Stein, 'but there is no disgrace when you lose to a team like Brazil. They played magnificently in the second half. Until half-time we had as much of the game as Brazil but after we lost that second goal it was impossible to come back. Brazil are a great team and I think they will win the tournament.' Stein was now concerned about lifting his players before the match he always said was the big one, 'The players were very satisfied with the first half; a wee bit disappointed with the first two goals. Some of the players felt they could have been averted. But they're great players and their finishing was clinical and to be beaten by what I think'll be the world champions after giving them such a great first half ... it left a wee bit of joy with us anyway.'

There were some comforting words for the Scots in the face of their loss from Hugh McIlvaney. He wrote, 'The hurt [Scotland] feel over the four goals dazzlingly inflicted on them by Brazil should be no more tinged with shame than the sense of inadequacy experienced by every golfer who has been buried under a flood of birdies from Jack Nicklaus, every fighter overwhelmed by Sugar Ray Robinson or all the [Formula 1] grand prix drivers who have ever had Juan Fangio's exhaust fumes blowing in their faces. When you lose to the best, self-recrimination is a graceless irrelevance.'

In the Sunday newspapers back home, ex-pros had their say and, in some cases, it wasn't pretty. 'How Asa Hartford ever gets picked I'll never know,' Jim Baxter said. 'He can't shoot, he can't pass the ball well and he can't win tackles. All he can do is run and most of the time that's just a waste of energy in his case. Graeme Souness would stop posing and start showing us he's as good as he's supposed to be.' Ex-Aberdeen man Joe Harper was also critical of the Liverpool captain, 'I've been disappointed in Graeme Souness. He likes a big stage and there isn't any bigger than the World Cup but he has not shown the class expected of him and against the Brazilians, he threw too many long balls forward to Steve Archibald when he was surrounded by three men.' Souness wasn't the only Liverpool player who former Everton striker Harper found fault with. He added, 'Alan Hansen has had too many chances. He's too casual – he seems to think he's a Brazilian, and he's not. I would go back to the Miller-McLeish combination in defence.' But one former player protected rather than criticised the man in his old position. Ronnie Simpson, who won four caps for Scotland in 1967 and 1968, said, 'Don't blame Alan Rough for any of the goals – he couldn't do anything about them. He really didn't have any saves to make or crosses to cut out, yet the ball went past him four times. He had no chance of getting to them. The free kick from Zico couldn't have been placed more accurately. I think he did the right thing at the third goal. Any goalkeeper in Britain would have done the same – advance on Éder and try to cut down his shooting space. But what can you do about a player who hits such precision chips?'

Perhaps the most insightful commentary from outside the camp came from Alex Ferguson. He pinpointed Cerezo as the Brazilian who made the real difference, 'He made some incredibly long runs which simply tore the guts out of our defence. There was not a single Scottish player who could match them in physique.' Ferguson also singled out Sócrates, 'He played in at least six different positions for spells of five minutes each. He played wide on the right, next he was drifting about on the left. Then he would drop back into midfield. It was a performance which marked him as one of the all-time greats along with Pelé and Rivellino.' Ferguson also disagreed with Stein's substitution of Strachan for Dalglish, insisting that Paul Sturrock would have been the better option. Like other observers, he also thought Souness was far from the finished article, 'He had the ball a lot, but when the Brazilians got it they went past him and they presented most problems from midfield.'

All the Scottish players who have commented were of the same opinion that the Brazilian side was probably the greatest team they've played against. 'I have always considered myself a good professional and a winner but even through the disappointment of defeat, I could see that this game was a great and memorable experience,' Graeme Souness would say, while Hansen wrote, 'I felt privileged to have been on the same pitch.'

Looking back on the game with the distance of years, both Strachan and McLeish have an interesting take on the Scottish mentality. 'We were playing a side of many gifts,' McLeish said to the *Daily Record* in 2010. 'Under those circumstances, we suffer from wee nation syndrome. We don't have the level of confidence that England might have when they're being similarly tested.' Strachan wrote, 'I was left with one outstanding impression of that match with Brazil. It was always the fact that, while we in this country play from fear, always looking to the dugout and wondering what criticism is going to come next, those South Americans get on with their game and play from joy.' It's hard to offer an argument to the contrary, and even the cavalier Scotland sides of days gone by have fallen foul of critics and bad fortune alike. Comedian Andy Cameron, however, put forward an alternative view, 'We're a wee nation but we'll take on the world, you know? There's something in your psyche that just says we're not giving up. We'll go and try. Invariably it doesn't work out.'

Narey's goal would go down in Scottish folklore, just like Archie Gemmill's against the Dutch four years earlier. Narey himself was typically modest when reminded about it by Bill McFarlane of the *Sunday Post* in 1987. 'My wife taped the game at the time,' Narey said. 'However, I haven't seen the replay for some time. I'm sure I must have taped over it.'

11

The Collision: USSR

'In the past, Scottish footballers,
especially those who have reached the
World Cup finals, have courted disaster
with enough enthusiasm to make the
behaviour of Evel Knievel look like a model
of belt-and-braces caution.'

Hugh McIlvanney

DESPITE ACCEPTING that a win was never likely, there was some fallout in the Scottish camp over the defeat to Brazil. Rough's positioning for that Zico free kick came under scrutiny. In training, it had been decided he should stand to the left and leave the rest of the goal to the defensive wall. He didn't do so, and now Jock Stein was seriously considering dropping him for the game against Russia. In his autobiography, Jim Leighton wrote about how close he came to making his international debut, 'Stein was not happy at all with Alan Rough's display against Brazil and wasted no time in conveying his feelings to his assistant Jim McLean. He told the Tannadice boss that Rough would not play again for Scotland as long as he was manager. Stein said that, despite my inexperience, I would be promoted above both Rough and Wood and play in our last group tie against Russia.'

Jim McLean talked Stein out of dropping Rough, arguing that it would be unfair on Leighton to make his Scotland debut in such a crucial match. 'I would have loved to have played in that tie, of course, but I think McLean was right. Facing Russia in such a vital encounter could have killed off my international career before it had even started,' said Leighton.

As expected, this was a must-win match. The Soviet Union had beaten New Zealand 3-0 with goals from Spartak Moscow's Yuri Gavrilov, and Dynamo Kyiv pair Oleg Blokhin and Sergei Baltacha. That gave the Russians a goal difference of plus two having scored four and conceded two, while Scotland had scored six and conceded the same number. A draw would be enough to see Russia progress on goal difference. 'In the early stages of the match they looked a bit apprehensive and beatable,' Stein said. 'Although they settled down once they had scored. It's a cup final and we'll have to treat it as such. We will have to be at our best to get a result but if we are we could make it.'

Beskov was content but not thrilled at his side's results so far. 'It is good when we win, but I am not satisfied with our form,' he said. 'We must play better against Scotland.' Needing only a point would seemingly be the more favourable situation to be in, but Stein wasn't so sure. He felt that wouldn't have suited Scotland's make-up. 'We have to go out and win the match and that suits our natural style,' he said to Jim Reynolds of the *Glasgow Herald*. He went on to make a statement that would become somewhat prescient, 'If we had only to draw we could have gone out with a defensive setup and tossed it away, for history proves that nobody beats us better than ourselves.'

The need for a win would influence Stein's team selection. He would go back to playing two up front, but Alan Brazil was still suffering from his experience in the sun against New Zealand, while Stein hinted that Kenny Dalglish and Danny McGrain might be left out. The manager said, 'Study Russia's record and it's obvious they must be favourites when they play us. So it is important to go for men in form. Reputations are not important. It's no sin nor a crime if a player's touch has gone or his confidence is wavering. It happens to everyone at some stage because of one thing or another. But we have players here who have come a long way and they are entitled to a game if they are in touch at the moment.'

Despite players like Blokhin and Shengelia, Stein felt one of Russia's biggest threats would come from Anatoliy Demyanenko. Playing on the left flank, Demyanenko began his career at hometown club Dnipro Dnipropetrovsk before joining Dynamo Kyiv, where he had won league titles in 1980 and 1981. Stein said, 'He could be a real danger man with the way he surges forward and causes all sorts of problems, but I would think the Russians are just as concerned about some of my players.' None of the Russian squad had played in a World Cup finals before. It was the nation's first appearance in the tournament since 1970 when they topped their group on goal difference ahead of hosts Mexico. They would lose to Uruguay in the quarter-finals thanks to a goal three minutes from the end of extra time. In qualifying for the 1982 World Cup, Russia topped UEFA Group Three, winning six of their eight games and drawing the other two. In a group containing fellow qualifiers Czechoslovakia, along with Wales, Iceland and Turkey, they had scored 20 goals and conceded only two. Blokhin was their top scorer with five.

Born in Moscow in 1920, as a player the Russian manager Konstantin Beskov was an intelligent forward, beginning his career at 16 with FC Serp i Molot Moscow, who would then become Metallurg Moscow. In 1940 he was drafted for the Red Army, where he was assigned to a special motor brigade in Moscow. In 1941 he signed for Dynamo Moscow, but it would be after the war's end in 1945 before he began training with them. He was part of the team that toured Great Britain in the autumn of that year. They drew 3-3 with Chelsea, hammered Cardiff 10-1, and in thick fog defeated Arsenal 4-3.

The system Dynamo used would beguile fans, media and opposition alike. Their short passing style – *passovotchka* – was combined with players interchanging positions throughout the game. Beskov himself started in the centre-forward position in a 3-2-2-3, or W-M formation, but drifted back to create a 3-2-3-2 system. The final match of their tour was on 28 November against Rangers at Ibrox. The Corporation of Glasgow laid on an extensive tour for Beskov and his team-mates. They sailed down the Clyde before visiting Glasgow University, Jordanhill Training College, the Mitchell Library and Kelvingrove Art Galleries. A crowd of 90,000 turned up to see the friendly match. The Russians went into a two-goal lead early on, but, despite missing a penalty, Rangers came back into the game to secure a 2-2 draw.

Beskov represented the Soviet Union at the 1952 Olympics in Finland, where he played twice, both games being against Yugoslavia in the competition's first round. The Tito-Stalin split, resulting in Yugoslavia's expulsion from the Communist Information Bureau in 1948, meant that the contest between the two nations was politically sensitive. Both Josip Broz Tito and Joseph Stalin sent telegrams to their respective teams ahead of the game. The first meeting saw the Soviets amazingly come back from 5-1 down to draw 5-5. In the replay, Yugoslavia won 3-1. The result was kept secret by the regime in Moscow until after Stalin's death a year later. They were the only two games where Beskov would represent his country.

Beskov played with Dynamo until 1954 before going into management in 1956, beginning his career with Torpedo Moscow. In 1960 he took over at CSKA Moscow, with whom he finished fourth in the championship of the USSR twice. His first spell in charge of the national team was in 1963. He took the Soviets to the final of the 1964 European Championship where he claimed he was using a 4-2-4 system, based on Brazilian tactics, although in Jonathan Wilson's book, *Inverting the Pyramid*, Wilson notes that, despite this insistence, Beskov had actually reverted to a W-M formation. He did retain the passing, collective style Soviet teams were known for, but also encouraged individual talent in order to build attacks. They reached the final where they played hosts Spain, losing a tight match 2-1. Once again the game was a political hot potato, and a defeat to General Franco's Spain was seen as a disgrace which led to Beskov's dismissal.

After a brief spell in charge of Lokomotiv, he returned to Dynamo in 1967. Here, he renewed acquaintances with

Rangers as Dynamo became the first Soviet side to reach a European final when in 1972 they took on the Ibrox side in Barcelona in the European Cup Winners' Cup Final. Beskov would receive some criticism by changing Dynamo's usual attacking style into a defensive one for the match. Rangers went into a three-goal lead by early in the second half, forcing Beskov to return to an attacking approach. The Soviets pulled two goals back but couldn't get the equaliser. His second term in charge of the national team began in 1974, but after a shock 3-0 defeat by the Republic of Ireland in October of that year he was dismissed once again. In 1977 he became manager of Spartak Moscow, and he would take them to the Soviet Top League title in 1979. It was in that year he once again took over as boss of the Soviet football team, alongside his club role, taking over from Nikita Simonyan. Beskov guided the national team to the bronze medal in the 1980 Moscow Olympics, although they finished bottom of their qualifying group for the 1980 European Championship.

In Spain, the behaviour of the Scots fans was continuing to delight the officials, with Ernie Walker saying, 'They are simply marvellous. They are singing and dancing and having a good time which is what it should be all about. We've never been in trouble before abroad as a national support and I only hope it stays that way.' With tongues firmly in cheeks, the Scottish support was now referring to themselves as 'Ernie's Angels'. 'That whole tournament we saw very little trouble,' Chic Brogan said. 'We saw one guy getting a doing, in Malaga. The polis are leathering him with their batons. We're like, "Oh, wait a minute here." The guy says, "It's a pickpocket." Okay, wire in. We were all warned about pickpockets. That's how when you've got your kilt on the sporran's great. You've got nothing else, just your sporran.'

The fans had one illustrious guest with them, St Etienne winger Johnny Rep, who had scored against Scotland in the 1978 World Cup for Holland. 'These supporters can win you the game,' he told the *Record*. 'When I hear them the hairs stand up on the back of my neck. They must be the best in the world. It makes me want to finish my playing career back in Britain.' Rep was hopeful that Scotland could get past Russia, 'But Scotland will have to play with the passion they showed against us in Mendoza four years ago. If they are like that then they can go through. Of course, Jock Stein has to pick the right team, one which will approach the game with the fire they showed in the first match. I hope Alan Brazil will be able to play for you. He is an exciting talent just as Strachan is. Your team has been steadily building towards a climax and this is it.'

Rep had enjoyed his time on the terracing with the Scots supporters, 'It was an incredible night to be in Seville with these Scottish fans. They never gave up for a moment supporting their own team and they cheered the Brazilians when they saw how well they were playing. It was a carnival night. I'm going with them again to the Russian match. They can help you. Let's remember there will be 20,000 Scots and about 12 Russians who will be at the match.'

Whatever the result of the final match, the fans were intent on making the most of their stay in Spain, although for Stuart Russell it was a working trip, 'My dad, myself and my big cousin Robert would be waiting for the papers in the morning at the airport then we'd go round all the vendors in Malaga, Torremolinos, Benalmádena, Marbella. All the vendors were there on time. All really professional, and I think they all got a really good turn out of it too.' One of their customers was Kevin Donnelly. 'The *Daily Record* was shipping in papers,' Kevin said to me, 'you could actually buy a *Daily Record* on the day. You're sitting around the pool and you're looking at the TV section and you're thinking, "Oh, that looks quite interesting." Then you suddenly realise you're in bloody Spain and you're never going to see it.'

After going around the vendors, Stuart and his father Frank would take the papers to the team hotel. Stuart said, 'My dad knew a few of the players and there were a few occasions we sat and had breakfast with them. I'm 15 at this time. I knew my dad played football but I didn't know he knew these people. He'd played with Kenny Dalglish at Cumbernauld. "Awright Kenny." "Aw, how you doing Frank?" I was gobsmacked. "You actually know this guy?" They're having a wee conversation. It was some experience. Our trip was more or less paid for and to be fair to my dad he liked a good bevvy but in that two-week cycle he was doing his paper run he never touched it.'

Iain McAuley was also awestruck to meet a Scottish football great, 'We met Billy McNeill and his family in Torremolinos. That was amazing because he was a total gentleman. I was 19 years old and played junior football at the time. I remember him taking me aside and taking an interest in who I was playing for.' However, the Celtic manager wasn't the only celebrity Iain bumped into. He continued, 'With the hotel we went to these baby bull fights up in the mountains. So you get a bus trip up to the mountains. [*Gregory's Girl* actress] Dee Hepburn was there with her boyfriend who was from England. He wasn't keen on us cos we kept calling him Gregory. We kept saying to her, "Why are you going out with an English guy? You'd be better with a Scottish guy."'

The trip wasn't the only activity Iain's hotel laid on, as he explained, 'They had a drinking wine competition out of a tube, which was like a bull's bawsack. They fill it full of wine and they get people from each nationality right in the middle of the wee baby bull ring. We had this guy called Bucket, who was like 28 and me being 19 he was really old, but Bucket could drink like a fish. Bucket won every round of the drinking wine competition. It was just like pouring it down the sink, down his throat. The Dutch and the Germans are going, "How does he do it?" We're like, "Well, he's called Bucket."' The trip also offered a chance for new experiences. 'In the hotel pool, we had a water polo competition. We'd never played water polo in our lives. We're from an estate in Dunfermline. You don't play water polo in Dunfermline. Here we are taking on semi-professionals,' said McAuley.

Brian Doran's masterplan to buy and sell World Cup tickets hadn't worked out as well as he had initially anticipated. He couldn't sell them to Scots fans in any kind of number. On the night of the Brazil game, he was arrested outside the gates of the Benito Villamarín Stadium, accused of touting tickets, and spent a night in the cells. Glasgow lawyer Len Murray said, 'No charges have been brought. The whole affair has been closed.' Local police said that Doran, Robert Torrance and Steven Roche had nearly 800 tickets and over £1,300 in Spanish money on them when arrested outside the stadium before the match. On the Monday after the game, Doran told the *Evening Times*, 'We were simply distributing tickets to our clients, some of whom had flown in that day from other parts of

Spain. Suddenly we were surrounded by police and taken to headquarters. There, the police officer in charge told me that hundreds of people were outside still looking for tickets. He suggested I go out and start selling my tickets. We went back with two policemen to sell the tickets, but the crowd became a bit rough and the policemen took us back to headquarters. Then the police chief came in and said, "Put them in jail."' Doran faced drugs charges back home, accused of supplying cocaine in Glasgow. He decided to remain in Spain after the tournament.

Ticket sales were still a matter of concern overall in Spain. Juan Garcia, the Costa del Sol delegate for Mundiespana, spoke to the *Evening Times*, 'I am very disappointed the way things have gone, and I have told Mundiespana I will not be going to Barcelona for the second phase.' Garcia was furious at the ticket distribution which contributed to empty terraces in Malaga. The original plan to only sell tickets within package holiday deals failed, 'They only sold about 1,200 holidays, and quite frankly it's still a big mystery to me what has happened to the ticket distribution. Mundiespana must have lost a lot of money because if they don't sell a package then there is no real profit for them. And Sportsworld could not have made very much money either, even though they made an agreement to start selling tickets off without the holidays. They were making no profit on the tickets.' Garcia was also annoyed that many Scots fans had made self-catering arrangements when they could have been in the many Spanish hotel rooms lying empty due to Mundiespana taking over a huge number of rooms then hiking up the prices. 'This is not the way we normally work,' Garcia said, 'and what has happened in the World Cup is totally against our normal policy in tourism on the Costa del Sol.'

The New Zealand management were united on the outcome of who would join Brazil in the second phase. 'I think the Scots will lose,' assistant boss Kevin Fallon said. 'The Russians are mechanical, but they are great athletes who can run at you all day. They do not have the flair of the Scottish team. Players like Strachan and Souness have more variety about their play, but the Russian team is so technically composed that they will sit on the Scottish lads, especially Souness.'

Manager John Adshead didn't hold out much hope that Scotland could get the win required, 'Principally because I am British I would have loved to do Scotland a favour by getting a goal or two that would let Jock Stein prepare for the match knowing that a draw would do the Scots. But in all honesty, I've got to go for Russia, because I believe that they are going to pose the same problems for Scotland's defence as they did for ours on Saturday.' Those problems were primarily the pace of Oleg Blokhin and Ramaz Shengelia. 'They will go out for a point and I think rely on Blokhin, who could catch the Scots out at the back, to get a goal,' said Adshead.

Blokhin had been golden boy of Soviet football for several years. First breaking into the Dynamo Kyiv team in 1972, he finished the season as the top scorer in the league as Kyiv claimed second place. They won the title in 1974, thanks in no small part to Blokhin's 20 goals. He would really arrive in 1975 as he won the Ballon D'Or, polling 122 points, with all 26 voters placing him – 20 in first place. Blokhin was then 23 years old. His Dynamo Kyiv team had won the Russian league and on 14 May 1975 beat Ferencváros of Hungary 3-0 to lift the European Cup Winners' Cup in Basel, becoming the first Russian team to win a European trophy. In the autumn, Kyiv went on to beat Bayern Munich 3-0 on aggregate to win the European Super Cup with Blokhin scoring all the goals. It was also a year when he was Soviet footballer of the year for the third year in a row and the Russian league's top scorer for the fourth year in a row.

The following year he won an Olympic bronze medal as the Soviet Union team beat Brazil 2-0 in Montreal. Blokhin had also won bronze in 1972 at the Munich Olympics. He added more Soviet titles in 1977, 1980 and 1981, and played in the 1977 European Cup semi-final as Kyiv narrowly lost to Borussia Monchengladbach. In 1981 he finished fifth in the Ballon D'Or.

Earlier in 1982, Blokhin's threat to Aston Villa in the European Cup was nullified by a Scot. Under-21 international Andy Blair was the man selected to mark him in Villa's quarter-final first leg in Kyiv. 'What I remember most is the excitement of playing in such an important game, knowing I was going to be pitting my wits against a man who was, at the time, one of the best players in Europe,' Blair told Aston Villa's website in 2012. 'I was absolutely thrilled about the chance of playing against Blokhin. He was an absolutely superb player and it was great for me to be part of the team who drew 0-0 in such a difficult game. That result was vital because it meant we started level in the home leg. Although I was in midfield, I played more as a right-back that day because Blokhin was such an effective player. We set our team pattern out according to the opposition and my job was to make sure he didn't score or create too many chances. He hit the post early on but apart from that I kept him pretty quiet and I felt I played my part in the team plan. I kept talking to Blokhin to put him off his game. I'm sure he didn't understand a word I was saying. Most of it was accompanied by the word "off".'

* * *

As Prince William was born to Princess Diana and Prince Charles in London, Jock Stein finalised his team selection with only one change from the Brazil game. Asa Hartford was out and Joe Jordan was in, shifting the formation from 4-4-2 to 4-4-3. 'Now [Stein] didn't tell me about his plans for me in Spain,' Jordan said to Archie Macpherson. 'Not once. But I think he was waiting for the last game. I would go back in the afternoons for special striker sessions with the coaches, like shooting, movement in the box, all that stuff which I had never done in any national squad before. I kept telling myself, he's not going to all that bother just for me to come here to make up the numbers. I felt I would get a chance in the last game, and I was right.'

Born in Clelland in December 1951, Jordan started out his playing days at Clelland Boys Guild. Playing with North Motherwell Amateurs at inside-left, he had trials at West Bromwich Albion. He joined Blantyre Vics as a 16-year-old; however, the officials there had reservations about him as being too small. After only two games in junior football he was off to Morton in November 1968. In the summer of 1969, Bobby Collins, a Scotland international and formerly of Celtic and Leeds, joined Morton. 'He was held in high esteem by everyone because he'd made his mark in Scottish football history,' Jordan told mightyleeds.co.uk. 'When he arrived at Morton, Bobby was the elder statesman of the team and it was a privilege to play with him.' Although Joe was at Cappielow for two years, he had only played eight league games when Leeds came in for him. Collins had tipped off Leeds boss Don Revie. 'Revie was still in awe of his instincts for the game,' Jordan said. 'Collins was living with his parents in Glasgow and travelling back to see his family in Leeds whenever he could. From time to time he trained with his old team-mates and one morning Revie asked him if he had seen any likely lads north of the border.'

'It was clear to me he had tremendous potential. I didn't think twice about letting Leeds know about him,' Collins said in 1974. 'He's fantastic in the air – the best header of a ball I've seen in a long time.' Revie paid Morton £15,000 and Jordan was away. At Leeds, his career really got going. He made his debut in March 1971 as a substitute in an Inter-Cities Fairs Cup quarter-final first leg with Vitória Setubal. He played 33 league games in the 1973/74 season as Leeds won the First Division. At Leeds, Jordan played and lost in two European finals: the 1973 European Cup Winners' Cup Final against AC Milan and the 1975 European Cup Final against Bayern Munich. 'Joe was one of the best signings I ever made,' Revie said in 1977.

Jordan's Scotland debut came in May 1973 in front of 95,950 at Wembley as a 70th-minute substitute for Lou Macari. A Martin Peters goal gave England a 1-0 win. His first start came in his third cap, against Brazil at Hampden in June 1973. Jordan won an under-23 cap in the second leg of a European Championship play-off against Holland in March 1976. That night, 32,523 fans at Easter Road saw Scotland come back from a 2-0 first-leg defeat to win 2-0 on the night. Jordan was one of the two players to miss in the penalty shoot-out as Holland won 4-3. Willie Miller and Frank Gray scored. 'Strong in the air and his style will upset a lot of defenders,' former Liverpool, Coventry and Nottingham Forest centre-back Larry Lloyd said. 'I've had many a running battle with Joe. If you hit him hard he just turns around and smiles – then hits you even harder. When you face Joe you expect a scrap.' In early 1978 Jordan made the move to Manchester United. 'I really feel ten feet tall when playing for Scotland,' Jordan said in 1977, 'and I just cannot understand those players who, over some grievance or other, say they are no longer interested in playing for their country. In my opinion, they're just plain daft. Pulling that dark blue jersey over my head is still for me, the biggest thrill in football.'

'So far in this competition, the Russians haven't been tested at the back,' Jock Stein said, 'and we want to put pressure on them there. If we play to our form then we can do it.' Stein wanted to see how Alan Brazil was recovering, but he ultimately felt the Ipswich striker wasn't ready for a starting place. 'This is a match which requires players to be 100 per cent fit for 90 minutes and that is paramount in my decision,' he added. Kenny Dalglish being omitted from the side entirely made ripples among the media. 'When I was left out the papers printed the usual rubbish,' Dalglish wrote in his 1997 book, 'this time alleging that I stormed out of the dressing room. That was nonsense. I left Scotland's dressing room to hand the players' tickets to their guests. I was going off on errands for the team, not in a huff. I went back to the dressing room to help the players change their studs. There was no demonstrations of anger. I never let it show, but inwardly I was disappointed, not just because Jock had dropped me but because of the manner in which he did it. It would have been courteous for him to have explained why he was dropping me. Some people thought it was the end of my Scotland career but I never did. I was hardly in decline.'

'Jock was the manager and he made the decisions,' Dalglish said to the *Sunday Times* in 1999. 'He had made enough decisions that were beneficial to Kenny Dalglish for me to know he did what he felt was best for the team. I had a lot to thank him for. He never gave me a reason, but then he never gave me a reason when he picked me for my Old Firm debut at Ibrox either.'

At the Soviets' press conference in the Atalya Park Hotel, Beskov was giving nothing away on his team selection. 'It is not a secret, but we have a habit of deciding on the day of the game,' he said. The Scots were an example of 'the British game', Beskov felt. 'The Scots have qualified for almost all post-war World Cup finals,' he said, not entirely accurately, 'and that is evidence they are a great football power.' He anticipated a physical, but not dirty, Scots side, claiming, 'A combination of technique and strategy will count. I think it will be a sporting encounter.' The Scottish journalists asked the Spartak Moscow manager if the noise of the travelling fans in the ground would put his players off. 'This is football,' Beskov said, 'every team has to play away from home and players of international sides should not be affected by the noise of the crowd.'

The journalists speaking to Stein wanted to know how he would approach the game. 'Of course, we must take the initiative,' Stein said, 'but be sensible about it. Can we afford to gamble everything on, say 20 minutes of all-out aggression? I don't think so, for it could all be thrown away with those tactics. A goal in the first minute is no more valuable than a goal in the final minute, provided it's the only one of the game. Of course, we would love that kind of a start, but it is more important we give a controlled performance.' Stein finished by saying his team wouldn't be worrying too much about the Soviets, 'Let them worry about our good players.'

Whatever happened at the end of 90 minutes, Stein had the backing of the SFA. President Willie Harkness said, 'Jock Stein lifted us from the ashes of Argentina when we were at our lowest-ever ebb. The fact that he rebuilt a side to take us through to the World Cup finals is an achievement in itself. I'm hopeful he can take us even further tomorrow, and that will be no more than he deserves. I would love to see Jock become the first man to take us through to the later stages of the competition. When the SFA appointed him we were convinced he was the right man for the job, and since then he has proved us right. Obviously, we were unhappy to lose by as much as 4-1 to Brazil, but our section is the toughest of the lot. I still feel we can win against the Russians. It's the kind of do-or-die situation our team likes. Jock Stein's side will be the right one for the occasion and my colleagues and myself are completely behind him.'

In addition to the talent the Russians had in midfield and up front, Stein was aware that one of their most gifted players was the goalkeeper Rinat Dasayev. 'He is an exceptional goalkeeper, the best in the competition,' Stein said. 'We will have to be imaginative to beat him. We will not get anywhere by pumping in cross balls because that just makes his life simpler.' Beskov was also Dasayev's club manager. 'He could be as good as [Lev] Yashin,' Beskov said, referencing the Soviets' greatest-ever goalkeeper, who had won the Ballon d'Or in 1963. 'He has all the qualities of a world-class goalkeeper.' Both Yashin, who spent his whole career at Dynamo Moscow, and Dasayev were noted not just for their shot-stopping but also their abilities to begin counterattacks with their quick throws. Dasayev had just turned 25 and had started his career with his local club Astrakhan as a teenager. Like Blokhin, a part of the Olympic team that won bronze in 1980, he won the Soviet championship in 1979 and was on his way to being named the Soviet Player of the Year for 1982.

Russia's defeat to Brazil was their first loss in 20 matches going back to a 3-1 loss to West Germany in November 1979. They had always made the quarter-finals of every World Cup they qualified for.

Alongside Allan Evans, Alan Hansen was another of the Scotland squad who had come up against some of the Russians in European competition. Liverpool had gone down 4-2 on aggregate to Dinamo Tbilisi in the first round of the 1979/80 European Cup. Despite being knocked out, and the fact that Liverpool were comprehensively outclassed in the 3-0 second-leg defeat in front of 90,000 fans in the Boris Paichadze National Stadium, Hansen felt Scotland had nothing to worry about. 'In fact,' he told the *Evening Times*, 'Tbilisi's best player was the midfield man Kipiani. He was magnificent. But he didn't make the squad because of injury, which is a bit of a bonus for us.'

Kipiani's footwork turned Hansen one way and then the other as he set up the first goal for Tbilisi that day. 'Chivadze played sweeper and looked very useful, while Shengelia I remember as a very pacy, tricky forward,' said Hansen. Shengelia chipped Ray Clemence for the second after defender Giorgi Chilaya bulldozed his way up half the pitch to play him in. Aleksandr Chivadze added the third from the penalty spot. Hansen played the result down claiming Liverpool were unfortunate, having to chase an equaliser after going a goal down due to the loss of an away goal at Anfield. The truth was that Liverpool were uncharacteristically outclassed in Tbilisi, manager Bob Paisley conceding as much after the match.

Robertson was switched from the left wing to the right as Stein felt that was where the Russians were more dangerous. Beskov warned his side that the Scots were a typically British team: physical, good in the air and keen to play some long balls. He highlighted that his defenders should be cautious in maintaining their position. To nullify the Scots' strength in the air he urged his players to keep the ball on the floor.

* * *

The match was live on BBC One with STV putting up the 1977 feature film *Sinbad and the Eye of the Tiger* followed by an episode of *The Sweeney* from 1976 called 'Visiting Fireman'. The lead-in to BBC's coverage was the 18th episode of series two of *Triangle*, the drama series set on a North Sea ferry. Barry Davies would be the BBC commentator, with Jimmy Hill alongside him. Russia's side was: Rinat Dasayev (Spartak Moscow), Tengiz Sulakvelidze (Dinamo Tbilisi), Aleksandr Chivadze (captain, Dinamo Tbilisi), Anatoliy Demyanenko (Dynamo Kyiv), Sergei Baltacha (Dynamo Kyiv), Sergei Borovsky (Dinamo Minsk), Ramaz Shengelia (Dinamo Tbilisi), Vladimir Bessonov (Dynamo Kyiv), Yuri Gavrilov (Spartak Moscow), Andriy Bal (Dynamo Kyiv), Oleg Blokhin (Dynamo Kyiv). It was a young Russian side with an average age of 25, Blokhin the elder statesman at 29 years and seven months. Scotland lined up as: Alan Rough, Willie Miller, David Narey, Alan Hansen, Frank Gray, Gordon Strachan, Graeme Souness (captain), John Wark, Steve Archibald, Joe Jordan, John Robertson.

Out on the pitch, Souness cracked a smile as the TV cameras passed him while the team stood as 'Scotland the Brave' played. Scotland kicked off and were on the attack from the beginning as Frank Gray marauded down the wing. Strachan showed his composure by deftly back-flicking the ball to a team-mate in the centre of the pitch. John Robertson won a corner as Scotland made their intentions to nab an early goal clear, but the first setback wasn't slow in coming. Souness found himself receiving a caution with only five minutes played, for nothing more than giving Romanian referee Nicolae Rainea some backchat after Jordan had been fouled. Rainea had officiated Souness and Hansen previously, taking charge of Liverpool's European Super Cup second leg with Anderlecht in 1978. Controversially, he allowed that game to go ahead despite Anfield being consumed by thick fog. Rainea also took charge of the 1980 European Championship Final between West Germany and Belgium. Rainea displayed the yellow card with a theatrical flourish. Souness, Scotland's most physical presence in the centre of the pitch, was now walking a tightrope. The booking, though, Patrick Barclay wrote, 'had the desirable effect of making football surface earlier than might have been the case'. In the *Glasgow Herald*, Jim Reynolds would refer to Rainea, who spoke Russian, as the Russians' 'strong and willing ally'. Twice, throw-ins that looked like a Scottish ball were awarded to the Soviets, as the Scots fans booed the decisions. Willie Miller was the next player to be pulled up, this time for a soft tackle. ITV Commentator John Helm remarked, 'Great concern for the Scots here that the Iron Curtain referee may just tend to favour the Russians, as he is doing here.' The Russians had been awarded five free kicks in the first eight minutes.

The first chance came in the tenth minute when Robertson fired in a cross. Jordan met it with his head, steering the ball low to Dasayev's left, which the keeper managed to tip round the post. Two minutes later Rough made a comfortable save down low from Blokhin. The Scottish fans behind Rough's goal roared. 'Two encouraging things from Scotland's point of view,' Jimmy Hill said on the BBC commentary. 'That was a first-class save from Alan Rough. He did get the right angle. It was tight but that ball was thumped really hard and he did well to get it out. But also that Joe Jordan has played a part in the game already. He's linked the line-up quite well. Not everything's gone right, but quite a few things have, and that's going to encourage him, that he's been on target with a header.'

Scotland's breakthrough in the 16th minute began with a long ball out of defence from David Narey. The Russian skipper Aleksandr Chivadze, a noted libero, tried to bring the ball down but failed to trap it. As he attempted to recover he slipped, leaving Steve Archibald the chance to nip in. Archibald knocked the ball on for Jordan to run on to and the big AC Milan striker slipped it low and left-footed past Dasayev's right hand and into the net to give Scotland an early lead. Jordan recalled the goal for BBC Scotland in 2020, 'Stevie Archibald got on to a mistake from their centre-half but I had a good 35 yards to go. I still had a decent turn of pace for a 30-year-old and although I didn't like having that much time to think, the keeper left me just enough room at the near post.' He told Macpherson, 'As soon as I got into the box, I knew exactly what I was going to do. I saw the space at the near post. Most people would think you put it across the keeper. I kept my eye on that space and I think it might have surprised the keeper because I kept it down and squeezed it in. It was a marvellous feeling.'

The Russians had a chance to equalise minutes later when Souness gave away a free kick but Blokhin fired his shot over the bar. Scotland had a shout for a penalty kick when Baltacha appeared to brush his left arm against the ball. 'That was deliberate,' Barry Davies said on reviewing the incident. 'No doubt about that. That was deliberate. And the referee missed it.' Rainea chose instead to award a corner and Jordan headed wide from Robertson's crossed ball.

From 20 yards out on the wing, Jordan floated a shot over the bar. Although Scotland had the bulk of the possession, they had to be careful of the sharp, quick breakaways the Russians were obviously capable of. On 29 minutes, as Blokhin bore down on the Scottish goal, Souness lunged in but failed to make a proper connection. Blokhin carried on his run, firing his shot diagonally across Rough's goal and past the post. 'Things just didn't click for us,' Rough wrote of the first half in his book *Rough at the Top*. 'There was a tension in the air, which had surfaced earlier and which did not dissipate, even when Joe Jordan opened the scoring. From then on we should have been masters of our own destiny, but our captain had already been booked, which restricted the level of aggression which he could display, and where we should have been fired up by taking the lead, it was as if we slunk back in our shells. This is one instance where I certainly don't take the blame for our problems, but although we quickly discovered that our opponents were no world-beaters we lacked cohesion and toiled to crank up the momentum which might have brought us a decisive second goal. We were tense, bloody tense, and the butterflies wouldn't budge.'

Strachan worked his way through the defence to fire in a cross, and only Dasayev's fingers took it away from the inrushing Wark. Archibald then hit a shot that Dasayev collected easily. Borovsky pulled down Archibald 25 yards out but Frank Gray hit the free kick straight at the keeper. Jordan turned and shot in the box, but it was saved down low by Dasayev. 'Not quite the venom in the shot he was hoping for,' remarked Barry Davies. At half-time Scotland were still in front. Russia had been awarded 14 free kicks to Scotland's six. The heat was always going to take its toll and there was a question of how long Scotland could keep their hard work going. 'Miller and Hansen outstanding in defence,' said commentator John Helm.

Scotland started the second half strongly. Early on, Archibald hit a shot which Dasayev got down to save. Next, it was Wark's turn as from the edge of the box he stung the keeper's hands with a shot. Moments later Robertson picked the pockets of the defence and fired narrowly over. Russia mounted an attack of their own as Blokhin fired a low ball across the six-yard box. Rough seemed at a loss for what to do, but the ball drifted past the danger area and out of play. Blokhin was in again moments later but Narey closed him down and forced the Soviet to fire high over the bar. Scotland chased the second goal they knew they were good for, but anxiety began to creep in and that led to some sloppy passing.

With just under an hour gone, Russia built from their own half. Gavrilov moved forward, playing into Shengelia at the edge of the box. Shengelia turned and knocked the ball sideways for Gavrilov, who had continued his run. Gavrilov touched with his left foot on to his right, then back to his left again. He shot; it was blocked on the line by

Narey, bounced off Wark and fell to Chivadze who leaned back and sent an inelegant shot into the ground. The ball bounced up and over the floored Rough into the net. 'At the interval, Jock advised us to get the basics right, and forget elaboration,' Rough wrote. 'But his message went unheeded, the malaise continued and it was symptomatic of the match that Alexandr Chivadze should level matters when he unwittingly swerved his shot past me after failing to strike it properly. One or two of our lads looked disconsolate when they should have fathomed there was ample time to retrieve the situation. It was almost as if we were preparing for the roof to cave in.'

Although perhaps his physical presence had been diluted, the early booking didn't stop Souness from dictating the play in midfield as Scotland had plenty of the ball in the centre of the pitch. At the other end, Anatoliy Demyanenko fired a shot past the post from 20 yards after being teed up by Blokhin. The FIFA official looked around for the substitute numbers board as McGrain and Brazil waited to get on. Finally, on 74 minutes, they were able to replace Strachan and Jordan.

After dropping a shoulder, Robertson crossed from the left, and the ball looped over Dasayev. Wark went up for it but Demyanenko had his right arm over him, holding him down as he attempted to rise. As Wark remonstrated to no avail with the referee, the Russians broke down the pitch. 'The referee quite unmoved, although there did look to be a push in the box,' said Barry Davies. Russia were now strolling around the pitch with the ball. 'Scotland throughout are a little short of running power at the moment,' remarked Jimmy Hill, 'and that's why they haven't got the fluidity that they had early on in the game.' Robertson flighted in a cross.

John Helm thought it was a penalty for a foul on Archibald, but the referee had actually awarded a free kick against him.

Momentum was now about to swing firmly in the Soviets' favour.

Brazil had the ball tight on the touchline down near the Russians' corner flag. McGrain came in behind him to take possession but only succeeded in knocking the ball out of play as the two bumped into each other. The resultant throw-in was played back to the thrower, who launched a long ball down the left flank. Just inside the Russian half of the field, Hansen rose to head the ball back. The Liverpool man made contact with the top of his head, not sending the ball back, but continuing it on in its journey into the Scottish half of the field. Hansen turned on his heels and gave chase as Shengelia looked to latch on to the ball, which took a bounce as Willie Miller moved towards it from his position in the centre of defence. At this point Hansen was still ahead of the Russian, and favourite to reach the ball. Hansen and Miller both seem to arrive at the same time. Hansen got his foot to the ball first, knocking it in the direction he was facing, towards the Scottish goal. As he did so the two Scots collided. Miller was knocked to the floor but Hansen kept running although he was now yards behind Shengelia. A horrified Alan Rough began to advance but had second thoughts and back-pedalled a few steps. Shengelia, now in possession, had enough time to weigh up his options. The Russian weaved to his right as Rough's upper body moved in the opposite direction. The keeper threw his left leg out as he went to ground, leaving Shengelia with an empty net to tap the ball into from 12 yards. It was now 2-1 to Russia and Scotland had yet another catastrophe to join those they had created in

Argentina four years earlier. Danny McGrain referred to it as 'a goal that would cause a fight among schoolboys on Glasgow Green'.

'What a disastrous way for it all to end,' said Davies. 'No question now that the Soviet Union will go on to Barcelona and a sad Scotland will go home.'

'It was like a pub goal,' John Wark would later say.

Brazil was penalised for a foul on the keeper as the Russians removed a bottle from their penalty area. Scotland weren't out of the match yet as Robertson knocked the ball to Souness, who drove forward and cracked a low shot from 18 yards that trundled outside of Dasayev's right hand for an equaliser. Had the goal come earlier and been more significant, the tenacity and skill Souness showed would be more fondly remembered by the Scottish support. But it was 2-2 and time was running out. 'Suddenly there is hope on the Scottish team bench,' said Davies. 'Suddenly the dream is alive again.'

Archibald burst forward as the Scots fans roared the team on, but the Spurs man was soon crowded out by three defenders. The Soviets defended desperately as Scotland fired hopeful balls into the penalty area in the last minute. Despite the referee making a show of indicating to the Russians that he would add on time for their late time wasting, there were less than 20 seconds added. 'His final act of treachery,' Reynolds wrote in his match report. In *The Guardian*, Patrick Barclay was also critical of the match official. 'An unpleasant taste was left in the mouth,' he wrote. 'Mr Rainea seemed to be adopting an admirably even-handed approach in the early stages when he strictly punished the excesses of Scotland's attempts to unsettle their opponents, but after the Scots had tempered their challenges and the whistle kept blowing – though not when Wark appealed reasonably for a penalty – another interpretation suggested itself.'

A bare-chested Souness stopped to speak with television reporters as he was leaving the pitch. 'It is a bit heartbreaking,' he said, 'not for the players, but for the supporters. Just listen to them. They've spent a lot of hard cash to come here. Disappointed for them more than anything really.' The skipper looked down at the floor despondently as he gathered his thoughts. 'I think we lost it really on the game against Brazil,' he said.

'You were in what everybody considered the most difficult group,' the interviewer said. Souness replied, 'Yeah, we came close. A small nation came close to what I regard as the best team in the world, and potentially one of the best teams; that's Russia.'

'It was a great game. A great game,' the interviewer said.

'I thought it was our night tonight at half-time,' said Souness. 'I thought we were going to go through at half-time, because really the Russians did not cause us a lot of problems, and we knew they would tire as much as we were going to tire in the second half. But they got the goals.'

'A marvellous match though.'

'It might have been a marvellous match. In a year's time, I might sit and watch it and think it was a marvellous match, but at the moment I don't think so. I am very disappointed; as I said, without sounding too corny, these are the ones we feel sorry for,' Souness said, as he pointed up to the stands.

'They've done terrifically well here,' the interviewer said of the Scots fans. 'Everyone thought that they wouldn't behave at all.'

'Yeah, they've behaved themselves,' replied Souness. 'They've been a credit to Scotland. I just hope some people at home think we have as well.'

'Russia was an anti-climax,' Chic Brogan said. 'The atmosphere had just went. It transfers on to the park and vice versa; if they give up it transfers back on to the terracing.'

'We were so shattered we didn't even know the score,' Alan Brazil said. 'I thought we had lost 3-2. I just knew we were out.' In 2006, Brazil recalled, 'They were crying inside the ground but they weren't tears of despair. One old guy grabbed me as I left the pitch and said, "All that effort and all that fight for nothing, but your mammy will be proud of you."'

Willie Miller spoke to the *Aberdeen Evening Express*'s Alastair Guthrie after the match, to offer his explanation for the collision leading to the goal, 'I went to volley the ball into touch as I had been doing. The instructions were to clear our lines. But Alan got a touch to it before me and this left Shengalia with the ball.'

'It was a bit of a misunderstanding,' Stein said.

Disappointed Scots fans now made their way either off to their hotels or out to the town. 'When we left the Russia game we were confused why the locals were slagging us in the taxis going back to Torremolinos,' recalled Iain McAuley. 'They were shouting at us and jeering and all that. I chucked my tammy out 'cos I thought they were just saying cheerio. But then they were stamping on it. I think it was to do with this Argentina-Falklands thing. There certainly was a bit of trouble going back to Torremolinos that night.'

Brogan's party were also heading back to Torremolinos but found a way to avoid any trouble. He said, 'We all jumped in the van, there's no car parks, it's just parked on a bit of waste ground. The motorway's shut. What they did was they shut the whole motorway and the team bus goes back, so it's clear and it doesn't take long. So, imagine the Scotland team bus with the polis in front of it. Then the other bus with the SFA. So Malky looks as the bus went by and he just swung out and filed in behind it. Now there's motorbikes behind us and the polis are looking but they're not sure because there's Scotland flags hanging out the van. The team bus is maybe going two junctions, but we were only going one junction so we got out the junction and away. Took us about five minutes to get back into the pub.'

* * *

The biggest talking point after the match, and for many years to come, was the calamitous collision between Hansen and Miller which led to the second goal. In *The Guardian*, Patrick Barclay was under no illusions when writing about whose fault it was, 'A moment's foolishness by Hansen, who barged into Miller when his colleague was about to make a simple clearance.' Hansen and Miller had first played together in a defensive partnership for Scotland in November 1979 against Belgium in a 2-0 defeat at the Heysel Stadium. Before the World Cup they had been on the pitch together five times, achieving clean sheets in 0-0 draws with Portugal and Northern Ireland, plus the 1-0 win over Sweden when Miller played in midfield.

'The Hansen-Miller incident happened away out on the touchline and should not have caused any problem at all,' Gordon Strachan wrote in his first autobiography, 'but it sparked off a great argument as to who was at fault. With Hansen facing his own goal and Miller heading away from it, the majority verdict was that Willie was at least going in the right direction. Putting my Aberdeen bias aside, however, I must admit I thought they were both at fault because nobody took command of the situation and shouted, "It's mine!"' Miller has stated publicly that he did give Hansen a shout, and he felt that his position on the field made him the perfect candidate to clear the danger.

The two defenders themselves have differing views on which of them was at fault.

'It was a simple misjudgement of the type which could occur in any game,' Miller wrote in 1989's *The Miller's Tale*, 'but it gained everlasting notoriety from a combination of circumstances; its consequences in the loss of a goal and the degree to which it influenced the outcome of a game so vital to Scotland's qualifying chances.' Having missed the New Zealand fixture, Miller was intent on doing well in the crucial match, 'I was even more involved in the play than usual for a sweeper, getting in good tackles and maintaining my concentration. Everything seemed to be going for me. My memory of the clash with Alan Hansen is that he went to meet a high ball down the touchline. It seemed to me that the ball was going over his head, so I went to cover it, but, by running backwards, Alan just managed to get a touch to the ball – just enough to deflect it past me – before he himself crashed into me and we both went down, allowing Shengelia freedom to run on and score.'

What made the error more annoying for Miller was that he felt he had performed well up until that point, 'I had put in worthwhile tackles, broken up play and linked well with the midfield, but I'm probably the only human being who remembers that I had done well. Well, I think my mum thought that too.' Miller felt the experience showed him that he and Hansen were not suited to playing together, that they were too similar in their approach. Despite an exemplary career in the game, people still delight in reminding Miller of the unfortunate event, 'I still get taxi drivers, those born comedians, asking if I've bumped into Alan Hansen recently. Alan gets the same treatment. It will never stop.'

Hansen wrote in his book *Tall, Dark and Hansen – Ten Years at Anfield*, 'It was one of those unbelievable happenings, a crazy incident. Yet, even after our spectacular crash, the team manager Jock Stein came out and said that two of his best players had collided, and by saying that he was making it clear publicly, as he did to us personally, that he was not ready to write us off as a partnership.' Hansen felt the problem was down to the differing ways the two defenders operated with their clubs, 'It isn't always easy to adapt. I would be playing one way for 70-odd games and then would have to try to make a little alteration here and there for a handful of internationals. You can do it – and Willie and I did do it and have done it since then – but unless you have absolutely superhuman concentration then there are always moments where you slip back into your club style.' Hansen was used to the Liverpool way where a defender stood his ground, and when a forward was attempting to run past then the defence allowed that to happen before the ball was played through because they knew he would be offside. 'With Scotland, I couldn't do that because Willie was used to a defensive setup where he tucked in behind and played as the last man in defence. Basically, the problem was that we came from such differing styles so that if I did let someone run on, instead of finding him offside I would see Willie standing around ten yards behind me.'

Hansen stated that the approach caused both players worries and admitted he should possibly have changed his style completely, and sat back alongside Miller, 'But it isn't as easy as it sounds to break the habits of a near-lifetime.' Hansen also wrote that he cannot accept responsibility for the collision, 'The consensus of opinion among Scottish pundits was that I was mainly to blame, but the more I have thought about what happened, the more I have struggled to pinpoint something to support their view.' He did concede that he didn't get proper contact on the initial headed clearance, 'However, I was able to turn quickly enough to stay in front of Shengelia in the chase for it and I felt I was in control of the situation. I saw Willie moving towards me, but all I needed him to do was take up a position to receive a pass from me.' Hansen felt with time running out it was important to keep the ball in play, so couldn't understand Miller looking to put the ball out of play. 'I'm not trying to knock Willie, but I'm absolutely convinced that had our positions been reversed – had I been the sweeper – there is no way we would have collided,' he added.

On hearing Hansen's explanation, Patrick Barclay had a different opinion, 'Once you see Miller's body language you don't say, "If I had my way differently I'd expect him to drop off for the short ball." You say, "He's going to kick the fucking ball so I'll get out of the way." You don't tackle him.'

Of his own part in the goal, Alan Rough wrote in 1988, 'In hindsight, I probably should have pulled down the scorer and risked the possibility of a red card but that would have been disastrous too.' In his 2006 book, he added, 'It was the sort of one in a million years collision which appeared to be *de rigueur* for the Scots in World Cup combat. I stood there, watching the debacle unfold and it was simply a lack of communication between the pair. I had plenty of time to weigh up the situation and ponder my choices, but these essentially entailed either running out of the box and hauling the striker down, which would have brought a red card, or wait until he neared me, after which it was in the lap of the gods. Unfortunately, nobody else put any pressure on Shengelia, he was clean through in acres of empty space, and the question was whether he might lose his cool and blast wide or give me an opportunity to dive at his feet. To his credit, though, he remained calm, converted the chance, and our aspirations had vanished in a pratfall straight from a *Carry On* film.'

'I've always said I thought Roughie could have done a bit more to stop the ball hitting the back of the net,' Miller said to the *Sunday Mail* in 2007, 'but you've got to take responsibility for your actions.'

Hansen was rooming with Davie Provan, and the Celtic winger attempted to console him with a few beers. 'Even now, though it's such a long time ago,' Hansen wrote in 1988, 'it's hard to push the incident to the back of my mind. Whenever I talk about it I can still see Willie coming towards me, and then I can remember, too, the realisation hitting me that a collision was unavoidable.'

'Although I'd always been a believer in the sweeper system,' Patrick Barclay said to me, 'I don't remember losing faith in Hansen. I didn't feel that we were great defensively. And I didn't often get proved right but it was proved right in the Russia game where we did enough to *sneak* a victory I think. But Hansen just lumbered. Instead of being the elegant faultless flawless Hansen that played for Liverpool – and Partick Thistle before – he was this donkey that knocked Willie Miller out of the way. I could never believe it you know when I read in the papers – even in some of the Scottish ones – "A collision between Miller and Hansen".

I mean, Hansen should have got at least the yellow for that challenge on Willie Miller.'

While Barclay lays the blame for the collision firmly at the Liverpool player's door, he is at pains to stress Hansen's qualities, which perhaps weren't always in evidence when he pulled on a Scotland jersey, 'I was a great fan of Hansen. I thought Hansen was the best footballing defender that Britain had produced since Bobby Moore. I wish he'd played more often in his natural position as a playmaker. He could do anything. He actually had more sweeper credentials than anybody except [Franz] Beckenbauer. He was quicker than Morten Olsen, so if he came forward he could beat a man, which Morten Olsen couldn't. He was more adventurous than [Italian international Gaetano] Scirea, he had everything. Only Beckenbauer I would say of any footballer I've ever seen had better natural ability to be a libero. I suppose Bobby Moore. If you look at Bobby Moore in 1966 he was sensational.'

Barclay feels that British managers have traditionally been reluctant to fully deploy a libero, but Hansen's qualities – his strength, reading of the game and his speed – made him a perfect candidate to play regularly in that position. He said, 'I always used to wish they would just let the player go because if the player is allowed it's quite easy. People say you leave a gap at the back, but you don't leave a gap at the back because the holding midfield player drops in. If that centre-half keeps running no one quite knows who's picking him up. And by the way, once Alan Hansen's gained speed, pity the poor bastard who has to try and stop him because he can drop the shoulder as well.'

Barclay recalls the reaction in the press box being one of, 'How many new ways are we going to find to go out?' David

Begg can also remember watching on with astonishment, 'Just a shambles. I wasn't doing the commentary so what I said at the time I can't remember. But I just couldn't believe it. To me it was Hansen on Miller, not the other way round. Both of them will give you the different versions. And he [scorer Shengelia] just walked round Roughie. It was just such a sickener.'

Kevin Donnelly recalls his reaction well, 'I remember standing up after Hansen had barged into Miller and just shouting, "No! No!"'

'I can visualise it now,' says Stuart Russell. 'If you look at a clock I'm looking at them probably at ten o'clock. I'm looking almost right on the halfway line and I'm looking at the two at ten o'clock. The ironic thing about it is those two – especially Willie Miller – must have been the best central defenders in the world. He was a fantastic football player, Willie Miller, and Hansen was silky smooth. But just that lack of communication. If Jock Stein had stuck to the partnership of McLeish and Miller I don't think that would have happened, because they played [together] week in week out.'

'I always liked Willie Miller and Alex McLeish as a central defensive partnership because there was a ruthlessness about them,' assistant manager Jim McLean said to the *Daily Record* in 2005. 'Perhaps we should have gone with the Aberdeen pairing but Hansen and Miller were the perfect partnership in many ways as one was a terrific player from defence and the other the type who would cover everything.'

'Willie Miller's mum, stepdad and wee sister were in our hotel,' Chic Brogan said, 'and big Malky got talking to them. So they just hung about with us and went in the van. She would sit in the front with his sister and his stepdad sat in the back with us. The next day at the hotel the game from the night before would be on the telly just on a loop. So we're watching it when Willie Miller and Hansen bang into each other and she's watching it going, "Aw naw," and big Malky's going, "That's your fuckin boy!" and I'm going, "Malky, calm down. It's nothing to do with her." Poor woman.'

Although the general consensus is that Hansen was much more at fault than Miller, the two players are intrinsically linked by the incident and share a collective ownership in the mind of any Scotland fan left dumbfounded at that moment. Collectively the pair played over 1,000 league games, won every domestic honour in English and Scottish football and both claimed European medals, yet the first thing any Scots fan of the 1980s will mention when their names come up is that comedy pratfall.

Hansen and Miller did play alongside each other internationally again. They were the central defensive partnership in Scotland's next game against East Germany in the European Championship qualifiers. They played as a partnership twice more, both times against Switzerland, in November 1982 and March 1983. 'I don't think that particular goal loss and the daft way it happened scarred my career too much,' said Hansen. 'I certainly had no qualms about lining up with Willie again and I don't think he had any about playing alongside me. But then the talking started and there were suggestions that the two of us just couldn't get things going between us. That made it harder for both of us. Strangely though, Willie and I have never talked about that clash. It's as if the memory still hurts too much.'

After Spain, Hansen made nine more appearances in dark blue. He played his last Scotland match against the Republic of Ireland in February 1987, and remained a stalwart of the Liverpool defence, captaining the Reds to the English First Division championship in 1990. He was inducted into the Scottish Football Hall of Fame in 2007. The USSR game was Miller's 19th appearance for Scotland. He went on to win a total of 65 caps, playing his final game against Norway in November 1989, the night Scotland sealed qualification for the 1990 World Cup in Italy. A late Norwegian tackle that night forced Miller out of the match, and out of contention for the finals. The bone damage sustained in the challenge led to Miller's retirement from the game in 1990. Willie was one of the original 20 inductees into the Scottish Football Hall of Fame in 2004.

* * *

A glum-looking Jock Stein sat in the BBC studio and spoke with Archie Macpherson. 'Everyone watching that at home will be sorely pained,' Macpherson remarked. 'I don't think you're any different are you?' Stein shook his head, 'No. I don't feel any better than that. We're just sorry that 13 players there played so hard, have worked so hard, all 22 of the squad, their attitude, their physical approach to the game, their tactical approach to the game was as good as their opponents. Just a couple of bad breaks at the goals. We never got a break. We've discussed a wee bit about the game and John Wark assures us he was pushed right off the ball for a penalty kick as well.'

'From your three performances, did you think you deserved to be in the final phase?' Macpherson asked. Stein said, 'I think if we were in another section, any other of the five sections, we would undoubtedly be in the next phase of the competition. We've came here against Brazil and Russia. They've 22 out of 23 wins, beaten against Brazil their only [defeat] ... and we've needed to chase the game, against them here, which is ideal for their style of play. We've done that tonight and we only got a draw in the match certainly but I think, okay, I think we deserved to win the match.'

Macpherson asked about the collision between Miller and Hansen 'which effectively put you out of the World Cup'. For an incident that has gained notoriety over the years, it's interesting to see that Stein, who wasn't shy about calling out his players' errors, didn't attach any major significance to it in the immediate aftermath. 'I think that was anxiousness as well,' Stein replied. 'A wee bit of a misunderstanding between Willie Miller and Alan Hansen. Shouting to each other would have helped. But I think at 1-0 a quarter of an hour after half-time was the best spell in the game, we played well. We had some tremendous shots on target. Unfortunately for us, I think we were against the best goalkeeper in the competition.'

Macpherson asked Stein what he was most proud of. The manager replied, 'I think the main thing we're proud of is we can compete at this level. We won't necessarily win anything at this level, at World Cup level, there's only two or three teams who could honestly say they could come and win a World Cup, but I think we've proved we can compete at this level. And tonight I think we've done Scotland proud, both on and off the field.'

'Do you feel it's been worthwhile?' Macpherson asked. 'All the pain, all the agony?'

'Oh, it's always worthwhile,' Stein said, 'the people that follow you get value for money, and they got 90 minutes there, value for money. I think with a wee bit break at all we might have come out of it on the right side.'

WE MADE THEM ANGRY

In the TV studio, David Coleman asked Lawrie McMenemy, who was a personal friend of Stein's, what he thought Stein would do now. 'I think he'll find what the players did for him personally very satisfying. I think the stick he'll start getting off some of the media will make him wonder if it's worth carrying on,' said McMenemy.

'But not deserved stick,' Coleman qualified.

'Undeserved. Totally undeserved. The man is the best manager that Scotland's ever had and one of the best in the history of British football, and yet he will get undeniable criticism. From the media's point of view, they will think that Dalglish should have played; he should have changed the goalkeeper; and yet if it hadn't been for the mix-up he could have come out a hero. And that's this game, you're on a very thin tightrope.'

Stein's sympathies lay with the players. There was no finger-pointing or laying of blame. He praised the players for their positive and professional attitudes, saying, 'They all wanted to do well for their country.' The boss was satisfied that the Brazil and Russia matches proved that Scotland could at least compete at the same level with the best in the world. He was also pleased that, after concern over where the goals were coming from, Scotland managed to score eight of them in their three games, even if they did concede the same number. At the end of the first phase, the only teams who had scored more were Hungary with 12 and Brazil with ten. The tournament's eventual winners Italy had only managed to score twice in qualifying from Group One on goal difference after three draws.

One person Stein felt was worthy of his criticism was the referee. 'We feel he definitely denied us one penalty kick,' he said. 'The referee tried early on to intimidate our lads and get the game down to a slow pace, but they refused to allow it and went on to produce some great play. We feel we were again on the wrong end of the referee's decisions which would have been vital in our game. The players assured me that John Wark was blatantly pushed inside the box. They had no doubts about it.'

The failure to get the required result brought into focus the fact Dalglish wasn't even given a place on the bench. 'Those who have seen Dalglish play know why he wasn't in the 16,' Stein said to the press. 'A lot of people close to me said I would be leaving myself wide open, but I knew I had to do what was right, not what was popular. I could have put him on the bench as some kind of appeasement but it wouldn't have been right.' Speaking to the *Belfast Telegraph*, Stein praised Frank Gray and John Robertson, who played in all three matches, 'They came to Spain as unfit players, but they were ready when it counted. I have never seen Gray play three better games for Scotland.' Of Robertson, Stein said, 'He has improved out of all recognition. He worked hard for his place, and for someone who looked absolutely hopeless before we left, his displays were top-class.' Stein also had praise for the SFA, 'The arrangements made by the association were perfect. They did not scrimp on anything. Only the best was good enough and they did a first-class job.'

Asked about the wisdom of playing David Narey at right-back, Stein gave an insight into how he saw his tactics as Scotland boss evolving. 'We are not talking in terms of a right-back in the old sense,' he said. 'We are speaking of people who can come from a deep position and get into the opposition penalty box. Look how Chivadze, who was playing at the back for Russia, was in a position to score their equalising goal. The continentals all play with a free man who can see the game and knows when to break forward. They play like that all the time, and that's the way ahead for us, as I see it.' Stein was asked if in hindsight he would have changed anything regarding Scotland's campaign. 'Yes,' he replied, 'I would have kept Harry Cavan away from the draw.'

Although disappointed, Gordon Strachan admitted he had enjoyed the Russia game. 'Yes, I would say that was my best performance for Scotland,' Strachan said to journalist Alastair Guthrie. 'It was all right playing well against New Zealand but Russia are a world-class side and it counts when you can do it against that kind of opposition. At half-time, our hopes were high that we would be moving on to Barcelona. I think the whole team played as well as they possibly could and I wouldn't like to think we let anyone down.' Strachan highlighted Dasayev as Russia's best man, saying, 'That save he had from Joe early in the game was the best I have ever seen.'

Joe Jordan also thought Dasayev was the man of the match, 'I thought the header was in and I don't know how he got to it. I think he must have touched the ball with a fingernail as it was the slightest of touches. I thought it was in. If we had scored then, or even just after my goal, I know we would have gone on to qualify.' Jordan's goal made him the first and as yet only Scot to have scored in three World Cup finals tournaments. He said, 'Brazil and Russia this time were of a higher standard of opposition from those we faced in 1974 and again in 1978. We had a better squad here and we're leaving Spain with pride. We are all obviously sick at going out on goal difference again. No, I don't think it was the goals against New Zealand which put us out. It is all right saying Brazil had a daft night in Seville but I think those four Brazilian goals were more damaging.'

Stein was asked about Scotland's next game, a European Championship qualifier at Hampden against East Germany. 'It really is too early to start talking about this one; it is still far away. Let's allow the wounds from last night to heal first,' he replied. Stein was happy to be drawn on the players who may still be involved with the squad, 'We have a lot of fine players, such as Jim Leighton, Alex McLeish and Miller, to get working with.' Inevitably, the press asked if Stein was ready to step down. 'I have no thoughts of calling it a day. If I was thinking that way the people I am working for would be involved from the start anyway,' he said.

In May 2020, BBC Scotland re-ran the Russia game in full. John Wark watched it, and reflected, 'I'd forgotten how much we battered them. We just had to win, any win, and we were good enough to win three games against them, honestly. But the goals we lost? Man ... The first one's horrible, we've got about four defenders round it, but Chivadze sclaffs it off the ground and it bounces up and over Roughie. And the second, the infamous mix-up between Miller and Hansen, even watching it again, even knowing exactly when it's coming, you can't stop yourself shouting "What the fuck are they doing???" at the telly.'

'The goals we lost were hard to take,' said Jordan. 'When you get to that level, and you're playing the best, you should still make them work for it, to score with quality the way Brazil did, say. But these were cheap. The thing is, the goal Graeme scores to pull us level again is a cracker as well, but it almost made it feel worse – touching distance again.'

'This was much worse than Argentina,' Rough said to Archie Macpherson. 'Much worse because we felt it's a game we expected to win. We didn't really expect to beat Holland in the final game in '78, although we did. But this one was really doable. It just made it like we'd taken a real beating. And what's more, if we had made it through, we had been promised £500 a man as a bonus and some of us were planning to go to Morocco before the next round. Now it was just back hame.'

The pair selected for the random dope testing this time were Strachan and Robertson. Many hours later they pulled up in a taxi at Snoopy's Scottish Bar in Torremolinos. Already there was Rod Stewart, sitting with Scots fans who sang his hit 'Sailing'.

It wasn't just the players heading for home; the fans were also departing. Andalucia's governor, Don Jose Estevez Mendez, told the *Evening Times*, 'We wanted the Scottish fans to come here to enjoy the sunshine and the football, and that is exactly what they have done. They have been marvellous.' The head of Malaga's World Cup security team, Bernabe Mediano Carrasco, was also pleased, 'We couldn't possibly have expected everything to be so good. They have been no problem at all to our policemen, who were trained on how to treat the fans with good humour.' Thomas Tuite at the British Consulate said, 'I am very happy for Scotland that the fans have been such a credit to their country.' SFA president Willie Harkness added, 'This shows once and for all that the fans who follow the national team do not cause problems. We have been delighted with their behaviour and it is just a pity they were disappointed in the end.'

'The Scots can come back here any time,' a senior official at the British Consulate in Malaga was quoted as saying. 'Their behaviour has been absolutely superb.' Jock Stein was also in full praise of the supporters. 'Those people who followed us out here were really magnificent. Their behaviour was excellent and their backing during matches fantastic. I just wish we could have given them more to cheer about.'

Iain McAuley's party didn't fancy travelling back to Dunfermline in the old van they had arrived in. He said, 'We got friendly with one of the Spanish guys in the bar. We decided we're going to sell the van and fly home. We're not going home in that; it's falling to bits. So we had a raffle in the local taverna in Torremolinos. The guy that bought it used it for keeping his chickens in.'

Scotland finished the tournament sixth in the Fair Play list, having had only one caution, for Graeme Souness. Brazil topped the table, with New Zealand second.

* * *

It had been rumoured that Motherwell would attempt to lure Jock Stein to Fir Park to replace Davie Hay. Club officials were staying in the Andalucia Plaza Hotel some 30 miles from Scotland's base in Sotogrande. 'I just want to have a holiday,' Stein said when asked by journalists of Motherwell's interest. 'No one has spoken to me about my future with the SFA. I read about hints and the like but nothing has been said. It is foolish of people to speak about the future without talking to those directly involved, but that's up to them. Anyway, this is the wrong time to make decisions about the future. It's the morning after the worst day of my life. Of course, not too many managers survive World Cups. It's a miracle if you do. But my position with the SFA is open.'

Speculation also turned to the future of players within the Scotland squad. It was suggested that a few of them had played their last game for their country, and this would prove to be accurate. Danny McGrain went off to join his wife and family in Marbella, telling the *Record*'s Ken Gallacher, 'I must now think long and hard about my football future. All my thoughts have been on the World Cup, but now that's over other things have to be considered. My position with Celtic is one of them. Whether I stay depends on the club and not myself. But I have made no demands. This was my last World Cup, and the game against Russia was my last game for Scotland. I don't have any illusions. The manager has to look for younger players and I don't see myself playing in the European Championships. There is no point kidding myself. I am 32 years old and I knew when I went on last night that it was the last time I would wear a Scotland jersey.

'This is the best Scotland squad I've been with. It's been marvellous. If the Russia game had gone just five minutes more we would have won it. It was a very sad dressing room. Worse than in 1974 when something similar happened against Yugoslavia. How can any country go out of the tournament on goal difference three times in a row? Incidentally, I have to mention the supporters. They were magnificent. They backed us all the way and behaved superbly.'

McGrain asked Stein for a private discussion before they went their separate ways. He said, 'I told him that to make it easier for all concerned I considered my time as an internationalist to be at an end and that I did not want to be picked anymore.' Stein asked his captain not to go public with his decision as he might want to use McGrain's experience in the opening internationals of the following season. McGrain added, 'Jock was not the kind of man you argued with, but I had not taken the decision lightly and I knew deep down that I did not want that. Becoming a full internationalist had made me a better player but I did not want an established reputation to be sullied by going into decline in full view of the spectating public.'

'He is the most complete professional I have ever dealt with,' Stein said of McGrain. 'Even though he wasn't fit for the last two games, he played a real captain's role and offered advice and encouragement. That's the type of player we need playing for Scotland.' Although McGrain suggested he may leave Celtic, he carried on with them until 1987, finishing his career with a season at Hamilton Accies. He was one of the initial 20 players inducted into the Scottish Football Hall of Fame in 2004.

Asa Hartford's ten-year international career was also at an end. 'When Jock Stein shook my hand at the airport I knew that was it,' Hartford told *The Scotsman* in 2016. 'We were better organised [than in 1978] under Jock Stein in 1982. But the squad just wasn't as good.' Asa would have another couple of seasons in England's top flight with Manchester City and with Norwich City before spending several years in the bottom two leagues with Bolton Wanderers, Stockport County, Oldham Athletic and Shrewsbury Town. By the time he called it a day in 1991, he had started over 900 games in English football. Hartford's 50 caps led to him being in the initial 11 players inducted into the Scottish FA International Roll of Honour when it was established in 1988.

It would be the end too for Joe Jordan. A scorer of vital goals for his country, not to mention winning a crucial penalty against Wales in 1977, he had written his name into Scottish folklore. It's fair to say that even today Jordan is still held up as everything a good Scottish international player should be; he displayed commitment, loyalty and passion every time he pulled on the dark blue.

In his autobiography *Behind the Dream*, Jordan reflected on his third World Cup finals and the end of his time with Scotland, 'At 31 I could not reasonably expect to play in another one and, denied that possibility, I could hardly expect to add to my collection of Scottish caps. I could only reflect on my good fortune down the years – and express disbelief when I read of the complaints of some players that Jock never called them up to thank them for their services. Surely, when it is over you know it in your bones, and why would a manager have reason to thank you? He had already thanked you by handing you the Scottish jersey.'

Jordan's AC Milan team-mate Franco Baresi found him tickets for the 1982 World Cup Final, and the forward, dressed in T-shirt and flip-flops, attended with best friend Gordon McQueen as Italy beat West Germany 3-1. Despite his international career being over, Jordan had cause to contact the SFA one final time. 'Scotland gave you a cap for every year, not for every game,' he told the *Daily Mail* in 2018. 'I've got ten caps and the last one went missing. I'd played in the World Cup in Spain and waited three or four months and it didn't come so I phoned the SFA. The guy says, "Oh, we sent it. It's gone." I said, "Well, I haven't received it." So he goes, "Yeah, we sent it to Inter [Milan]." Inter? No, not Inter. They had it on the wall at Inter. I had to go and get it.' Jordan was inducted into the Scottish Football Hall of Fame in 2005.

The brief international career of Allan Evans would also come to an end, with his four caps all coming between March and June of 1982. Evans would go on to win the European Super Cup with Aston Villa in January of 1983.

Of his experience in Spain, Evans told Aston Villa's match programme in 1983, 'I didn't enjoy it totally, partly because the hotel was not to my liking, and more than anything, because I missed my family. I am very much a family man and, after all the season's travelling with Villa, being away another three and a half weeks was a bit too long for me. Don't get me wrong – I was proud to be involved and enjoyed playing in the first game with New Zealand. Being left out of the Brazil match was not a setback because Jock Stein had told us the team he intended to use even before the New Zealand game. He wanted to use Willie Miller in the back four because of the Brazilians' type of football suited him more than me. I must admit I half expected to play in the last game against Russia, largely because I had played against half their team in the European Cup, but I could see the manager's point. He didn't want to change the side after they had done well against Brazil. And if I was disappointed, I only had to look at Kenny Dalglish. He was left out as well and that must have been a much bigger blow for an established international of his class.'

Of the non-playing members of the squad, George Wood, Davie Provan and George Burley had all won their last caps. Wood won all four of his caps under Stein, his last coming in that game against Northern Ireland in April 1982. After 23 league appearances for Arsenal in the 1982/83 season, he moved to Crystal Palace where he was their first-choice goalkeeper for four seasons in the Second Division. 'I only got four Scotland caps and I felt that I should have had more,' he said in 2013. 'Dai Davies got caps for Wales when he was playing for Everton reserves. I'm always grateful for the four caps.' Davie Provan also made his final international appearance in that match against the Irish. Provan played for another five seasons with Celtic before the illness myalgic encephalomyelitis (ME) forced him to call time on his career. He went on to become a prominent pundit and co-commentator. Burley's 11th and final cap came against England in May 1982. He had another three seasons as a regular choice in the First Division with Ipswich before stepping down a division with Sunderland. Burley became Scotland manager in 2008, leading his country in 14 internationals and winning only three before stepping down in November 2009.

The media were proved wrong on the two other players they had speculated had reached the end of the national line. Although no longer the first choice, Alan Rough would go on to gain a further two Scotland caps. His next appearance came in September 1985 as a half-time substitute against Wales in Cardiff on the night Stein died. 'He just walked up to me and said, "Right, you are on you fat bastard," Rough said to the *Herald* in 2015. 'The bell calling us back on the pitch rang so I just put on my jersey and got on with it. That was the last time I ever spoke to him.' Rough's inauguration into the Scottish Football Hall of Fame came in 2013.

Kenny Dalglish also continued, earning a further 14 caps. Kenny took his record appearance total to 102 in the 3-0 win against Luxembourg under Andy Roxburgh in November 1986. It's a record that still stands today and won't be surpassed for many years to come, if it ever is. Dalglish was one of the inaugural inductees into the Scottish Football Hall of Fame in 2004.

The rest of that Scotland squad had international careers of varying lengths. Alan Brazil's international career ended just under a year later with another four caps and scoring one goal, against Wales. Frank Gray earned seven more caps, the last against Canada in June 1983. John Robertson would win only another four caps for his country, the last while playing in England's second tier with Derby County in a 1-1 draw with Belgium in October 1983. Steve Archibald would play ten more times for Scotland without scoring again, his 27th and final cap coming as a Barcelona player in the 1986 World Cup finals. He was inducted into the Hall of Fame in 2009. John Wark earned a further 11 caps, all under Stein, scoring twice more. Despite not playing in Spain, Paul Sturrock would add to his seven caps over the next five years. He would play twice in the Mexico World Cup of 1986 and finish his Scotland career in a 4-1 defeat to Belgium in April 1987 with 20 caps and four goals. David Narey wouldn't score another goal for Scotland but he would go on to play 35 times, making his last international appearance in a 3-2 win over Cyprus in 1989. The USSR game was Graeme Souness's 28th cap and he would go on to play in the 1986 World Cup finals, the 2-1 loss to West Germany there becoming his 54th and final outing. Gordon Strachan's Scotland career ended in March 1992 with his 50th cap, a 1-1 draw with Finland at Hampden.

Alex McLeish would become a mainstay of the Scotland side for the next decade, earning 77 caps and finishing up in February 1993 with a 3-0 win over Malta. Jim Leighton took over the gloves from Rough, making his debut in the next international against East Germany in October 1982. Only Kenny Dalglish would play more games for Scotland than Leighton, as he claimed 91 caps in an international career that lasted three days short of 16 years. He was inducted into the Scottish Football Hall of Fame in 2008.

Miller, McLeish and Archibald all went on holiday together to Marbella after the 1982 finals. 'There's plenty of glamour with Spurs,' Archibald said to the *Daily Record*, 'but I love playing for Scotland. Last season I had a run of injuries and it affected my scoring rate. However, I never lost my confidence. I've always been ready to have a go for goal, even if I've missed. The one I headed against New Zealand gave me a special pleasure. The job I had to do against Brazil was a lonely one and perhaps not very attractive, but it was the right way to play. It was good to team up with Joe Jordan in the Russia match. I thought Scotland did everything right and we were just unlucky in the end.'

Miller was seen as one of the best players in the Scottish side. Celtic boss Billy McNeill said, 'The biggest success. Defended immaculately against Brazil and Russia. The mix-up leading to the second goal wasn't his fault.' Miller's club manager Alex Ferguson hailed his performances as 'magnificent'.

John Wark summed up the campaign in an interview with the *Northern Echo*, 'I suppose our team was a bit like the one in *Escape to Victory* – we had lots of good outfield players but the goalkeeper was lousy.' In 2020 he said to the BBC, 'It must be the best squad we've ever taken to a finals – and the best manager. We had players who'd won everything in the game, they needed someone who commanded their respect and big Jock did it just by walking into the room. To this day I believe that was our chance.'

Shortly after the tournament, Jim McLean stepped down as assistant to Stein. In his autobiography *Jousting With Giants*, he was critical of his own performance in the role. He wrote that, during the four years or so he spent as assistant manager to Jock with the international squad, 'I was nothing more than a hanger-on in almost all of that time. I'm ashamed today of the way I did that job, and ashamed that I might have let Jock Stein down after he had shown a great deal of faith in me and my ability as a coach. Quite honestly, I was a disgrace as an assistant manager.'

In *Adventures in the Golden Age*, Archie Macpherson addressed those claims, 'He [McLean] said that because he did not realise until it was too late that he had not spoken up when he should have about tactics and team selection. He was too much in awe of the man to take issue with him, and because of his own domination of Tannadice, he simply did not know how to handle being a subsidiary.'

McLean went on, 'There was no way I contributed enough to the role Jock handed me. If anything I gained more from taking the job than either Jock or Scotland did.

'Looking back, I realise now that I approached the job in the wrong way. Possibly, because of my own lack of confidence, I didn't try to assert myself. It was in my mind that I was asked to be assistant manager, number two, and therefore I did not want to ever be accused of undermining Jock ... We had occasional disagreements but they were between us.

McLean continues, 'I deferred to Jock because I reckoned that was what the assistant manager's job should be – simply to be there to help the manager when he needed help and to exchange views with him when he wanted that. We disagreed on some things, on the approach to some of the games, or tactics used in some of them. If I thought he was wrong then I would tell him.'

McLean recalls Stein's response when suggested appointing someone in his place, who would agree more on the matters relating to the squad and its setup, 'I don't want a yes man. It would be very easy for me to go out and get a yes man – but what good would he be to me?

'At the end of the day, I'll listen to you but I'll make up my own mind. I would not have you here if you weren't ready to state your views plainly and honestly. That's what I need.'"

Stein would appoint Aberdeen boss Alex Ferguson as his new assistant. 'He phoned on a Friday night and said he'd like me to join him,' Ferguson said in *The Official Celtic Opus*. 'I was delighted, but I asked Jock what would be my responsibilities. He said he wanted me to do all the training and physical preparation. I don't know where I got the cheek, but I asked him what about picking the team and he said, "Let's not get carried away." I was killing myself laughing.'

Ferguson would be Stein's assistant for the rest of his reign, which continued for another 25 internationals. His final game was on 10 September 1985, where a 1-1 draw sealed a place in the 1986 World Cup play-offs, but Stein died suddenly moments after the final whistle sounded. Ferguson took over the team for the two play-off games against Australia, where a 2-0 win in the first leg at Hampden was enough to seal a fourth World Cup finals in a row.

* * *

All the signs should have been good for Scotland going into the 1982 World Cup. They had the manager that the SFA, the players and the fans wanted. That manager had the squad of players he wanted, players who were all fit and free from suspension. They were also all largely on form. The squad contained players who had won that season's European Cup, English First Division, Scottish Premier Division, English FA Cup, Scottish Cup and English League Cup. Several of them went on to be included in the

Scottish Football Hall of Fame. So why did that group of players fall at the first hurdle?

'It's the first time I ever heard the abbreviation NGE,' Patrick Barclay said to me by way of some sort of explanation. 'The first time I ever heard NGE was in the days following the Soviet game, and it was the great argument about whether we were just unlucky or whether we were just Not Good Enough – NGE. And now a lot of people use it. I can remember people like Brian Scott, Jim Reynolds, Jim Traynor probably was starting out about then, Ronnie Scott all those guys having that argument; are we just not good enough or do we keep having bad luck? You know, somebody has to lose and it's us. I can very much remember the heart-searching that went on among the media after that defeat.'

There's no question it was a tough group. Scotland will never be expected to beat Brazil no matter the relative qualities of the particular era of players, and while the likes of England and Germany can hand out thrashings to minnows with relative ease, Scottish teams over the years never can seem to put the smaller nations to the sword without some stumbling blocks along the way. Over the 90 minutes in the last group game in Malaga, Scotland were more than a match for a strong Soviet team, but was it through indiscipline, inability, poor officiating, bad luck or just one of those things that they didn't find the result they needed? Was elimination already in the post due to the first two group games? 'Because of those two goals we probably stuffed you up qualifying,' Wynton Rufer said. Willie Miller also believed it was the two goals conceded against New Zealand that put Scotland out, while Joe Jordan stated it was the capitulation to Brazil that cost them. Had Scotland gone into the USSR match with a 5-0 win over the Kiwis behind them and a 6-4 goal difference, requiring only a draw and the Soviets needing a win, a very different game would have played out, so it's no indication that would have been the key to qualification.

Were the team selections to blame? Did Stein tinker too much? Was there a need to bring Allan Evans into the squad? What was the wisdom in dropping Dalglish for the last game? Did Stein have too many good players at his disposal meaning he couldn't settle on who his best 11 was? Should Alan Rough have had more competition for the gloves? They were all subjects for bar room debates at the time and the only definitive answers are the results Scotland had on the pitch.

Stein's thinking that he needed three teams for the tournament was probably correct and in a way he may even have been ahead of his time. In tournament football played in 80 to 90-degree heat against three very different sides, it makes perfect sense to use a variety from the 22-man squad allowed. 'You play your best 11 in every game' is an obvious rejoinder, but Hansen and Evans should have been as good a central partnership as McLeish and Miller while Scottish fans should have been as happy with Dalglish and Brazil up front as Archibald and Jordan. Scotland had a wealth of talent available at the time, and idea of the 'best 11' kept the press and punters alike occupied in a debate over that era, and even now, with hindsight, I don't think there's a definitive selection or formation that should have been played over any other.

Stein's insistence on squeezing Allan Evans in is curious. He clearly liked the Aston Villa man's ability and his attitude, and the fact he had won an English title and a European Cup surely gave him the qualifications. Alex

McLeish had suffered some injuries, so perhaps it made sense having quality cover. But neither of Evans's Scottish colleagues at Villa Park, Ken McNaught and Des Bremner, who both had the same medals, were capped by Stein, and the fact he never played for Scotland again perhaps shows that the flirtation with Evans came just at the wrong time.

Alan Rough never really had a serious contender for the number one jersey until the autumn of 1982 when Jim Leighton took over. Stein awarded Rough 30 caps, including the two subsequent to Spain '82. Over Stein's period in charge, Billy Thomson won seven caps, George Wood won four and Jim Stewart was capped once. Who could have challenged Rough? Thomson was young, Wood was in and out of the Everton and Arsenal sides, and, although, Stewart was Rangers' first choice in the early 1980s, his form was not noteworthy enough to warrant displacing Rough, who by that time had gained plenty of international experience. The 17 times capped Bobby Clark had been Aberdeen's goalkeeper when they won the league in 1979/80 but by that time he was 34, and Dundee United's Hamish McAlpine was also the wrong side of 30. Celtic couldn't offer competition as their goalkeepers of the era were Englishman Peter Latchford and Irish international Pat Bonner. It was noted at the time that Rough could have done with full-time training, startling as it is now from a modern perspective to think he played with a part-time club in the period when he was Scotland's first choice.

Dalglish's drop to the bench against Brazil and exclusion from the squad entirely for the must-win Russia match is certainly puzzling, but Stein was nothing if not strong-willed and was prepared to take whatever decision he felt was best. It certainly can't be said he didn't rate Dalglish, as no Scotland player earned more caps under Stein than Kenny. Of his 102, Stein awarded him 39, the same number he granted to Graeme Souness and Willie Miller, with Alex McLeish claiming 38.

There's no definitive reason why Scotland couldn't qualify for the second phase in 1982; failing again on goal difference makes it just all that more heartbreaking for players and fans alike, but, as Stein said, the Scotland team offered the fans value for money. Scotland are still waiting to qualify for the second stage of a tournament, although over the last 20 or so years the wait has been just to qualify, a need sated by the squad's play-off wins to make Euro 2020. Going out on goal difference, self-inflicted errors and putting minor football nations on the map is part and parcel of Scotland's place in tournament football. But Scotland fans get over these disappointments very quickly. I've never heard anyone who's been at any of the tournaments Scotland have played in express regret at being there. They know fine they'll do it again. So here's to the next finals Scotland qualify for to the roars of delight at a goal out of nothing, a goal-line clearance that defies belief and to the shouts of 'Here we go', 'What's he doing?', 'Oh no, not again' and 'We'll support you evermore.'

Acknowledgments

THANKS TO the Scotland fans who told me about their experiences in Spain – Chic Brogan, David Dewar, Kevin Donnelly, Bobby Jamieson, Iain McAuley and Stuart Russell. Thanks to Sam Malcolmson and Wynton Rufer for telling me what it was like playing against Scotland. Thanks to Patrick Barclay and David Begg for their thoughts and experiences on covering Scotland at that World Cup. Thanks to Andy Bollen for advice and encouragement. Thanks also to Jane and all the staff at Pitch Publishing.

Bibliography

Books

Brazil, Alan; Parry, Mike. *There's an Awful Lot of Bubbly in Brazil: The Life and Times of a Bon Viveur* (Newbury: Highdown, 2006)

Brown, Gordon: editor; Campbell, Bill: editor. *The Scotsport guide to Spain World Cup '82* (Edinburgh: Mainstream Publishing in conjunction with STV, 1982)

Burns, Kenny; Yeomans, Ron. *No Ifs or Butts* (Nottingham: Kenny Burns Promotions, 2009)

Burns, Thomas; Keevins, Hugh. *Twists and Turns: The Tommy Burns Story* (Edinburgh: Sportsprint Publishing, 1989)

Crampsey, Robert A. *Mr. Stein – a Biography of Jock Stein, 1922–85* (Edinburgh: Mainstream, 1986)

Dalglish, Kenny; Gallacher, Ken. *King Kenny: an Autobiography* (London: Stanley Paul, 1982)

Dalglish, Kenny; Winter, Henry. *Dalglish: My Autobiography* (London: Coronet Books, Hodder and Stoughton, 1997)

Dalglish, Kenny; Winter, Henry. *My Liverpool Home* (London: Hodder & Stoughton, 2010)

Downie, Andrew. *Doctor Sócrates: Footballer, Philosopher, Legend* (London: Simon & Schuster UK Ltd, 2017)

Ferguson, Alex. *A Light in the North: Seven Years with Aberdeen* (London: Mainstream Digital, 2013)

Gemmill, Archie; Price, Will. *Both Sides of the Border: My Autobiography* (London: Hodder & Stoughton 2005)

Glanville, Brian. *The Story of the World Cup* (revised edition, London: Faber and Faber, 1997)

Goodwin, Bob. *The Spurs Alphabet* (Robwin Publishing House, 2017)

Gray, Andy. *Gray Matters* (London: Macmillan, 2004)

Hansen, Alan; Gallacher, Ken. *Tall, Dark and Hansen – Ten Years at Anfield* (Edinburgh: Mainstream, 1988)

Hansen, Alan; Tomas, Jason. *A Matter of Opinion* (London: Partridge, 1999)

Horsfield, Stuart. *1982 Brazil The Glorious Failure* (Worthing: Pitch, 2020)

Jordan, Joe; Lawton, James. *Joe Jordan: Behind the Dream: My Autobiography* (London: Hodder, 2004)

Leighton, Jim; Robertson, Ken. *In the Firing Line: The Jim Leighton Story* (Edinburgh: Mainstream, 2000)

Macpherson, Archie. *Action Replays* (London: Chapmans, 1991)

Macpherson, Archie. *Jock Stein: The Definitive Biography* (Newbury: Racing Post, 2014)

Macpherson, Archie. *Adventures in the Golden Age: Scotland in the World Cup Finals 1974–1998* (Edinburgh: Black & White Publishing, 2018)

McColl, Graham. *'78 – How a Nation Lost the World Cup* (London: Headline, 2006)

McGrain, Danny; Keevins, Hugh. *Danny McGrain: In Sunshine or in Shadow* (Edinburgh: John Donald, 1987)

McLean, Jim; Gallacher, Ken. *Jousting with Giants: The Jim McLean Story* (Edinburgh: Mainstream, 1987)

McLeish, Alex; MacDonald, Alastair. *The Don of an Era* (Edinburgh: J. Donald, 1988)

Miller, Willie; MacDonald, Alastair. *The Miller's Tale: An Autobiography* (Edinburgh: Mainstream, 1989)

Miller, Willie; Robertson, Rob. *The Don, The Willie Miller Story* (Edinburgh: Birlinn, 2007)

Redshaw, David. *Malaga Football Club: The Story* (Leicester: Matador, 2010)

Robertson, John; Lawson, John. *Super Tramp: My Autobiography* (Edinburgh: Mainstream Publishing, 2011)

Rough, Alan; Brown, Stewart. *Rough at the Top* (Edinburgh: John Donald, 1988)

Rough, Alan. *My Story: The Rough and the Smooth* (London: Headline, 2006)

Souness, Graeme; Harris, Bob. *No Half Measures* (London: Collins 1985)

Souness, Graeme. *Football – My Life, My Passion* (London: Headline, 2017)

Strachan, Gordon; Webster, Jack. *Gordon Strachan: An Autobiography* (London: Stanley Paul, 1984)

Strachan, Gordon. *Strachan: My Life in Football* (London: Time Warner, 2006)

Sturrock, Paul; Duddy, Charlie; Rundo, Peter. *Forward Thinking: the Paul Sturrock Story* (Edinburgh: Mainstream, 1989)

Sumner, Steve; Almond, Bobby; Mansbridge, Derrick. *To Spain, The Hard Way* (Christchurch, New Zealand: London Whitcoulls, 1982)

Taylor, Hugh: editor. *The Scottish Football Book. No. 18* (London: Stanley Paul, 1972)

Ward, Andrew. *Scotland the Team* (Derby: Breedon Books, 1987)

Wark, John; Henderson, Mel. *Wark On: the Autobiography of John Wark* (Studley: Know the Score! 2009)

Williams, John; Dunning, Eric; Murphy, Patrick. *Hooligans Abroad: The Behaviour and Control of English fans in Continental Europe* (Place of publication not identified: Routledge, 2014)

Wilson, Jonathan. *Inverting the Pyramid: A History of Football Tactics* (New edition. London: Orion Books, 2014)

Wilson, Mike. *Don't Cry For Me Argentina: Scotland's 1978 World Cup Adventure* (Edinburgh: Mainstream, 1998)

Yallop, David A. *How They Stole the Game* (London: Constable, 2011)

Newspapers
Aberdeen Evening Express
The Age
Belfast Telegraph
Daily Express
Daily Mirror
Daily Record
Evening Times
Financial Times
Glasgow Herald
The Guardian
Independent on Sunday
Irish Times
Liverpool Echo
Lancashire Post
New York Times
Northern Echo
Press and Journal
The Observer
The Scotsman
The Times
Sunday Mail
Sunday Mirror
Sunday People
Sunday Post
Sunday Standard
Sunday Telegraph
Sunday Times
Sydney Morning Herald

Websites
scottishfa.co.uk
englandfootballonline.com
rsssf.com
punditarena.com

theceltlicwiki.com
readingfc.co.uk
londonhearts.com
youtube.com
eu-football.info
uk.globaldatabase.com
allmediascotland.com
news.bbc.co.uk/1/hi/uk/6499565.stm
upi.com
officialcharts.com
imdb.com
calcio.com
forzaitalianfootball.com
telegraph.co.uk
blog.nationalarchives.gov.uk
theblizzard.co.uk
englishfootballleaguetables.co.uk
glencampbell.com
fifa.com
runnersworld.com
oxforddnb.com
hamishogston.co.uk
nzsoccer.com
malagacf.com
thecourier.co.uk
surinenglish.com
superhotspur.com
eveningtelegraph.co.uk
star.kiwi
dafc.co.uk
lep.co.uk
fifamuseum.com
fourfourtwo.com
gameofthepeople.com
saopaulofc.net

terceirotempo.uol.com.br
tricolornaweb.com.br
universidadedofutebol.com.br
stadiumguide.com/benitovillamarin
sports.ru/tribuna/blogs/sovietfootball
russianfootballnews.com
taleoftwohalves.uk
avfc.co.uk
transfermarkt.co.uk
lfchistory.net
umbro.com
footballshirtculture.com
letslookagain.com
manchestereveningnews.co.uk
dailymail.co.uk
barobertsongs.com
discogs.com
dailyecho.co.uk
holmesotogrande.com
lareservaclubsotogrande.com
scottishfootballhalloffame.co.uk
www.independent.co.uk
www.arabarchive.co.uk
www.ipswichstar.co.uk
irishtimes.com
mfc.co.uk
escapetovictory.spodrum.co.uk
thecourier.co.uk
fitbastats.com
afcheritage.org
unscr.com/en/resolutions/doc/502
allybegg.com
www.mightyleeds.co.uk
thisisopus.com
screenonline.org.uk

rcir.org.uk/?page_id=2579
scottishfootballmuseum.org.uk/resources/news/how-scotland-
brought-football-to-brazil/

Scholarly works
Wright, Caleb. *The Beautiful Game as a Soviet Game:
Sportsmanship, Style, and Statecraft during the Golden
Age of Soviet Soccer* (2018). Graduate Student Theses,
Dissertations, & Professional Papers. 11198.

Periodicals
Football Pictorial
1982 FIFA World Cup in Spain, FIFA report, English edition
Evening Times Scotland World Cup Scrapbook (Glasgow:
Outram, 1982)
Scottish Football Association annual minutes
When Saturday Comes
Match
Shoot!

Match programmes
Scotland vs Brazil, June 1973
Celtic vs Manchester United, Jimmy Johnstone and Bobby
Lennox testimonial, May 1976
Ipswich Town vs Liverpool, September 1977
Liverpool vs Ipswich Town, February 1978
Scotland vs Northern Ireland, May 1979
Celtic vs Manchester United, Danny McGrain
testimonial, August 1980
Scotland vs Portugal, March 1980
Scotland vs Wales, May 1980
Scotland vs England, May 1980
John Robertson testimonial, 1980
Scotland vs Portugal, October 1980
Ipswich Town vs Manchester United, October 1980

Israel vs Scotland, February 1981
Scotland vs Israel, April 1981
Scotland vs Sweden, September 1981
Ipswich Town vs Liverpool, February 1982
Scotland vs Holland, March 1982
Scotland U21 vs Italy U21, March 1982
Scotland U21 vs England U21, April 1982
Scotland vs Wales, May 1982
Scotland vs England, May 1982
FIFA World Cup Official Programme, España '82 UK edition
Scotland vs East Germany, October 1982
Aston Villa vs Barcelona, January 1983
Scotland vs East Germany, October 1985
Scotland vs Romania, March 1986
Scotland vs Brazil, May 1987
Scotland vs France, March 1989

Television programmes
Top of the Pops (BBC, 6 May 1982)
World Cup Grandstand: Brazil v USSR (BBC, 14 June 1982)
Match Time (Granada, 8 January 1983)
The *Boys From Maybole* (STV, 1983)
Are You Watching Jimmy Hill? (BBC, 1998)
The Football Years: Viva España (STV, 2010)
Jimmy Hill: A Man for All Seasons (BBC, 2016)

Films
G'olé! (FIFA, 1983)

Podcasts
Official Scotland Podcast
Between the Lines